Immigration and Bureaucratic Control

Language, Power and Social Process 20

Editors
Monica Heller
Richard J. Watts

Mouton de Gruyter
Berlin · New York

Immigration and Bureaucratic Control

Language Practices
in Public Administration

by
Eva Codó

Mouton de Gruyter
Berlin · New York

Mouton de Gruyter (formerly Mouton, The Hague)
is a Division of Walter de Gruyter GmbH & Co. KG, Berlin.

Library of Congress Cataloging-in-Publication Data

> Codó, Eva, 1971−
> Immigration and bureaucratic control : language practices in public administration / by Eva Codó.
> p. cm. − (Language, power and social process ; 20)
> Includes bibliographical references and index.
> ISBN 978-3-11-019589-7 (hardcover : alk. paper)
> ISBN 978-3-11-019590-3 (pbk. : alk. paper)
> 1. Sociolinguistics − Spain. 2. Communication in public administration − Spain. 3. Spain − Emigration and immigration. 4. Immigrants − Spain − Language. 5. Multilingualism − Spain. I. Title.
> P40.45.S7C63 2008
> 306.440946−dc22
>
> 2008005115

♾ Printed on acid-free paper which falls within the guidelines of the ANSI to ensure permanence and durability.

ISBN 978-3-11-019589-7 hb
ISBN 978-3-11-019590-3 pb

Bibliographic information published by the Deutsche Nationalbibliothek

The Deutsche Nationalbibliothek lists this publication in the Deutsche Nationalbibliografie; detailed bibliographic data are available in the Internet at http://dnb.d-nb.de.

© Copyright 2008 by Walter de Gruyter GmbH & Co. KG, D-10785 Berlin.
All rights reserved, including those of translation into foreign languages. No part of this book may be reproduced in any form or by any means, electronic or mechanical, including photocopy, recording, or any information storage and retrieval system, without permission in writing from the publisher.
Cover design: Christopher Schneider.
Printed in Germany.

To Martí and Pol for their love

Acknowledgements

My first expression of gratitude goes to Melissa G. Moyer. She was the person who guided me throughout this research project and also the one who encouraged me to submit the proposal for this publication. Her support and enthusiasm have been unfailing over the years. She is responsible for much of what I am as a researcher.

Other people have also contributed in valuable ways to the completion of this book. First of all, I want to thank the efforts of Virgina Unamuno, who offered to throw light on the process of data analysis at a moment when I needed a listening ear. She has been an endless source of encouragement and support. Secondly, I am indebted to Joan A. Argenter, Josep M. Cots, Hortènsia Curell, Monica Heller, Joan Pujolar, Amparo Tusón and Jef Verschueren for the many insightful comments and suggestions they made when this research was first presented in the form of a PhD thesis. In particular, my most heartfelt thanks go to Amparo Tusón because of the great personal effort she made to be present at the thesis defence. Mark Sebba and Gabi Budach kindly agreed to be external examiners and to write a report on this work. Many thanks go to them for their thoughtful reviews.

Obviously, without the help of numerous people at the site where I gathered my data, this book would not have been possible. I do not mention their real names here for confidentiality reasons. In particular, I want to thank the senior official who gave me permission to do fieldwork for his aid and personal commitment to what I was doing. I am also grateful to Miquel and Rosa for their kindness and help. It was through the many conversations I had with them that I began to understand how the office functioned. My greatest debt of gratitude goes, of course, to Hussain, but especially, to all the undocumented migrants that went through the legalisation process and on whose words and silences this book is based.

Finally, I would like to mention the generosity of two people: Michael Kennedy, who carefully proofed this book; and secondly and most importantly, my editor, Monica Heller, who patiently read the different drafts, provided challenging ideas and was always extremely supportive. Thanks also to two anonymous reviewers for their thorough readings of the manuscript and for the many insightful comments they made. Any remaining shortcomings are, of course, my own.

Two bodies gave financial assistance to this project: the Autonomous Government of Catalonia (predoctoral research grant 1997FI 00381), and the Spanish

Ministry of Education and Science (funded research project BFF2001–2576). I thankfully acknowledge their support here.

List of Figures

Figure 1. Areas of main concentration of foreigners holding legal residence permits in 2003 (source: Observatorio Permanente de la Inmigración [2004])   16
Figure 2. General floor plan of the administrative unit   22
Figure 3. Detailed plan of the information desk service and recording arrangements   23
Figure 4. Actors and stages in the bureaucratic procedure   46
Figure 5. Structural organisation of service interactions   55

Transcription procedures

The data extracts presented in this book have been transcribed following a slightly adapted version of the LIDES (Language Interaction Data Exchange System) proposal. LIDES aims to develop a standard for the transcription and coding of multilingual data with a view to creating an international database. It is based on the CHILDES system (MacWhinney 2000), a widely used standard for handling language acquisition data.

The main difference between standard LIDES and the transcription conventions I have employed concerns the way in which distinct linguistic codes are signalled. In my corpus I have used different typefaces instead of language tags in order to enhance the readability of the transcripts. Another transcription practice not included in the LIDES Coding Manual (LIPPS Group 2000) is the use of the UUU speaker code, which stands for "undecidable speaker", to represent periods of non-speech. The need for such a speaker code stems from the fact that, for technical reasons, the system requires whatever occurs on a main tier to be assigned to a speaker. Yet assigning a silence to one of the participants implies a particular interpretation of the ongoing talk (Levinson 1983). The UUU speaker code enables researchers to represent silences without having to make such attributions. This convention, however, needs to be distinguished from the XXX speaker code, which is used when a speaker cannot be identified (the transcriber is also not sure whether the speaker is a participant in the interaction or not).

The participants involved in the exchanges analysed have been identified as follows. The bureaucrats are: MIQ (Miquel), TER (Teresa), RAM (Ramon), JUA (Juan), ROS (Rosa) and LOL (Loli). Obviously, these are all ficticious names. As for clients, and given the large number of them, they are referred to in the transcripts as ENQ (enquirer) if there is only one in the exchange or EN and a number (e.g. EN1) if there are several of them. These are generic speaker codes derived from clients' discursive role. Other speaker codes that appear are:

AGE	Advisory agent
PEN	Previous enquirer
DOO	Door staff
RES	Researcher
ST4	Student four

A translation for the turns in languages other than English is provided in a dependent tier located below the main tier. Because of the foreign language nature of most of the data presented, an effort has been made to reproduce "broken" language use on the %tra tier. Dependent tiers are employed to include researcher's comments or relevant linguistic and situational information. They

xii   *Transcription procedures*

begin with a % symbol followed by a three-letter code. The following dependent tiers are used in this book:

%act:	participants' actions while talk is produced
%add:	addressee or addressees of a particular turn
%com:	researcher's comments about the main tier
%tra:	free English translation of the main tier

When situational information cannot be associated to a specific speaker turn, it is provided by means of the @Situation file header.

Language coding

Although LIDES recommends the use of special language tags for identifying different languages, different typefaces have been employed in this book to facilitate the reading of the transcripts. These are presented below.

Underlined	Undecidable language
Plain	Spanish
Italics	Catalan
Bold	English
`Courier`	French
CAPITALS	German
Double underlining	Italian

Transcription conventions

Below is the list of the symbols that can be found in the transcripts of spoken data.

+^	quick uptake or latching
+...	trailing off
0	nonverbal activity
xxx	unintelligible material
www	untranscribed material because of confidential information or irrelevance to excerpt
#	pause
##	longer pause (but shorter than 1 sec)
#figure	length of pause in seconds (minimum 1 sec)
[=! text]	paralinguistics, prosodics
[>]	overlap follows
[<]	overlap precedes
[?]	best guess
<>	scope symbols

[!]	stressing
:	lengthened vowel
::	longer lengthening of vowel

Intonation contours

.	end-of-turn falling contour
?	end-of-turn rising contour
!	end-of-turn exclamation contour
-,.	end-of-turn fall-rise contour
-.	intra-turn falling contour
-?	intra-turn rising contour
-!	intra-turn exclamation contour
-,	intra-turn fall–rise contour

Contents

Acknowledgements	vii
List of Figures	ix
Transcription procedures	xi

Part I: Situating the study

Chapter 1
Immigration, bureaucracy and language ... 3
1. Migrations in a globalised world ... 3
2. Heterogeneity, equality and citizenship ... 5
   2.1. Linguistic diversity and opportunities of access ... 7
3. Immigrants, bureaucrats and the state ... 8
   3.1. Bureaucracy and language use ... 11
4. Goals of this research ... 12
5. Sociohistorical, legal and political background ... 13
   5.1. Immigration to Spain: A recent phenomenon ... 13
      5.1.1. Number and geographical distribution of migrants in Spain ... 15
      5.1.2. Social composition ... 16
   5.2. The legal framework ... 17
      5.2.1. Implementation and outcome of the legalisation campaign ... 18
6. Researching a state immigration office ... 19
   6.1. Negotiating access ... 20
   6.2. Collecting the data ... 21
   6.3. Types of data ... 25
   6.4. The participants ... 29
   6.5. Data transcription and analysis ... 31
7. Making sense of the data ... 32
   7.1. Situated talk and the shaping of society ... 32
   7.2. The analysis of face-to-face verbal interaction ... 37
8. How this book is organised ... 41

Chapter 2
Service activities and bureaucratic procedure ... 43
1. Introduction ... 43

xvi Contents

2.	The administrative procedure	44
	2.1. Applying for legal status: Documents and requirements	44
	2.2. Processing petitions: Stages and actors	45
3.	Characterisation of service exchanges	51
	3.1. Episodes and activities: An overview	54
	3.1.1. Service activities in detail	57
4.	Concluding remarks	66

Part II: Information as valuable capital

Chapter 3
An illusion of information

1.	Introduction	69
2.	Written vs. oral communication	70
3.	Front-line service talk	74
	3.1. Reporting the initial assessment of petitions	75
	3.1.1. *"Trámite"* and "three weeks"	76
	3.1.2. *"Falta"*	79
	3.2. Beyond initial assessments	81
4.	Extreme routinisation, equality and fairness	83
5.	The representation of the bureaucratic procedure	85
	5.1. Whose choice?	85
	5.2. Facilitating understanding	86
	5.3. Avoiding miscommunication	88
	5.4. Constructing an illusion	89
	5.5. Information and the exercise of power	93
6.	A crucial change in information policy	94
	6.1. Setting the scene	95
	6.2. Accepting managerial authority	96
	6.3. Justifying individual positions	99
	6.4. Team work and the lack of a unified front	107
7.	Concluding remarks	111

Chapter 4
Strategies of information management 115

1.	Introduction	115
2.	Handling clients' challenging moves	116
	2.1. Coping with contradictions	116
	2.2. Providing further information	118

		2.2.1. Teaching clients what *trámite* means	118
		2.2.2. Redefining role-identity	121
		2.2.3. Wavering between institutional and individual positions	125
	2.3.	Accounting for organisational arrangements	126
3.	Clients' strategies of contestation		127
	3.1.	From indirect challenges to the use of key insider knowledge	129
	3.2.	Open challenges	134
	3.3.	Offering solutions	137
	3.4.	Trying to change footing	140
4.	Concluding remarks		146

Part III: Regimented spaces

Chapter 5
The scrutinisation of behaviour — 151
1. Introduction — 151
2. The wish for absolute control — 152
   2.1. Regulating time and space, and defining norms of appropriate conduct — 152
   2.2. Managing interactional organisation — 164
3. Ramon's idiosyncratic forms of language use — 172
4. Concluding remarks — 185

Chapter 6
Language choice and multilingual practice — 187
1. Introduction — 187
2. Spanish and Catalan: Different languages, different spaces — 188
3. The other languages — 192
   3.1. Lingua franca English — 198
4. Concluding remarks — 221

By way of conclusion — 223

Notes — 233
References — 237
Index — 247

Part I

Situating the study

Chapter 1
Immigration, bureaucracy and language

1. Migrations in a globalised world

One of the hallmarks of the societies we live in is the generalised movement of peoples and capitals across the globe. Indeed, the human experience of living in the twenty-first century is, in many ways, defined by the daily realities of displacement and migration.

There are certainly different forms of migration, as different as the various motivations and socioeconomic circumstances leading to the decision to abandon one's place of residence and settle in a new country. In this book, I shall concentrate on the study of the realities of people who migrate from the economically less developed countries of Africa, Asia and Latin America to the industrialised, rich nations of Western Europe. Economic immigrants, as they are usually called, leave their countries of origin driven by a desire to improve their living conditions and move upwards socially.

The social and economic contexts of economic immigrants are radically different from the circumstances of other types of migrants, like the retired individuals who relocate to milder climates or the young developed-world professionals who take up well-paid jobs abroad. Also different are the family situations, professional prospects, and above all, sets of capitals (cultural, linguistic and educational) that these three groups may draw upon in their process of accommodation to new social and cultural spaces.

Today, economic immigrants are a major socioeconomic force in the societies in which they settle (Massey et al. 1993). From an economic perspective, the workforce supplied by immigration is essential to the functioning of most Western economies; from a social standpoint, immigrants are the driving force behind social change; from cultural, religious and linguistic perspectives, newcomers' different practices are calling into question accepted views of citizenship, national identity and cultural homogeneity. Foreign immigration is, thus, an active agent in the shaping of Western societies at present.

There are multiple facets to the economic immigrant experience. In this book I shall concentrate on the institutional side; I shall analyse the complex bureaucratic process foreigners must go through to be authorised to reside legally in a new country. Beyond legal status, but largely conditioned by it, are the material circumstances of their lives. These are basically defined by work opportunities, housing conditions and possibilities of access to health care and education. On a more symbolic level, although with clear bearings on the material realities of everyday life, are the stigmatisation of migrants' distinctive cultural, linguistic and religious practices, the attribution of blame for the negative in society, and the restrictions in their access to, participation in and definition of the public arena.

Those of us who are concerned with the ways in which social inequalities get produced and reproduced in daily life encounters cannot but see the study of immigration as central to our undertakings. The social transformations brought about by the arrival of migrants cannot obscure the pervasiveness of group boundaries and the operation of old and new mechanisms of social exclusion.

To expose the inequalities affecting immigrants and the multiple mechanisms of exclusion to which they are subject (including the fundamental role of language and linguistic practices in this exclusion), it is essential to examine the circumstances in which their daily lives unfold, the kinds of experiences they go through and the ways in which they are (or are not) being incorporated into the host societies. At stake are the values we live by, namely, democracy, equality, freedom and the goodness of the welfare state. One of the key questions that arises when we examine the treatment given to immigrants is precisely the extent to which these values guide state policies and practices in this area.

To answer this question, we need to focus on the ways in which states deal with immigration. This can be done at two levels. At a broad level, we can examine the nature of state laws and regulations; we can focus, for example, on what elements of the immigrant phenomenon, such as social welfare policies or security and control, they emphasise most. An examination of the broad legal and political frame, however, cannot give us the full picture of the ways in which immigration is being handled. Underlying the legal and political spheres, there is the level of daily practices at key state institutions. The examination of what happens at those key sites is important because they are the places where policies become practices and where newcomers meet the state. It is in real-life encounters at those sites that the state becomes a tangible agent in the migratory experience, an agent with specific effects on the lives of individuals.

This is precisely what this book is about. It deals with the connections between macrolevel legal processes regulating access to citizenship and the situated experiences of petitioners in a bureaucratic context. The data analysed comes from one such site: a state immigration office located in the city of Barcelona, Catalonia, Spain. But before presenting the data and its sociohistorical background, I want to situate this book within wider debates on immigration, the politics of equality and the management of social heterogeneity.

2. Heterogeneity, equality and citizenship

The increasingly multiethnic composition of most industrialised societies as a result of transnational migration has opened a number of debates in political and scholarly circles. The majority of those debates try to answer the question of how best to deal with the demands of cultural diversity within the framework of present-day liberal democracies. The emphases vary, depending on what the causes and the mechanisms underlying contemporary migration processes are taken to be (Massey et al. 1993). However, at the heart of most public discussions on immigration there is a common set of ideas and arguments, the most important of which are summarised below.

One key theme is the issue of security. Transnational migrations are conceptualised as an element of threat, essentially because of their perceptually uncontrolled nature and their potential for creating social instability (Gould 2005). Since the late 1980s, in most Western European countries there has been growing political and social pressure to tighten the regulation and control of immigrant flows. In the background are criminalising views of (especially undocumented) immigration. That is, in the political and media arenas, the arrival of migrants is conceptualised as essentially a phenomenon to be regulated by means of the law and the police (Wodak and van Dijk 2000).

The heterogeneity of beliefs and sociocultural practices that migrants bring to Western societies has sparked intense and ongoing debate on how to deal with diversity in ways that ensure equality and fairness. Different models have been proposed. The assimilationist view takes the Herderian notion of the nation-state as the baseline and claims that no society can be cohesive without its members sharing a common set of beliefs, values and practices. Migrants have to assimilate in order to be treated equally. A less strong version of this approach is what Parekh (2001) has called the *civic assimilationist view*. This model advocates the strict separation of the public and private realms, that is, official state neutrality and a depoliticisation of differences. While diversity is possible and even welcome in the private arena, a system of uniform laws must govern public life (Barry 2001).

Against views of civic equality emerges the multiculturalist position, often also labelled the *politics of difference*. The multiculturalist position argues that culture is fundamental to identity creation, that is, that cultures are the context out of which our identities unavoidably emerge. Thus, respecting one another involves respecting significant cultural differences. This translates into the need for minority groups' rights to be recognised at the political level (Kymlicka 1995; Parekh 2001). For multiculturalists, equality is tantamount to a differential treatment of individuals, or an "equality of difference". Treating everybody equally requires taking into account and recognising each person's legitimate differences. This may translate itself, for example, into the exemption for certain groups of the obligation to abide by certain laws that may enter into open conflict with their cultural practices. According to this view, officially recognising the right to a distinctive cultural identity of different minority groups is not incompatible with social cohesion; on the contrary, the former is a requisite for the latter. In principle, a "multicultural" culture constituted out of the interaction of different cultures will emerge as a result of this mode of political integration.

Behind these models are various definitions of national identity and citizenship. Interestingly, the ideological distinction between the political right and left often gets blurred in this area. In many discourses, migrants are perceived to be a threat to a perceived homogeneous national identity. The current trend to make immigrants pass language competence tests in order to acquire citizenship reflects public fears in this area (Stevenson 2005). There seems to be a tension, though, between insistence on the protection of essential national values on the one hand and the formulation of a set of civic citizenship rights on the other. Both discourses coexist at national and European levels, with emphases varying according to circumstances and country. The idea of *civic citizenship* has been advocated by, among others, Delanty (1995). His idea of inclusive postnational citizenship transcends national understandings of citizenship based on ethnic and cultural homogeneity. In Delanty's view, postnational citizenship, which he claims should be based solely on place of residence, must be linked to the institutionalisation of pluralism, the recognition of migrants' social and civil rights, and their right to democratic participation in political institutions. Along similar lines, a project supported by the European Commission discusses a basic set of social and welfare rights like residence rights, access to nationality and family reunion, and the right not to be discriminated against for reasons of race, religion and nationality, all of which are encompassed by the concept of civic citizenship (Niessen et al. 2005).

The idea of defining a set of European Union standards with regard to immigrants' basic civic rights stems from the belief that integration is and should be facilitated by public policy, and that state policies within the Union need to converge. The concept of integration emerges as central to public endeavours because it is taken to be the key to harmonious coexistence within social heterogeneity. It is believed that immigrants must integrate in order for social harmony, equality and access to be guaranteed. But what exactly is meant by integration is in most cases left underdefined. This allows the dominant majority to retain control over the process (Blommaert and Verschueren 1998). As this book will show, migrants are expected to think and behave appropriately, but they are allowed no say in the definition of what appropriate behaviour exactly means and yet they are often blamed for not wanting to integrate. The extent to which recipient societies open spaces for immigrants to integrate emerges as a highly relevant question here (Giménez 2003). What is often singled out as the element preventing migrants from integrating is their culture. Many scholars have denounced what they see as a culturalization of the other (Barry 2001) and a view of culture which is static, essentialist and indexical of antagonistic positions towards the majority group (Blommaert and Verschueren 1998).

Underlying many a view of integration is a solid belief in homogeneity as the condition sine qua non for social stability and cohesion (Moyer and Martín Rojo 2007). This stems from monocultural and monolingual conceptions of the nation-state. It is by undermining the ideological bases on which the nation-state is built that transnational migrations call into question the significance of national boundaries. But current migrants also challenge national framings of the migrant phenomenon by establishing transnational networks of legal and affective support outside their countries of origin and travelling back and forth rather regularly. Paradoxically, the transnational pull is counteracted by the still decisive role that individual states play in the definition of the legal framework and by the differing nature of public policies in this area. The ideological tension between the national and the transnational is most evident in Europe because of the European integration project. Apart from the legal terrain, this tension is apparent in the field of language policy (Mar-Molinero and Stevenson 2005). While European multilingualism is strongly promoted, it is only of an elite type; that is, the many languages that migrant populations bring with them are not considered part of the kind of multilingualism that is desired and desirable.

The strong tendency to uniformisation of nation-states is being called into question by migrants' practices. The institutions and services of our developed societies have, increasingly, a highly heterogenous clientele to serve. If Western European states are to follow the democratic principles of fairness and equality, they must rethink themselves and their institutions in ways which ensure that social diversity is respected and that difference is not turned into inequality.

2.1. *Linguistic diversity and opportunities of access*

The effects of cultural and linguistic diversity on individuals' life chances were first studied by John Gumperz (1982a, 1982b). His seminal studies of gatekeeping interactions were the starting point for an impressive body of research. For the first time, the connection was established between details of speech that were linked to speakers' different sociocultural backgrounds and their real-life opportunities. The notion of *gatekeeping*, a term first coined by Erickson and

Schutz (1982), defines a type of interactional activity in which an institutional representative defines which candidates should be allowed through the gate, that is, should be given access to limited socioeconomic resources such as work or legal residence.

Many studies followed Gumperz' insights. Some involved mainly South Asian migrants in the UK (Roberts and Sayers 1987; Gumperz and Roberts 1991; Roberts and Sarangi 1995; Sarangi 1996), while others focused on different minority groups and/or social activities (see Erickson 1975, 2001; Roberts and Sarangi 1999; Trinch 2001 and Kerekes 2006).

This book connects up naturally with research on gatekeeping, firstly, because of the gatekeeping nature of the encounters it analyses, and secondly, because of its focus on the connection between linguistic heterogeneity and opportunities of access. However, the theoretical stance I adopt, in line with reseachers like Heller (2001b), tries to take interactional sociolinguistic analysis a step further. I aim to develop a more general understanding of the way in which social inequalities are produced and reproduced in and through language use in our postmodern societies. The study of migrants in bureaucratic contexts is a fruitful terrain for that purpose, especially when what comes under scrutiny are the mechanisms of legal entry into our developed societies. Thus, this book seeks to contribute to recent research on language, bureaucracy, immigration and social exclusion. Especially relevant to this case study is the work conducted by Maryns (2005, 2006) and Jacquemet (2005). They investigate how the regulation to which both the production and the interpretation of asylum seekers' narratives are subjected constitutes a fundamental source of inequality. The institutions' requirements regarding genre and appropriate forms of evidence constrain what is sayable and what is interpretable. Further, the tight restrictions imposed on access to spaces of contextualisation and sense-making undermine the credibility of the agency in charge of granting asylum.

3. Immigrants, bureaucrats and the state

Like the studies by Maryns and Jacquemet, the present work focuses on the bureaucratic side of state control over immigrants. Although some steps have been taken towards a common immigration framework for the EU (through the Treaties of Schengen and Amsterdam), the legal regulation of migrant flows continues to be largely in the hands of individual states.

At a broader level, each state attempts to exert control through its laws. When immigration laws are perceived to have become obsolete or to no longer regulate migration flows efficiently, new laws are passed. These give the state new legal mechanisms to intervene as a major organising agent in the migratory process. States strive to make immigration an orderly phenomenon, but as a social force, it can hardly be orderly. In this book, I shall examine the state's urge to exercise control over immigrants on a more microscopic plane, dissecting the component elements of everyday interaction. I will investigate how states try to regulate the migrant phenomenon at a local level, through the daily practices of their representatives, that is, individual bureaucrats.

The work of these bureaucrats does not take place in a vacuum but is framed within the context of specific institutions. The bureaucracies that official representatives work for have habitual ways of doing things and specific policies and practices that employees get socialised into. For instance, over decades, the public administration in Spain has been notorious for its general malfunctioning and the lack of accountability of its institutional representatives (Nieto 1984, 1996). This book will seek to unveil what the nature of bureaucrats' practices is, how they come to have the shape they have, and in what ways this affects the services immigrants are provided. Another interesting aspect we shall consider is the tension between institutional policies and individual practices, and the ways in which the agents of the state manage to cope with the many contradictory elements informing their daily work.

The study of the functioning of a state bureaucracy and the connections between institutional processes and individual experiences is also relevant because it sheds light on contemporary social life. More and more aspects of our daily lives are becoming subject to institutional regulation (Chouliaraki and Fairclough 1999). Whole domains of social activity are being organised by state bureaucracies, which act as distributors and regulators of rights and obligations and thus exercise a considerable degree of control over the lives of individuals. This is nowhere more evident than within the domain of the regulation and control of foreign immigration.

Because of the status of institutions as mid-level structures mediating between the political realm and the daily realities of citizens, as Agar (1985) argues, the study of state organisations allows for the visualisation of the multiple connections between three levels of social analysis: the social, the institutional, and the local and situated. The way in which these three levels are interconnected and bear upon one another is of significance for an understanding of the processes whereby societies become structured. Moreover, the analysis of the position and functioning of institutions and especially of their practices will undoubtedly improve our understanding of the ways in which institutional life opens up opportunities for individuals, or on the contrary, limits participation and creates boundaries. This is particularly important when what is at stake is the incorporation and participation of social groups which, because of their different cultural backgrounds and straitened socioeconomic circumstances, are perceived to threaten the well-being of the recipient societies.

One of the main functions of state institutions is the socialisation of individuals into becoming "proper" citizens. This process takes place from the moment an individual is born and is initially effected by the family and school, with state institutions playing a greater role as the person advances into adulthood. It is hardly ever a conscious process but rather one which allows appropriate rules of conduct, or in Bourdieu's (1991) words, a given *habitus*, to gradually be absorbed. Studying a state bureaucracy dealing with immigrants allows us to observe at first hand the subtle (and not so subtle) mechanisms whereby the forces of this socialisation process are brought to bear on immigrants in an attempt to turn them into "proper" citizens. Clients are taught, among other things, who can ask what at what point, but also what the best way is to obtain a specific piece of information and how bureaucrats' answers have to be interpreted. This process of socialisation provides immigrants with valuable information which they are then able to use in their future dealings with state bureaucracies in the new country.

The actors whose experiences and practices this book examines fall into two clearly distinguished groups, namely local institutional representatives and their immigrant clients; both are interesting to study for different reasons.

The clients of the immigration offices are mostly foreigners, newcomers who strive to make sense of the bureaucratic realities they encounter. They draw on their background knowledge, which includes past experiences with bureaucracies at home, bureaucratic experiences throughout their migration trajectories, or previous experiences in the same host country. Not negligible is the role that their expectations of transparency, rationality and rigorous practice from a first world bureaucracy may play. We shall see how different clients draw on different resources to make sense of their bureaucratic encounters, resulting in very different outcomes; we shall also observe the different attitudes they take with regard to the experiences they undergo and how this informs their practices and affects their experiences.

On the other side of the counter, local bureaucrats serve the public. Their social practices play a fundamental role in the organisation and success of service communication; this is why I place a great deal of emphasis on the fine-grained analysis of their routines. A fundamental issue I seek to address in this regard is the question of how much room there is for individual agency in bureaucratic contexts. These settings function very much like systems, as Agar (1985) has claimed. Institutional incumbents do not have total freedom to act as they wish since they are bound by institutional pressures, but they do have a certain leeway to behave in modes that may be more or less constraining. An example of this would be the extent to which clients are allowed to question the legitimacy of institutional practices. This is only possible if institutional representatives make room for it, but in the light of the pressures of the institutional order and of the personal and professional circumstances in which their practices are embedded, this is highly unlikely to happen.

3.1. Bureaucracy and language use

This account of a bureaucracy is based on the study of communication within it. One of the first notions that comes to mind when we think of talk and bureaucratic practice is bureaucratic jargon. Yet the bureaucratic nature of certain encounters is not just defined by the use of a particular set of lexical items and syntactic structures; what makes an interaction bureaucratic is a distinctive whole way of proceeding. Srikant Sarangi and Stefaan Slembrouck (1996: 84) describe bureaucracy as a "mode of practice", that is, a set of procedures, a way of relating to cases and clients, a whole configuration of social roles speakers may take on, and a frame for interpreting moves and contributions. In this vein, the bureaucratic nature of an event cannot be defined by parameters external to it; it is jointly constructed by participants in the course of their interactional dealings. Bureaucracy is a "social event", a "process which happens to those involved" (1996: 3).

One specific focus which allows us to observe how bureaucracy gets "done" is the process of information exchange. Two chapters in this book, namely Chapter 3 and Chapter 4, are devoted to its examination. Information is important, on the one hand, because it is the raw material upon which bureaucratic cases are built, and on the other, because it is around the demand and supply of information that most bureaucratic encounters revolve. In the context of the present study, additionally, information is vital because it is through having access to specific details on the processing of their applications that immigrant clients may decide to supply supplementary documentation. These new documents may change the course of their applications, and consequently, the shape of their future lives.

The mechanics of information exchange are intimately interwoven with participants' positions of speaking. The analysis of the ways in which participants, especially local bureaucrats, draw creatively on various facets of their professional roles to negotiate particular positions of speaking and how this is accomplished verbally is a major theme in this book.

The transmission of information is, as I will show, also closely connected with the exercise of power and control. Indeed, the investigation of the connections between bureaucracy and control cannot proceed without paying due attention to the role of information in effecting control. Information exchange takes place discursively and in situated social interaction, hence the vital role of the study of language use to account for the multiple ways in which information can be represented and the extent to which it may be open to negotiation.

4. Goals of this research

The study of an immigration office enables a researcher to observe first-hand not only the practical implementation of policies, but also the ways in which such policies are represented to citizens and the significance they have in and for the lives of individual people. Although it is assumed that linguistic phenomena cannot be explained without an understanding of their institutional and social embedding, and that the social and institutional orders can only be accounted for by describing the ways in which they are produced and reproduced in daily social routines, for practical reasons the concerns of this book are divided into the primarily linguistic and the primarily social. Its primarily linguistic concerns are defined below:

1. to characterise the process of information exchange in terms of the organisation of encounters, sequences and topics, and of control over them; also, to depict bureaucrats' practices of information provision and explore how much of the information is understood by migrant clients.
2. to analyse the strategies employed by interlocutors to pursue their often conflicting goals; in particular, to explore the ways in which officials manage the tensions inherent in their situated position as information providers and institutional gatekeepers.
3. to investigate the hierarchical value of the different languages at play and explore their role in creating and/or perpetuating social inequalities.

With regard to the social concerns of the present study, they are the following:

1. to describe how adequately a state bureaucracy deals with the challenges posed by incipient social heterogeneity; also, to examine how a nation-state copes with the contradiction of having to regulate access to key socioeconomic resources and being committed to the values of equality and fairness.
2. to explore how social inclusion and exclusion are accomplished in situated talk and emerge as a consequence of specific discursive and categorisation practices; to understand how social inequality is produced and reproduced in the process of structuration of social life.

5. Sociohistorical, legal and political background

To understand the shape and nature of social actors' discursive practices, it is fundamental to examine the sociohistorical circumstances under which data is produced. Blommaert (1999), for instance, argues that the study of language use cannot proceed without taking due account of the intrinsic historicity of every linguistic fact.

Conducting research in a field like immigration thus requires the detailed investigation of the political and legal circumstances framing the research. Certain types of data, like the asylum seekers' narratives studied by Maryns (2005, 2006) or the data presented in this book, may only become available at specific legal and political moments.

5.1. Immigration to Spain: A recent phenomenon

This book focuses on the immigration phenomenon in Spain. Apart from the relevance of the case study itself for what it tells us about general bureaucratic and gatekeeping processes, the sociohistorical circumstances of international migration to Spain make the country a particularly attractive context to study. This is because Spain has only recently begun to experience immigration on a large scale.

Current large-scale immigration to Spain must be understood and framed within the context of changing patterns of migration on a European level. The Mediterranean countries of the south have gradually replaced the countries of the north as preferred destinations. Thus, in 2001, Spain was the member state which contributed the largest number of new immigrant residents to the European Union (Arango 2002). Like other southern European countries, Spain has been for many centuries a country of emigrants to different places in the world, mainly the Americas and northern Europe. The arrival of economic migrants is a rather recent phenomenon. In fact, the first immigration law dates back to 1985, and it was only in the 1990s that Spain began to attract significant numbers of immigrants from developing countries. A large proportion (over 70%) of its current foreign population has actually entered the country over the last seven years. Not surprisingly, this mass immigration is changing the composition of Spanish society rapidly and profoundly.

The recent sudden increase in the number of migrants is due to the significant socioeconomic changes that have taken place in the country over the last two decades: rapid economic growth and significant social and demographic changes, such as a sharp decline in birth rate and the incorporation of women into the labour market. Like most of the industrialised societies of the West, Spain is becoming more heterogeneous than ever. But because of the rapid nature of the changes that have taken place, Spaniards in general and Spanish institutions in particular are failing to acknowledge the country's new social realities. This study bears witness to that.

Giménez (2003) discusses two reasons that are frequently put forward to explain the country's inadequacy in dealing with the immigrant phenomenon. The first line of reasoning has it that the country is not "psychologically" prepared to receive immigrants, being as it was until recently an exporter of migrants. The second, which is closely linked to the first, argues that the country does not have enough economic resources to integrate foreigners in any adequate way. This argument is grounded on the limited and in many areas still incipient role of the welfare state in Spain. In fact, one of the features which distinguishes Spain from some of its neighbours, like France, is the fact that large-scale international immigration started at the same time as many welfare services began to be provided. Even as social diversity began to grow, there were still many uncertainties as to the nature and scope of the Spanish welfare state.

These two public discourses have framed Spanish policy-making in the area of immigration. De Lucas (2006) argues that the Spanish state has been "obsessed" with establishing quotas and regulating flows according to the often quite distorted needs of the labour market, constructing immigrants as, basically and exclusively, foreign workers. These ideas have also allowed politicians, especially right-wing leaders, to criticise certain immigration laws for being too progressive "for a country like Spain". Discussing law LO 4/2000, which frames the legalisation campaign analysed in this book, former Interior Minister Jaime Mayor Oreja, from the centre-right Popular Party, stated that "We, in Spain, cannot behave as if we were nouveaux riches. We cannot have the most progressive law in Europe. We must be sensible and cautious".[1] Those same arguments have also been used to justify the inadequacy of certain public services addressed to immigrants. As a latecomer in the group of receiving societies, Spain has had the chance to learn from the successes and failures of other countries in incorporating migrants. Yet the extent to which those experiences have been taken into account in Spanish policy-making in this area is arguable.

A feature which distinguishes southern European countries from historical immigrant destinations like the US, Canada or Britain is the fact that international migrations to southern Europe have begun at a time and in a sociopolitical context which is radically different from the context of previous migrations. Globalisation and the new information and communication technologies have influenced the shape and development of contemporary migration processes as well as the conditions of reception in the host societies. A clear example is the current spread of English as a global lingua franca and the opportunities it opens up for intergroup communication. Yet, as I will argue in this book, these new contexts also incorporate new mechanisms of social exclusion.

5.1.1. Number and geographical distribution of migrants in Spain

Due to the large proportion of undocumented migrants, it is difficult to determine in any accurate way the number of foreigners living in Spain. Official figures, such as those provided by the Spanish Ministry of the Interior, take into account only those individuals holding a work and/or residence permit and those who have the status of students. The number of undocumented migrants can be determined by taking into account the figures of municipal censuses, as municipalities do not require those who register to have legal status. Yet there are also some problems with these figures.[2]

In June 2004, there were said to be 1,977,291 foreigners residing legally in Spain.[3] Yet according to some estimates, the actual number could be higher by a million, thus rising to some 2,900,000 people (Pin et al. 2004). According to the official figures, foreigners represented around 5% of the population in 2004; if undocumented migrants were included, that percentage rose to some 7%. In some areas, like the province of Barcelona –where the study presented here was conducted– legal foreign residents accounted for 5.3% of the total population. If illegal foreign residents were included, that figure would rise to about 8.5%.

It seems clear, then, that the composition of Spanish society – in terms of the percentage of foreigners – is quickly coming to resemble that of neighbouring European countries. This is even more significant if we take into account that only seven years earlier, in 1997, foreigners constituted a mere 1.5% of the total Spanish population. In other words, in a period of seven years, immigration had moved from being a socially marginal phenomenon to becoming a significant one.

An important feature of the distribution of foreigners in Spain is that it is uneven across the territory. The foreign population tends to concentrate in a few areas, namely along the Mediterranean, in the Madrid metropolitan region and along the Andalusian coastline in the south (see Figure 1 below). Together, these areas accounted for 68.5% of the total number of foreign residents in 2003 (Observatorio Permanente de la Inmigración 2004).

With respect to nationalities, the largest group in 2003 was, by far, Moroccans (317,927), followed by Ecuadorians (170,652), Colombians (90,481) and Chinese (54,719). As the arrival of immigrants has, if anything, increased since that year, the figures presented in this section can only be taken as an approximation of current situation.

16 *Immigration, bureaucracy and language*

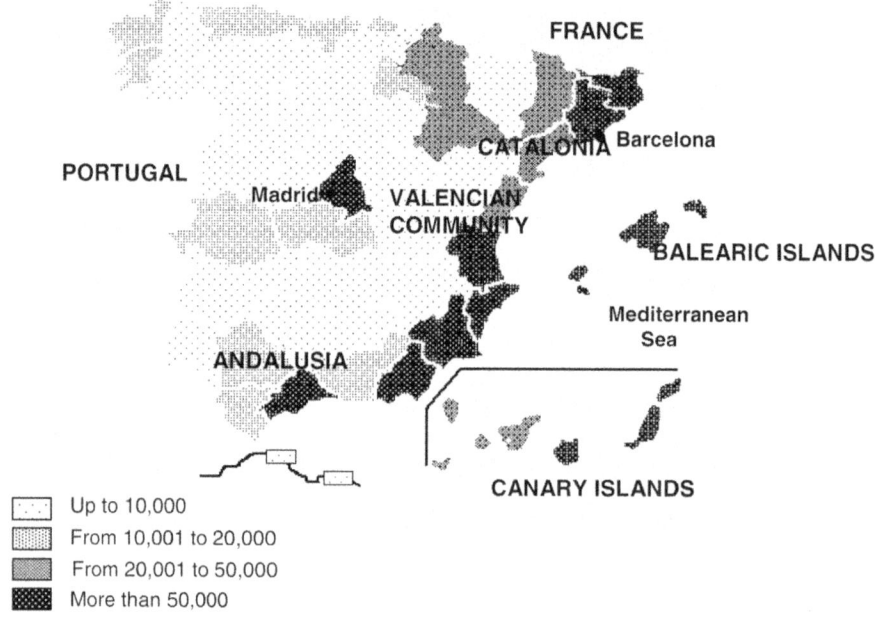

Figure 1. Areas of main concentration of foreigners holding legal residence permits in 2003 (source: Observatorio Permanente de la Inmigración [2004])

5.1.2. Social composition

Some of the characteristics of immigration into Spain are also typical of other southern European countries, such as Italy, Greece or Portugal. One of them is the high percentage of foreign residents without a proper work or residence permit. This is related to the similarities in these countries' economies on a macrostructural level, such as the existence of a loosely regulated labour market. This high percentage of undocumented immigrants has been a constant since the late 1980s. Immigrants' preference for initial periods of illegal residence is a good indicator of the restrictiveness of the immigration laws, and explains why "backdoor" methods are often resorted to.

Another characteristic of immigration to Spain is that it is fairly heterogeneous in terms of geographic origin, with people coming from North Africa, Latin America, Central and Eastern Europe, Asia and sub-Saharan Africa. This seems to be a distinctive feature of current international migrations. The high degree of interconnectedness between different parts of the world has a direct effect on the diverse composition of migrant populations. Another feature to be highlighted is the low proportion of asylum seekers and refugees fleeing conflict, a feature which Spain shares with other southern European countries.

Immigrants to Spain are predominantly young, ranging from 20 to 40 years of age (Pin et al. 2004). They tend to be starters in the migratory chain and are fairly mobile geographically (Arango 2002). The numbers of men and women are quite balanced. However, men tend to concentrate in rural areas, where agriculture is the main economic sector, whereas women are dominant in the Canary Islands and the northeast and northwest, where the predominant types of economic activities (the hotel trade and domestic service) facilitate their access to the labour market.

As far as level of education is concerned, it is fairly high on the whole and only slightly inferior to the Spanish average (Pin et al. 2004). Despite their good educational level, most immigrants take jobs for which they are overqualified. This is mainly due to the characteristics of the Spanish labour market and to immigrants' difficulties in having their educational certifications accepted. Occasionally, lack of competence in Spanish may also pose problems.

The tendency has been for immigrants to concentrate in a few occupational niches, mainly retail businesses, agriculture, construction, the hotel trade and domestic service. However, the current trend is towards diversification. One element that stands out is the high rate of unemployment among immigrants, attested by Díez and Ramírez (2001), in spite of the high demand for workers in certain sectors. This may be due to the lack of proper legal status in some cases, but it may also reflect the lack of flexibility of the job market.

5.2. The legal framework

Having drawn a picture of foreign immigration in Spain in terms of its geographical distribution and social composition, I will now move on to a discussion of the legal context regulating it. The reason is that the interactional data on which this research is centred was gathered at the time of a special legalisation campaign aimed at foreigners who were residing in Spain without proper legal authorisation.

By the late 1990s – some thirteen years after the passage of the first immigration law in 1985 – there was a significant consensus among the political forces in Spain that a broad legal reform was needed. As a result, a new immigration law was passed in December 1999. This law was known as Organic Law 4/2000. The political circumstances leading to its passage were highly controversial. Though the ruling centre-right Popular Party was opposed to it, the opposition managed to cobble together a majority in parliament to get the law passed. This had two important consequences. First, the political consensus with regard to immigration that had existed until then vanished. Secondly, the implementation of the new law was the responsibility of a government that had opposed it.

Organic Law 4/2000 introduced significant changes with regard to the previous law. Its most innovative aspects were its welfare provisions. Access to public health, education and legal aid became universal, even for those without legal documentation. As regards the mechanisms for controlling flows, Organic Law 4/2000 provided for a process of nearly automatic legalisation for those who could prove an uninterrupted two-year residence period in Spain, and for the launching of a one-shot legalisation campaign to take place during the year 2000. The data presented here was collected during that campaign.

5.2.1. Implementation and outcome of the legalisation campaign

The implementation period for the "2000 Legalisation Campaign", as it was referred to in the media, began on 21 March 2000 and ended on 31 July 2000. This was a campaign intended for nationals of countries not belonging to the European Union[4] or the European Economic Area (which included Iceland, Liechtenstein and Norway) who could prove arrival in Spain prior to 1 June 1999 and who had at some point during the three previous years held or applied for a work or residence permit.

The government spent some 16 million euros on the campaign. 150,000 information booklets were published in six different languages, namely Spanish, English, French, Arabic, Chinese and Russian. Application forms were also available in all these languages. A free call-in information service was offered. Calls were answered in Spanish, English and Arabic from 9:00 a.m. to 6:00 p.m. Information and applications were also available on the World Wide Web. Nearly a thousand new employees – including clerical staff, interpreters and technicians – were hired to assist in the campaign.[5]

The number of applications for legalisation dramatically exceeded the government's predictions. The final figure (246,392 applications) more than tripled the initial forecast. The regions where the largest number of applications were submitted were Catalonia in first place, Madrid in second place, and Andalusia in third place.

In relation to acceptance rate of applications, as of 31 December 2000, only 14,042 applications had been successful in Barcelona province, amounting to 27.2% of all applications submitted; 34,982 applications (67.8%) had been rejected. If we compare this percentage to the percentage of rejections on a national level, we observe that it was much higher in the case of Barcelona province – 67.8% for Barcelona vs. 34.4% for Spain as a whole.[6]

The figures released by the government on 31 July 2000 (the end of the application period) are even more illuminating. The way applications were being processed in the province of Barcelona seems to differ greatly from the way they were being handled in other provinces. With approximately the same number of applications submitted, as of 31 July 2000, 78% of applications (37,531) were still pending a final decision in Barcelona, as compared to only 30.4% in Madrid (14,855).[7] In general terms, it seems that the time immigrants were supposed to wait until a final decision was made was longer in Barcelona than elsewhere. Long waiting times together with the specific information practices implemented by officials partly explain the feelings of unrest that can be sensed in many of the interactions analysed in Chapter 4.

As might have been foreseen, the 2000 Legalisation Campaign did not do away with illegal residents. The centre-right government in power even argued that the campaign had had a "magnet effect" by attracting illegal immigrants who had been living in neighbouring countries. During 2001 two more such campaigns were implemented. However, due to the restrictiveness of the new law that came into being in 2001, the number of illegals continued to increase during the 2002–2004 period. The centre-left party which came into power in March 2005 decided to open yet one more legalisation campaign in 2005, but its effectiveness remains to be assessed.

6. Researching a state immigration office

Fieldwork for this research was undertaken between 2000 and 2002. Most of the ethnographic materials, as well as the interactional data examined here, were collected between April and August 2000. The interviews, by contrast, were carried out at a later stage (2001 and 2002).

This study centres around interactions taking place at the information desk of an immigration office in Barcelona. From the point of view of the type of service provided, information, as a verbal service (Ventola 1987), is of particular interest. Information can be given, negotiated, challenged, contested, misunderstood and hidden. An examination of who controlled information, how control was enacted and what the motivations behind it were appealed to me, especially because of the typology of the clients involved and the significance for their life projects of the information demanded. It was an ideal ground for the examination of the use of language as an instrument of social control.

The service I observed was part of a newly created administrative unit in charge of processing all applications for legalisation submitted in the whole Barcelona province within the framework of the legalisation campaign described above. Because of the exceptional nature of that campaign, this administrative unit was not located in the same building as the rest of the immigration services in Barcelona. This in itself represented an obstacle for many applicants, as they were not familiar with this new location.

The unit offered four services, two of which were run and staffed by the immigration department (the registry and the information desk), while the other two were under the responsibility of the police department (the services responsible for taking immigrants' fingerprints and distributing permits). There was, in addition, a small restricted zone, not accessible to the general public, where applications were processed (which I refer to as "the back office").

The door giving access to the general office was guarded by policemen at all times. Inside, access to the different services was regulated by door staff (*ordenanzas*). They were also in charge of handing out numbers when the office opened at 8 o'clock in the morning.

6.1. Negotiating access

Gaining access to the site was difficult, often frustrating and time-consuming, but as the existence of this study demonstrates, not impossible. Immigration is a highly sensitive field to study. In fact, it took me five months of almost full-time persuasion and several rejections to be able to gain access to a bureaucratic site connected with the legalisation of newly arrived immigrants in Spain.

As often happens in research, the opportunity to carry out my fieldwork in the site I investigated came up unexpectedly, while I was negotiating access to another site. The person to whom I was talking (who was in charge of the social welfare offices run by the Catalan regional government) was acquainted with a high-ranking civil servant at the Barcelona immigration services. He volunteered to put me in touch with that person, rang the civil servant immediately (much to my surprise), and arranged an appointment for me to speak to this person. What motivated this promptness is not clear, especially as the first part of our interview had been fairly tense.

My second stroke of luck was the coincidence that the civil servant to whom I was thus referred had previously lectured for a while at the university I was affiliated with. This common ground made him more amenable to allowing me access to the immigration offices. I started out by carrying out ethnographic observations and even audiorecorded service data at several departments within that site, but finally decided to concentrate on one only. I shall provide more details about this later.

Even though I had permission to carry out my research from a high-ranking official, I also had to negotiate access with the managers of individual offices.

Some of them welcomed me, others merely tolerated my presence, and one, who was in charge of the office that handled petitions for asylum and refugee status, refused to allow me to audiorecord talk. As Silverman (2000) highlights, obtaining bottom-up access can turn out to be at least as important (or even more) as obtaining top-down permission. I also attempted to audiorecord in some departments that were run by the police, but they did not allow me to.

It was through observing and listening to service talk in the different departments I visited that I was able to identify the site that would best suit my research purposes. I chose the information desk at the 2000 legalisation office for four reasons: firstly, because of its focus on one bureaucratic procedure only, which allowed me to examine it in close detail; secondly, because of its focus on providing information face-to-face; thirdly, because different languages were employed in service talk; and finally, because most of the staff had just been hired to work on the legalisation campaign. That gave me the opportunity to observe how they became socialised into appropriate modes of institutional conduct.

The manager of the information desk had a positive attitude towards my work. This was facilitated by the fact that the senior official mentioned before had phoned her to ensure my entry would be smooth (it was after my rejection by the asylum office manager). She kindly escorted me to the information desk and introduced me to most of her employees.

6.2. Collecting the data

In my interviews with the senior official, it had become apparent that making videorecordings would not be an option. Therefore, I decided to concentrate on audiorecordings. I told him how I would go about doing it, and what kind of equipment I would use. The only suggestion he made was that I should not ask clients for consent individually because the office was very busy, but that if anyone asked, I should handle any requests for information with extreme care. This was, he said, to prevent possible complaints from clients. Since the institution with which I was affiliated did not require me to obtain informed consent from informants either, it seemed to me that, given the circumstances, my best option was to follow the official's recommendations. I am aware that this may shock some readers, especially those working in North American contexts, where regulations for the protection of human beings in social science research are very strict. I myself found it unfair not to be able to ask undocumented migrants (an already vulnerable population) for consent. For that reason, I made sure that the microphone was always perfectly visible. I placed my recording equipment not

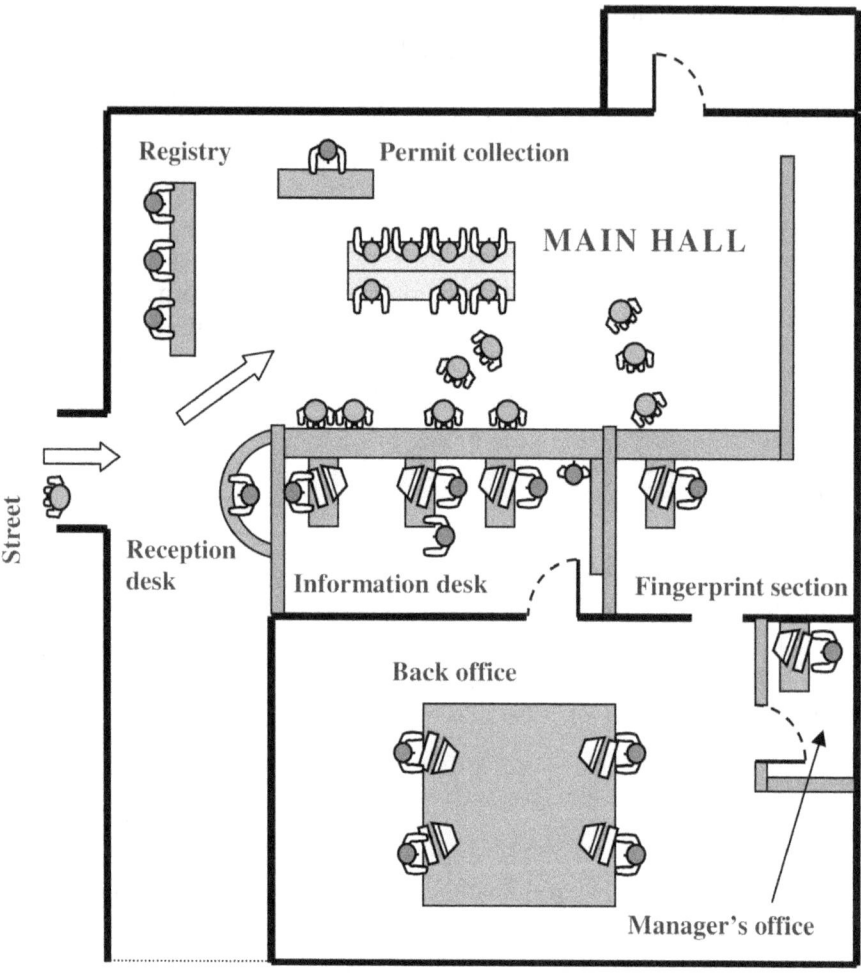

Figure 2. General floor plan of the administrative unit

on the counter (as it gets easily covered by documents and picks up the noise of rustling papers) but rather on the computer that information providers used to locate information on the status of petitions (see Figure 3 below). Recordings can thus be said to have been made in the clients' "knowing presence" (Lamoreux 1988/89). Interestingly, no one ever asked about the recording device. In fact, I think that because I was sitting next to officials making notes, some petitioners took me for some kind of supervisor checking on bureaucrats' work.

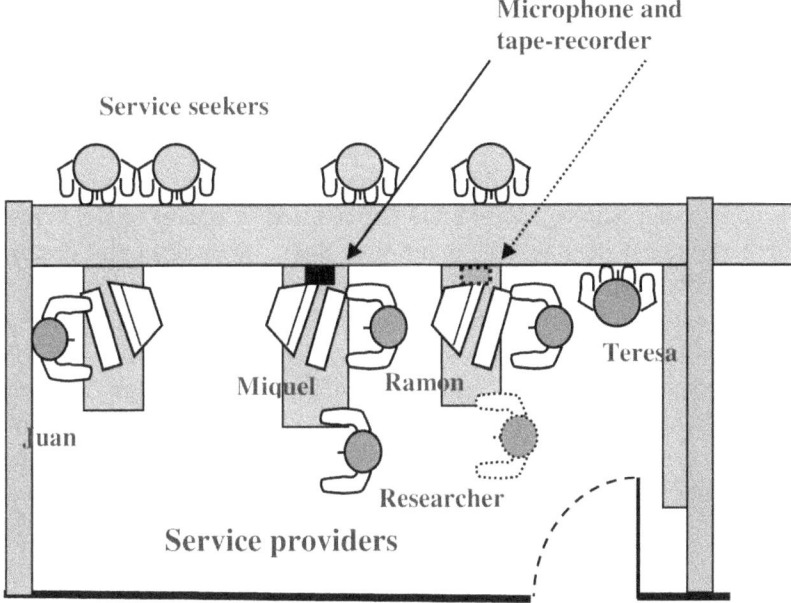

Figure 3. Detailed plan of the information desk service and recording arrangements

Apart from the visibility of the recording machine, I made sure that participants' anonymity was preserved when it came to transcribing what I had recorded. I changed all names, and especially addresses, that could be heard in the recordings so that no one could ever be identified or located.

Officials' attitude towards the recordings was, on the whole, favourable. At the beginning they were curious about what I was doing. Coming from an English department, some of them were concerned that I wanted to assess their expertise in English. I tried to calm these fears by emphasising that I was interested in communication in general, and that I wanted to see how their immigrant clients made themselves understood. That made sense to them, given their poor opinion of clients' language competences, and they soon forgot about their command of English.

Most of the officials found it actually stimulating to have somebody interested in their daily routines and willing to listen to their concerns, opinions, and complaints. They always told me anecdotes, linguistic and otherwise, which had happened in the intervals between my visits. In spite of this, one of the information providers, whom I shall call Juan, did not want to be recorded. He was a solitary person who rarely interacted with his workmates. In fact, he was one of the information providers to whom I was not introduced by the manager on my first visit. I decided not to insist on his participation in the project.

I was always present when interactions were taperecorded. As videorecordings were not possible, information on speakers' nonverbal activities, like gestures, body posture, use of objects, gaze, facial expressions, movements away from the counter and so on, as well as ethnographic details on number of enquirers, age, gender and ethnic group had to be recorded by means of field notes. To make recordings understandable to me later, it was necessary to number encounters and note down a few key words for each so that I could keep track of the beginning and end of conversations. I tried to be an "accepted bystander" or "professional overhearer" (Duranti 1997) at the site. For this purpose, I needed to find an unobtrusive spot, that is, a place which was near enough the events being examined but not so close that interlocutors would feel the need to include me. The best location proved to be a chair next to the official whose interactions with immigrants I was recording. It was a good location, for I had visual access to the information that came out on the computer screen, did not interfere with service talk, and was close enough to participants to overhear their verbal exchange.

My main difficulty was the management of gaze. Gaze, together with bodily posture, is one of the mechanisms whereby social actors display their mutual engagement in focused interaction. This is particularly relevant in service contexts, where eye-to-eye contact is the means employed by service seekers to attract servers' attention. If servers want to protect their territoriality, that is if they do not wish to be addressed by service seekers because they are engaged in some other undertaking, they have to carefully manage gaze and posture. Essentially, this involves refraining from looking up until availability for service is restored.

This is the dynamic that I experienced at the office. My presence behind the counter symbolically defined my status: I was categorised by information seekers as a member of the service team, and as such, likely to be engaged in service dealings. If I looked at information seekers for too long a time, I ran the risk of being addressed. This was something I did not want to happen because it would interfere with seeker–provider communication, distract me from documenting what was going on, and give the impression that I wanted to meddle in the functioning of the institution. I tried to reach a compromise between my need to look at information seekers regularly to be able to record their nonverbal activities in writing and my wish not to become an active participant. However, my condition as "expert" in English induced my active participation in a few exchanges. This happened in cases in which officials experienced difficulties in communicating with information seekers or in translating a specific Spanish word or expression into English. I would either volunteer or be asked for help.

Another effect of my presence was that occasionally, aware of my interest in language use, officials on their own initiative asked information seekers about their language abilities.

The fact that I was sitting next to officials gave me extensive opportunities to chat with them. This was also facilitated by the episodic structure of their service interactions, as most such exchanges required the official to search for information in the computer database. Typically, information providers would enter the number of the information seeker's file into the computer, and wait for the information to appear on the screen. I took advantage of those few seconds to ask for clarifications and make comments on the current or previous enquirer(s). Most of the officials took advantage of my questions to display their professional knowledge.

6.3. Types of data

Although this research considers various types of data, service interactions between petitioners and state officials constitute its backbone. A number of scholars, such as Sarangi and Roberts (1999), have argued for the need to broaden the focus of institutional communication research and go beyond the study of client–server talk, the reason being that service talk does not take place in a social vacuum, but is rather contingent upon a constellation of *backstage* (Goffman 1959) activities and interactions. A decontextualised, technical analysis of the data fails to grasp the complexity of the events examined. In keeping with the above, the frontstage interactional data gathered for this study is supplemented by extensive ethnographic observations made at the information desk and related settings, fieldnotes, backstage comments by officials, and informal and semi-informal interviews with members of both participant groups.

The corpus of service interactions which I have used for this study consists of 20 hours and 18 minutes of audiorecorded material. This is the spoken data which was gathered at the information desk. The whole corpus is, however, larger (60 hours). The 20 hours which I have concentrated on here contain 348 verbal encounters, involving approximately 417 information seekers and five information providers. A total of eight languages are employed, namely Catalan, Spanish, English, French, German, Arabic, Punjabi and Italian. Spanish, English and French are regular languages of communication between information seekers and information providers. Of those three languages, Spanish and English are the most frequently employed. As regards Arabic, only one service exchange unfolds (partially) in this language. In the rest of cases in which Arabic is employed, only single words or phrases are inserted into conversations.

This is also the case with German and Italian, which are used only by clients. Finally, Catalan and Punjabi are not used as languages of interaction between clients and officials. Only one instance of the use of Catalan by an information seeker is documented. As for Punjabi, it is exclusively employed among clients and was not generally picked up by my recordings. A detailed analysis of multilingual practice, language negotiation and language choice will be provided in Chapter 6.

Ethnographic observations also constitute an essential part of this study. Research on interaction in organisational settings requires extensive ethnographic fieldwork, as researchers who are outsiders to the institution know little about institutional practices and organisational conditions. They need to familiarise themselves with the social aspects of talk in order to be able to produce emic analyses of data, that is, analyses which account for participants' own contextual understandings and processes of sense making (Cicourel 1992).

Apart from the information desk I describe here, which was my primary data collection site, I carried out ethnographic observations and did audiorecordings at three other departments connected with the immigration services in Barcelona. I also visited an adult education centre located in the Barcelona inner city which was subsidised by the Spanish government and where Spanish classes for foreigners were taught.

I visited the various immigration departments on a regular basis, that is, at least three times a week, and spent the whole morning and part of the afternoon there. The ethnographic background of this study comprises the valuable contextual information I was able to gather in all of them. My experience in these bureaucratic settings allowed me to get acquainted with key bureaucratic terms, processes and procedures. I also became familiar with the work practices of the institution. Conversations with office staff proved to be a rich source of ethnographic data. In addition, I collected relevant printed material, such as application forms and information leaflets in several languages, supplementary forms such as the *expone* form, which had to be enclosed when supporting documentation was submitted, and in general any form of written communication between the institution and its clients.

My visits to the adult language classes occurred over eight months. I made fieldnotes, audiorecorded eleven sessions, and conversed informally with the students (most of whom were undocumented immigrants). I have not incorporated any of the classroom data into the study I present here, but I have used my regular chats with students as sources of ethnographic information. Our conversations centred basically on topics related to their experiences of living and working in Barcelona and Spain, and on questions connected with language learning, language use and intercultural communication. Because most of them were recent arrivals, they did not meet the requirements to apply for legalisation within the campaign that was taking place at the time. Occasionally, we talked about the campaign, though not in so much detail as with Hussain, whom I shall introduce later.

The third type of data that I have used for this study is "backstage comments". I use this term to refer to talk which is not produced "on stage", that is, not as part of the public activity of serving a client. Backstage comments are usually – but not exclusively – metacomments, that is, evaluative talk about the social interaction. Often, the events that occur during the exchange trigger participants' critical reflections on the institutional determinants of their talk. Backstage comments occur at different times, involve different participation frameworks, and take on different shapes (questions, imperatives, statements and exclamations). They can occur while the service encounter is taking place (during one of the frequent periods of non-speech), or right after it. They can be addressed to me or to a colleague; they can be volunteered or requested. As regards content, they may contain the official's interpretation of what is going on, comments on the information seeker's interactional or linguistic behaviour, official's accounts of his/her own communicative practices, and metalinguistic or metapragmatic comments. Since these comments took place interspersed throughout service talk, they were normally picked up by the taperecorder. Below is an instance of what I have referred to as backstage comments. Speakers MIQ, RAM and TER are office staff and RES is the researcher.

(1)

1	*MIQ:	no se han casado porque tiene que estar no sé cuánto tiempo sin
2		trabajar i *ara com està si no té papers ni res*!
	%tra:	they haven't got married because she is not allowed to work for I don't know how long but what about now she doesn't have legal documentation or anything!
3	*RES:	*ara deu estar treballant sense papers.*
	%tra:	well now she must be working without proper documentation.
4	*MIQ:	*pues per estar treballant sense papers es podrien casar*
5		*perfectament*!
	%tra:	in that case if she is working illegally they might as well get married!

In (1) above, Miquel questions the statement by the service seeker (who is Spanish) according to which he and his girlfriend (who is Polish) have not got married because she must wait for several months before she can work legally in Spain. It is interesting that Miquel uses Spanish to quote the man's words and then switches to Catalan to comment critically on them. In this case, backstage comments occur after the interaction has been completed and are addressed to me (RES).

Apart from the three sources of data mentioned, I also used the interview as a research technique to get to know participants' representations, values and attitudes. Admittedly, one of the limitations of this study is that the formal interview data available is rather restricted. That does not mean I did not casually converse with members of both speaker groups regularly, as I have noted above. However, it is true that the data I gathered contains, in general, more information on the perspective of bureaucrats than on the point of view of immigrant clients.

The formal interview data that I have (that is, aside from bureaucrats' abundant backstage comments and my ethnographic notes on migrants' opinions collected at the language centre), consists of two long interviews (one with a member of information desk staff and another with an immigrant client) and one short group group interview with three other migrants.

The staff member I interviewed was Miquel, the government official involved in the largest number of interactions analysed in this book. I interviewed him in 2001. The other long interview was with Hussain. After having lived illegally in Spain for two years, his status had been legalised in 2000 within the framework of the exceptional legalisation campaign described here. I interviewed him in 2002. The group interview was short (20 min), and in it I talked to three Pakistani students from the language centre. They had all recently arrived in Barcelona from Italy. They were in their mid-twenties and had university qualifications. This interview was gathered in 2000.

The three interviews were ethnographic in nature and therefore fairly unstructured. In the cases of Miquel and Hussain, I followed a previously prepared list of questions but allowed for – and whenever I considered fit, encouraged – digressions from the topics. The group interview was more spontaneous, as I had not anticipated being able to do it.

The major difference between the two long interviews is that one of them was audiorecorded whereas the other was not. Miquel explicitly requested that I not do so. As he also seemed reluctant to be interviewed in a formal way, I decided to turn our interview into a rather informal chat. This meant that, after our meeting, I had to hurriedly make notes of everything I could recall. During our conversation, I asked him about issues related to the distribution and organisation of work at the office, information providers' habitual language practices and his relationship with fellow workmates. In addition, I was interested in the reasons behind certain managerial decisions, such as the change in the institution's policy for providing information, and in the perceptions he had of the experience of communicating with individuals from different linguistic backgrounds. Our conversation unfolded in Catalan, as this was the language we regularly conversed in.

My interview with Hussain lasted for approximately 60 minutes. It was held in Spanish (the language we habitually employed) and took place at my home. The reasons were, on the one hand, that I needed a quiet environment for the recording, and on the other, that I wanted to give the impression that "I did not have anything to hide" (García Jorba 2000). On the whole, it was a relaxed event.

Hussain comes from a middle-class family in Lahore, where he attended primary and secondary school. Spain was his third choice after having tried to settle in Holland and Germany. He arrived by plane and entered the country on a "business visa", as he reported in the interview. The main topics discussed were Hussain's migratory experience, the situation of his family in Pakistan, his reasons for emigrating, his choice of Barcelona and Spain, his linguistic difficulties, his experiences at the immigration office, his view of bureaucrats' information-providing practices and his plans for the future.

6.4. The participants

The people that were involved in the service talk examined for this research can be broadly divided into two groups. On the one hand, there are the clients of the service. These are usually unregistered immigrants seeking to become legal residents. Their goal is to obtain either general information about the legalisation process as prescribed during the period of the campaign, or specific information on the progress of their applications. They will be referred to as "information/service seekers", "enquirers" or "clients". Some Spanish nationals also belong to this group, most notably solicitors and paralegal agents requiring information on behalf of their clients, or simply Spaniards accompanying a foreign acquaintance.

The other participant group is made up of local office staff whose task is to deal with immigrants' requests for information. Because of their official role as providers of information, they are often referred to as "information providers". Although in some interactions, a few other participants intervene (the researcher and a member of door staff, for example), this is the basic participant structure. Information providers are also referred to as "bureaucrats" and "officials".

A total of 417 immigrant clients were involved in the interactions recorded at the information desk. The majority came from countries not belonging to the European Union or the European Economic Area. Information on place of origin was mainly obtained through the researcher's visual access to the computer screen. This is because when clients demanded information on the status of their applications, officials called up their electronic files, and among the details that became available was information on their nationality.

The two largest groups of information seekers were, by far, North Africans (39.8%) and South Asians (31.9%). Latin Americans came in third place, but they formed a significantly smaller group (only 6.9% of the total number of enquirers). The fourth largest group was made up of Spanish nationals (6.7%), followed by East Asians (5.8%) and Africans from sub-Saharan countries (3.1%). The smallest group was that of citizens coming from the former Soviet Union and Eastern European countries (1.5%). The origin was unknown for 4.3% of information seekers.

As regards the distribution of clients by gender, the overwhelming majority (85.1%) were men. Interestingly, there were no female information seekers among the South Asian and sub-Saharan communities. Women outnumbered men only among Latin Americans (that is, if we only take into account foreign information seekers and exclude Spaniards).

With respect to the other participant group, that is, state bureaucrats, the information desk was regularly staffed by four officials, namely Juan, Miquel, Ramon and Teresa, with Teresa the only woman. Miquel and Ramon were in their late twenties or early thirties and each held a university degree in the Humanities. Juan and Teresa were somewhat older, in their late forties. As far as I could gather, neither of them had a university degree. The head of the information service was a female civil servant in her late thirties. I did not have the chance to meet up with her during fieldwork, as she was on sick leave. Apart from these four bureaucrats, two more from a different office are mentioned in one of the transcripts (extract [75] in Chapter 6). They are Rosa (ROS) and Loli (LOL).

In relation to employment conditions, all information providers were employed on a twelve-month contract basis. This was the case with most of the other employees, too, although a few of them even had even shorter six-month contracts.

As for their work obligations, the main tasks of these front-line bureaucrats were either to check the status of immigrants' applications or to take in supplementary certificates for files. The back office was in charge of processing paperwork. Miquel, Ramon and Juan were responsible for providing information. Each of them had access to a computer terminal to find out details about immigrants' applications. Teresa, by contrast, had no access to a terminal, as her main task consisted in receiving new documents for files. Teresa was assisted in this task by Ramon, who took over whenever she was absent. Unlike the other officials, Teresa moved around considerably. In fact, she often had to go to the restricted area to consult with the officials in charge of processing applications.

For these reasons, Teresa's interactions with clients – and often also Ramon's – were extremely difficult to taperecord.

It is worth mentioning that competence in foreign languages was not a requirement for government officials. However, most of the institutional representatives that feature in this study actually had some knowledge of at least one foreign language. Both Ramon and Teresa were quite reluctant to use any languages other than Spanish or Catalan in service communication. Both had a poor command of English, with competence limited to producing a few lexical items and short phrases. Their interactions (especially Teresa's) in that language were therefore infrequent and minimal. Apart from English, both of them could speak French. Whereas Ramon's competence was largely passive, Teresa was remarkably fluent with a native-like accent. This was because, as I found out, she had resided in France for a period of her life.

With regard to the linguistic abilities of Miquel and Juan – who had officially been employed as interpreters for the service but in fact worked as information providers – they were specialists in Arabic and Russian respectively. Apart from these languages, both of them had a working knowledge of English. In other words, though they were able to get their messages across, neither of them was really proficient in it. Miquel could also speak some French.

6.5. Data transcription and analysis

For the purposes of this study, 82 service exchanges were transcribed in full detail using a slightly adapted version of the LIDES transcription system (LIPPS Group 2000). These particular encounters were chosen either because of their multilingual nature or because they contained phenomena relevant to the process of information provision, such as long sequences during which meaning was negotiated. I also transcribed the interviews with Hussain and the three students at the language centre in their entirety, and attempted to reconstruct my conversation with Miquel, the official. From the detailed transcripts and my listening to the recordings time and again, I was able to produce a comprehensive classification of different interactional phenomena. These two elements served as the basis for my analysis.

The process of analysis was fairly circular in that I repeatedly moved from data to theory and vice versa. The most difficult task was identifying which elements I wanted to focus on from among the multiplicity of interesting aspects. Once I had identified broad themes, I scanned all the interactions transcribed, as well as my classification of phenomena. After that, I listened to all the tapes again, searching for non-transcribed material which might be relevant. New interesting interactions were often identified. Finally, I read through my ethnographic notes to search for further pertinent details on the themes identified.

7. Making sense of the data

In this section I present the theoretical tools I use to make sense of the language practices observed at the research site. My theoretical framework is, unavoidably, heterogeneous and interdisciplinary. Indeed, it incorporates and articulates concepts from contemporary critical social theory without losing sight of the important contributions made by the traditions of analysis of talk to the understanding of situated social interaction.

The reason why I use such a heterogeneous framework is that this is an "integrative" piece of research (Sarangi and Roberts 1999). It is integrative because it seeks to embed the understanding of the linguistic data examined in detail within a broader understanding of the policies and practices of the institution investigated; but it is also integrative because it tries to comprehend the sociopolitical import of situated linguistic practice, that is, the ways in which what we call social life gets shaped through the multiplicity of concrete encounters in which individuals engage. Such an undertaking requires drawing on sociological models to understand the macropicture of social life, while at the same time, resorting to theories of interaction to comprehend the intricacies of face-to-face talk.

7.1. Situated talk and the shaping of society

In this study I have drawn on different sociological models, most notably the work of Giddens (1979, 1984), Bourdieu (1977, 1991), and Foucault (1977, 1984; Gordon 1980; Fraser 1989; Rabinow and Rose 2003). I have taken concepts piecemeal from all three frameworks rather than restricting myself to any one because they each place emphasis on different aspects of the relationship between individual action, language use and societal structures. This allows me to explain the theoretical connections I try to establish in this book more fully. In what follows, I have made an effort to establish points of contact between the three models and to integrate concepts in a coherent fashion. The goal I have pursued is to come to an understanding of the deeper significance of situated social encounters, and in this endeavour, I have been aided by the notions of *structuration, agency, power, resources, habitus* and *field*, which have functioned as the magnifying lenses that have enabled me to visualise the processes by which of the fabric of our social life is configured.

I have drawn on both Giddens and Bourdieu because they share a common goal, that is, to go beyond the action-structure dichotomy and to try to integrate the individual and the societal within one single paradigm. The concepts posited by these authors have been useful to understand the ways in which the verbal encounters at the immigration office are not just instances of situated interactions between individual speakers, but the raw material out of which societies are constituted and organised. At an immigration office this is particularly clear because what is at stake is the granting of a work permit that gives access to crucial socioeconomic resources. This access (or lack of it) will define immigrants' lives in key ways and will determine their position in the social arena. Both Giddens and Bourdieu defend the view that individual actions shape the social world, but whereas Bourdieu emphasises the importance of structure in social processes, Giddens' theories underscore the local and situated nature of social life.

The most central notion in this book is Giddens' concept of *structuration*. It is so crucial because it serves to explain the relationship between situated actions and social structures. For Giddens, social structures do not exist. They are instantiated, that is, they come into being, in situated social practice. This is what renders situated events important. For instance, the power differential existing between two social groups becomes real and has specific effects on the lives of individuals every time the members of those groups interact. It is in these encounters, and the way they are conducted, that the unequal organisation of social life becomes visible. But how are social structures created? For Giddens, they are the result of processes of structuration that take place in individual encounters. Thus, the inequalities that shape our societies and, more specifically, the disadvantaged social position of certain actors are the actual outcome of processes of marginalisation and exclusion that take place in situated events, like job selection interviews, or in this case, information encounters at an immigration office.

Language plays a fundamental role in processes of structuration, as social activities are to a large extent constituted in language. This is evident at the immigration office, where information is transmitted verbally. Yet language is also important in another way: it is important because it is in and through linguistic usage that particular unequal representations of the social world, like relations of domination and subordination, are sustained and reproduced, or may be changed.

One of Giddens' most insightful claims is that structures are not only constraining, but also enabling. Structures give individuals the tools to carry out the practical activities of their daily lives, that is, it is by drawing on structures – like relationships of domination – that social actors get an idea of how to behave in specific social contexts. In addition, structures render speakers' actions intelligible, that is, they are the background against which it is possible to make sense of individuals' actions. Thus, Giddens depicts the relationship between daily life and social structures as dialogic. One cannot exist independently of the other. To act in situated social events, social actors draw on structures, and structures exist only insofar as they are reproduced in situated social events. Whether social actors reproduce structures intentionally or not is another matter, which we will address shortly.

Giddens' notion of structuration is intimately related to that of *social practice*, as structures are said to exist only in situated events. For him, the study of social life is the study of social practices ordered across space and time. It is in social practices that the relationship between actors and social structures gets articulated. A social practice is a habitual way of doing things. This idea is closely connected with Giddens' conceptualisation of social life as *routine*. I find the notion of routine, and its role in social reproduction, of particular interest for the institutional context I have analysed, where a great deal of what happens is defined by the routinised character of bureaucratic practice.

Giddens' notion of routine serves to explain the individual's role in social reproduction. According to him, the routinised, repetitive character of social endeavours is a necessary psychological mechanism to inspire a sense of "ontological security" in social actors' understanding of what they do. At the same time, routinised practices are the mechanisms of reproduction and continuity of social life. Thus, routine is not accidental; it is not something that happens, but something that is made to happen, albeit unintentionally. This links up with another fundamental notion in the study of socially reproductive processes, which is *agency*. I draw on Giddens' notion of agency to explain the role of bureaucrats in the recreation of relationships of social domination and subordination, and the ways in which they exercise power and social control.

For Giddens, agency is not related to considerations of intentionality. An agent is the "perpetrator" of an activity, independent of whether or not s/he is aware of the consequences of his/her actions. The implication of human agency in the continuity of social life does not mean that social actors set out to create social systems intentionally. Their agency role resides in their ability to reproduce social systems through their routine participation in social events.

Linked to this idea of unintentional social reproduction is the notion of power. Unintentionally, social actors may wield power. For Giddens, power is intimately bound up with the idea of agency. He understands power as a transformative capacity. In other words, it is the ability to get things done, to achieve outcomes, and as we shall see in Chapter 3, to create realities and truths. Yet power is not necessarily related to intentionality. A social actor, as we shall see in the analysis of the data, can wield power without consciously intending to do so. It is in its ability to bring about changes that power is conceptualised as enabling. In that sense, Gidden's notion of power relates closely to Foucault's. Foucault argues that modern power is "productive" rather than "prohibitive". Power produces reality; it creates groups and boundaries; it defines "domains of truth" and forms of knowledge. This understanding of power is crucial to grasp the ways in which control is exerted at an office whose main function is the supply of information, that is, the transmission of insider institutional knowledge about the administrative procedure regulating access to citizenship.

A fundamental idea from Foucault's understanding of power, and one that I find extremely appropriate for the context researched, is its web-like character. Foucault claims that it is misleading to think of power as the prerogative of certain social groups. It is more appropriate, as we shall see, to conceptualise power in terms of a complex network of relations of domination defined by specific local interests. Foucault claims that everybody is in a position to simultaneously exert and endure power, and this is certainly the case of the institutional representatives at the immigration office. They have to abide by institutional regulations that prescribe what they can or cannot do, so they endure power, and at the same time, they exert power by, among other ways, regulating clients' participation in the shaping of service communication and by devaluing the particular language varieties they speak.

Human beings are described by Foucault as "vehicles of power". Thus, researchers have to pay attention to the full complexities of power in the settings they investigate. Linked to the conception of power as a web of interests is the notion of the practical character of power. Foucault claims that power should not be understood as something that exists in a vacuum and can therefore be given or exchanged, but as something that is exercised. Power exists in action (Gordon 1980); it is "anchored" in the micropractices of everyday life. In that respect, Foucault argues for the need to examine the visible side of power, that is, its mechanics and effects, rather than its internal, invisible side, that is, individuals' motivations for exerting power. In keeping with Foucault's ideas, the microanalysis of talk in interaction that I undertake in this book will shed light on the many-sided strategies whereby power is exercised by the institution and the individual bureaucrats representing it.

Both Giddens and Bourdieu relate power in interaction to the ability to mobilise appropriate resources, like information, the appropriate language variety, jargon or interactional behaviour. The notion of *resources* as used here comes from Bourdieu's theory of practice (1977, 1985, 1991). Resources are fundamental social structuring devices in that they are unequally distributed among social actors. The consequence of the unequal distribution of resources is that not all social actors have the same opportunities for action, as they do not have equal access to appropriate resources. The production, distribution and access to valuable resources is strictly controlled, and so is the possibility of attaching value to them. This is usually the prerogative of socially dominant groups. As we shall see, controlling people's access to resources, like information, or at a broader level, legal residency, is a key way of exercising social and political control. In this book we shall focus on the regulation of access to key resources as a way of controlling people's opportunities for action, but also on the struggle over the value attached to specific linguistic resources.

Although social activities are situated in time and space and locally constructed, the resources employed in their construction are not local in origin but social; their acquisition depends, largely, on an individual's position in the social arena. Resources are socially ranked, so that differences among them are turned into elements of social distinction; social distinction creates boundaries and articulates processes of exclusion. Differences in resources are thus differences in power (Chouliaraki and Fairclough 1999).

The arenas where the value of resources is decided are what Bourdieu calls *fields of action* or markets. Fields are social spaces articulated by networks of social positions which are defined by particular distributions of resources. In the bureaucratic arena, for instance, state representatives have the upper hand because they have access to important forms of capital like insider information about administrative procedures and knowledge of the bureaucratic code. Yet, at the same time, fields are sites of struggle in which, as we have mentioned, social actors try to maintain or alter the distribution of capital, or fight over the value attached to different forms of capital, such as linguistic capital. We shall see the ways in which this happens when immigrant clients and local bureaucrats interact and what the outcomes of these struggles are. The notion of struggle is fundamental to come to an understanding of the dynamics of social processes. Actors' chances of success depend on their particular position within a given social field. Yet their resistance also has a symbolic dimension in that what is at stake is agents' ability to intervene in the definition of the social world and their position within it.

Bourdieu also claims that actors participating in a social field show specific *habituses*, that is, routinised ways of acting and perceiving. The habitus is the concept that he uses to explain how the social weaves its way into individual, local practice. The habitus is a set of dispositions acquired through socialisation into specific modes of behaviour and participation in social fields; what is important is that the habitus is a largely unconscious and unreflexive practical sense. In this respect, it is similar to Giddens' notion of routine, which guides individuals in their everyday-life endeavours, gives them "ontological security", and of which they are largely unaware. Because of its unreflexive character, the habitus is a key element in the reproduction of unequal modes of social organisation and of relationships of domination and subordination.

7.2. The analysis of face-to-face verbal interaction

I suggested earlier that talk is an instrument of both continuity and change. The social order is reproduced in local interactional practice, but it may also be contested. Whether participants' contributions in an exchange will work to sustain or challenge existing social practices can, to a certain extent, be predicted on the basis of their position in the social space. These predictions, however, may not be borne out in actual practice. This is because social interaction has its own rules, modes of conduct and organisation. In this sense, the postulation by Goffman of the interaction order as "a domain of study in its own right" (1983) is one of the most noteworthy contributions to the understanding of the complex relationship between language and the social world. Goffman tries to counter the argument that macrostructural variables such as social class, age or gender shape the interactional domain in a deterministic way by positing the "relatively autonomous nature of the interaction order". He postulates a "loose coupling" of the interactional realm with macrolevel social processes. The way in which structural arrangements bear upon verbal exchanges is described as "a membrane selecting how various externally relevant social distinctions will be managed within the interaction" (1983: 11). The loose coupling that he advocates enables him to account for the possibility of social change occurring.

Along similar lines, Erickson (2001: 175) claims that, while issues of power and ideology from the wider societal order may permeate a social encounter, participants will work at sustaining a "moral order indigenous to the encounter itself", in which issues of ritual and face play a prominent role. This is because interactions are multidimensional and social situations are never fully determined.

It seems clear, then, that sociolinguistics, because of its emphasis on the fine-grained analysis of interactional data, plays an important role in the study of social life and can contribute important insights to sociologists' understandings of it.

In this book, the methodological and theoretical tools that I have used for the analysis of situated talk are drawn from Conversation Analysis (henceforth CA) (Sacks et al. 1974; Schegloff et al. 1977; Atkinson and Heritage 1984; Boden and Zimmerman 1991; Drew and Heritage 1992; Hutchby and Wooffitt 1998; and ten Have 1998, among others), the dynamic conceptualisation of context posited by Gumperz (1982a, 1992a, 1992b) and later developed by Auer and di Luzio (1992) and Duranti and Goodwin (1992), and Goffman's microsociology (in particular his 1959 and 1983 works).

As I pointed out above, this study draws on a number of concepts and methodological procedures developed by CA. In what follows, I shall present the most important ones. All these notions shape the way I understand and investigate social interaction and they inform my analyses at all points, even if I do not always refer explicitly to them.

It is important to mention here that my approach differs from CA in one significant aspect, namely in the relationship between talk and social life. Because of the principle of *procedural consequentiality* (Schegloff 1991), within CA the influence of the social in talk has to be demonstrated in the actual features of the interaction. If it cannot be shown, it cannot be posited. Thus, the ways in which language mediates processes of inequality and exclusion are therefore not tackled by CA researchers. CA analyses concentrate on the ways in which interactions are organised, and on how specific organisations enable the accomplishment of social activities. What is never addressed is why certain social actors end up with more opportunities for action than others. CA-based studies, like a great deal of research in pragmatics, adopt an egalitarian stance in relation to language use (Fairclough 1989). Even when institutional discourse is examined, CA research falls short of providing an ideological critique of language use in key institutional sites.

Although in this study I do not align myself with the CA perspective on social life, I draw upon CA principles of interactional organisation to explain talk in local sequential contexts. One of the fundamental ideas is that language is a mode of social action. In other words, researchers are not interested in the purely formal features of talk, but in what talk is used to "do" in the social world. Another fundamental idea is that interaction is jointly constructed by speakers because following turns build on previously produced talk. Likewise, meaning is not the sole responsibility of an individual participant; meanings are coconstructed and emergent in the unfolding of interactional events.

CA also posits that talk is situated within a specific interactional context defined in terms of the kind of communicative event being accomplished by participants and within a specific sequential context. Within CA, a turn at talk is always uttered and interpreted in relation to previous talk, and that turn shapes a new context of action for ensuing talk. Put in other words, social actions are simultaneously context-shaped and context-renewing (Heritage 1984). The interactive nature of context came into sharp focus through the work of John

Gumperz and his associates (Gumperz 1982a; Auer and di Luzio 1992) and was later developed by Duranti and Goodwin (1992). Contextualisation is the process whereby any "brought along" element of the contextual background, be it social, cultural, material or situational, is "brought about" by participants in the course of an interactional event. Speakers' productions are intended to be understood against the background of this new brought about contextual framework.

Context is dynamic and in constant change rather than a static set of elements established before the social interaction begins. The context is not something that exists outside the interaction, but rather its creation is internal to the talk, in the minute-to-minute unfolding of interactional events. The notion of contextualisation enables researchers to dispense with the thorny question of how much context is relevant for linguistic analysis, because contextual relevancies are made available in the text itself by participants at talk. Following Duranti and Goodwin, I also understand the relationship between talk and context as mutually reflexive. The linguistic and nonlinguistic elements of communicative events shape each other in a dialogical manner. Talk is defined by the social context in which it occurs, but it also defines that context in crucial ways. Contextualisation as central to the process of meaning creation is dialogical (Blommaert 2005) in that it always involves the active participation of more than one speaker.

Participants' access to context is not unproblematic, however, because it is defined by issues of power and inequality. Gumperz (1982a) and others (Roberts and Sayers 1987; Gumperz and Roberts 1991; Sarangi 1996) demonstrated how conversational inference often relies on rather small features of talk whose meaning is socioculturally determined and access to which is contingent upon intensive engagement within particular kinds of social networks. This means that possibilities of access to both valuable indexical resources and the places where those resources acquire value are unequally distributed in society. The understanding of language as an unequally distributed indexical resource allows interesting insights into the investigation of the connections between talk and processes of social stratification. Building upon the interactional sociolinguistics tradition, authors like Blommaert (2001), Heller (1999, 2001a) and Maryns (Maryns 2005, 2006; Maryns and Blommaert 2002; Maryns and Blommaert 2005) use the notions of multilingual talk, contextualisation and categorisation to unveil the ways in which social inequality gets constructed and reproduced around issues related to the mobilisation of appropriate forms of talk and the definition of what counts as appropriate language in a given social context.

The last piece that completes my theoretical and methodological jigsaw is Erving Goffman. In *The presentation of self in everyday life* (1959), Goffman draws on a number of theatrical metaphors to describe and account for the various ways in which individuals behave in social establishments. I found Goffman's metaphors particularly useful to describe and establish relationships between the different social roles in the office and the variety of modes of behaving and linguistic practices that I observed.

Goffman (1959: 106) divides public establishments into two basic regions, namely *frontstage* and *backstage*. Regions are spaces bounded by "barriers to perception". These two regions comprise the whole range of activities that take place in social establishments. The front region is the space where the "performance" is given, where the "show" is staged. The back region is the place where the "performer" can relax and step out of character.

The backstage is not necessarily a physical space. As Goffman points out, any space can be transformed into a backstage region by invoking a backstage style. This style is characterised by, among other things, sloppy sitting, use of non-standard speech, playful aggressiveness, and such like. Another feature of backstage behaviour is that performers tend to ridicule, caricature and criticise their audiences. These derogatory practices may serve to create a bond of solidarity among actors to make up for frontstage situations in which the demands of the audience may force actors to show disregard for one another.

Goffman's distinction is helpful to understand how different forms of talk invoke or even create different social spaces with their corresponding sets of rights and obligations. What is interesting is that speakers may step in and out of these different spaces in the course of one single interaction. It is thus essential to note and analyse these changes of *footing* (Goffman 1981) in order to understand the function and import of speakers' linguistic productions.

In my data, the frontstage corresponds to those verbal productions that are directly linked to the service being requested and provided, and in which speakers take on the social roles associated with it (i.e. client and server). The notion of "backstage talk", in turn, encompasses all verbal material which does not have to do with the provision of the service, and in which different types of participation frameworks and speaker constellations are possible.

The process of fieldwork and my sitting behind the counter while recordings were being made gave me extensive access and even prompted service providers' backstage interactions and comments.

These backstage comments contain their perceptions of the client group, their ideological positionings with respect to the political and social aspects of immigration, and their views on modes of institutional practice. Crucially, they also give us information on the tensions existing in the office and on how each institutional actor tries to cope with them. Without access to the backstage, we would not be able to comprehend the reasons behind certain interactional practices and would have no way of elucidating the extent to which the backstage permeates the frontstage. This division into regions and their associated forms of talk and roles allows us to observe in detail the hybrid nature of frontstage talk, and the multiple positions of speaking and voices that get actualised in the course of service interactions.

Having discussed the main notions that inform my understanding of the nature of face-to-face verbal communication and of its relationship to social structures, I shall now move on to a description of the way in which this book is organised.

8. How this book is organised

This book is organised into three parts. Part I (Chapters 1 and 2) is essentially introductory. Chapter 1 situates the study thematically, theoretically and methodologically, introduces the research site and the social actors involved, and sketches out the processes of fieldwork, data collection, transcription and analysis. Chapter 2 describes in detail both the bureaucratic procedure that regulated the processing of paperwork and the interactional data gathered with a view to facilitating comprehension of the ensuing chapters.

Part II (Chapters 3 and 4) focuses on describing the process of information exchange, how it unfolded and the ways in which language was used to serve specific institutional purposes. Chapter 3 examines the ways in which information was presented and represented to clients. It centres on officials' practices of simplification and reformulation, and on the unintended consequences they had. An important part of the chapter is devoted to the analysis of a key decision made by the institution in connection with its information policy. This institutional decision put a strain on relationships among members of staff and on client–official communication. Whereas Chapter 3 deals with officials' linguistic practices and routines in a fairly decontextualised fashion, Chapter 4 examines in detail longer excerpts of data. It presents the strategies that the two participant groups deployed to accomplish their social and discursive objectives, and with what effects.

Part III (Chapters 5 and 6) centres on the theme of social control and the ways in which it was exerted in and through discursive practice. In Chapter 5 we shall see how, at this immigration office, the exercise of control became bound up with the regulation of social and physical spaces, and the definition of what counted as appropriate behaviour. Chapter 6 examines the issue of control from the perspective of multilingualism. It examines the office's regulated sociolinguistic regime, that is, how the use and value of the different languages and language varieties at play was strictly controlled by the office staff.

In the conclusion, the main analytical threads of Parts II and III are taken up. I wrap up the main arguments presented throughout the book in the light of the research questions formulated in Chapter 1. In particular, I examine the higher-level implications of the discursive phenomena depicted in terms of how they are linked to processes of exclusion and social stratification. I also focus on how the gatekeeping practices and ideologies of the officials researched and those of the bureaucracy they worked for served to enact the regulatory function of the state. Finally, I discuss the complex relationship between individual agency and institutional processes and how they fed into one another in imposing uniformity and exercising social control at the site examined.

Chapter 2
Service activities and bureaucratic procedure

1. Introduction

It is not possible to comprehend the talk exchanged at the information desk of a bureaucratic agency without having a clear understanding of the bureaucratic procedure set in place by the institution to process paperwork. This is because the defining feature of bureaucratic organisations is that individual citizens are reconceptualised into bureaucratic cases to which rational decision-making procedures are applied (Weber 1947, 1948).

A great deal of what goes on in front-line institutional encounters has to do bureaucrats' mediating between the real-life worlds of lay clients on the one hand and institutional procedures and practices on the other. A key theme that emerges in connection with this, and one which I explore in detail in Chapter 4, is, therefore, how the bureaucrats at this office understood and managed their roles, with the many contradictions and tensions inherent in them, and how they related to the specific bureaucratic procedure organised by the institution. However, it is impossible to gain a contextual understanding of front-line communication without having a clear idea of how petitions were processed in the back office.

In this chapter I present a detailed description of both the bureaucratic procedure and service talk. In the first part I focus on the administrative procedure, with detailed references to institutional labels, bureaucratic stages, actors and activities. I explain what happened to applications from the moment they were entered in the official registry until a residence permit was granted or denied; when and where decisions on entitlement were made and by whom; and what opportunities clients had for intervening in the decision-making process. I also briefly discuss the main requirements clients were asked to fulfil in order to be entitled to legal status. In the second part I present the main organisational features of the verbal interactions studied. I focus on how interactions were organised and the ways in which different activities were related to the accomplishment of actors' social goals.

2. The administrative procedure

2.1. Applying for legal status: Documents and requirements

The 2000 Legalisation Campaign began in March with the dissemination of information. The dissemination process was not on a very large scale: 15x13 cm advertisements were placed in newspapers with information on where to submit applications and a free phone number from which more details on the procedure could be obtained. There were also some articles on the campaign in newspapers the day it started and the topic featured in the Spanish and Catalan news media. Fifteen-page booklets and also shorter leaflets were published in Spanish, Arabic, Chinese, Russian, English and French. They contained general information on eligibility, requirements, documentation, submission offices and types of permits. I am not aware of how widely distributed they were, though four months into the campaign there were still piles of booklets lying around the office where I conducted my research.

All petitioners were required to fill in and sign an official form which had to be accompanied by three photocopies. These forms were available in the same six languages as the explanatory booklets. The forms that were in languages other than Spanish were bilingual, that is, they were in Arabic and Spanish, Chinese and Spanish, and so on, and could only be filled in "in Spanish" (sic). Immigrants were also asked to provide a photocopy of their passport, travel document or registration card, together with documents proving that their arrival in Spain had occurred prior to 1 June 1999, as this was one of the two requirements for eligibility. The other one was to have applied for a work permit in Spain before 31 March 2000.[8] Proof of previous work permit applications had to be submitted with the new one.

Petitioners were allowed to submit their applications at a variety of public offices. The main requirement was that the office in question had an official registry, where the submission of documents could be formally recorded. At such offices, the civil servant serving as registrar stamps a copy of whatever letter, official request or application is filed. This stamped copy works as a *resguardo* 'counterfoil slip' to prove submission. In their dealings with public administrations, Spanish citizens are always advised to keep a stamped copy of all documents presented. By means of this stamped copy, members of the public are safeguarded against documentary losses, as the public institution is legally responsible for all official submissions.

In the case of the legalisation campaign examined here, retention of this stamped copy was particularly essential because immigrants were asked to furnish it every time they wished to enquire about the status of their petitions. The information booklet published by the Spanish immigration service gave very specific indications as to this:

If presenting the application at the Registry of an Administrative Unit:
To request a **duly stamped copy** of the application showing the date, which will be valid as a counterfoil proof of presentation. (bold in the English original, Administración General del Estado 2000: 8)

2.2. Processing petitions: Stages and actors

The description of the bureaucratic procedure I provide in this section is based on the information I gathered during fieldwork, as the booklets published by the government provided no details on the administrative procedure or the way decision making was organised.

Three months was the minimum amount of time immigrants had to wait before a final decision on their applications was reached. In fact, successful applications were finalised at the end of three months. Unsuccessful applicants had to wait a minimum of six months before the authorities notified them that their applications had been turned down.

The first step after the reception of a petition was the creation of a new *expediente* 'file'. Files were created physically, that is by means of folders where documents were kept, and also electronically, with a new entry in the institution's computerised database. This process did not take place immediately or shortly after applications were submitted; it took a good three weeks or even a month before they started to be processed. In charge of these tasks was back-office staff. The majority did not have permanent positions with the civil service, but rather had been hired to handle the paperwork generated by this exceptional campaign. Thus, for most of them, it was a temporary job and a fairly low-paying one. The office was also clearly under understaffed for the workload they faced. As I mentioned in Chapter 1, the final number of applications was more than triple the government's initial forecast of 80,000 (some 250,000 applications were submitted in the whole of Spain). However, the department's workforce was not enlarged (at least in Barcelona). This scarcity of human resources was consequential for information provision at this site.

After a new file had been created, the officials' job was to examine all the documents provided by petitioners. If, in their view, everything was correct, the application moved forward. The officials' positive endorsement was recorded in the applicant's computerised file as *fase de instrucción* 'preparatory phase'. Whenever they judged that insufficient documentation had been provided (as would be the case if a previous application for a work permit by 31 March 2000

46 *Service activities and bureaucratic procedure*

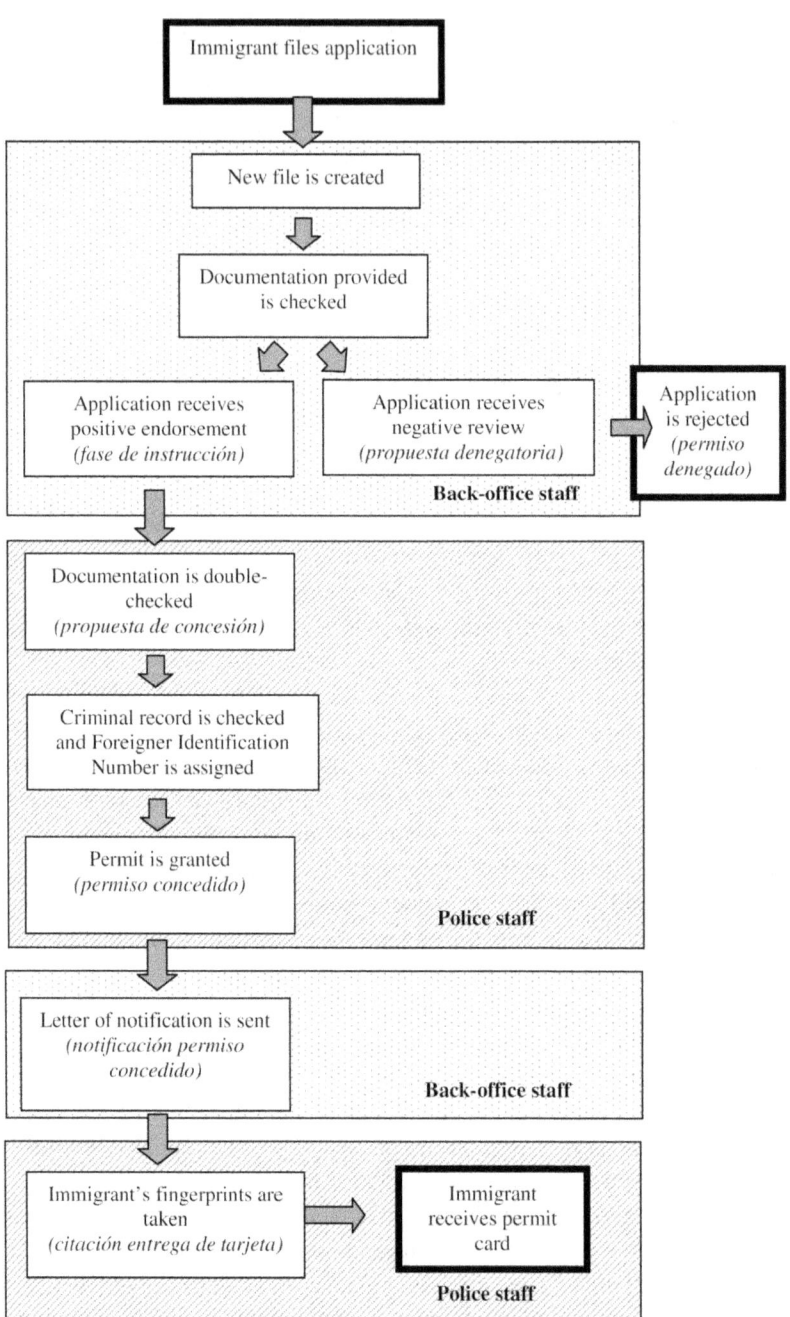

Figure 4. Actors and stages in the bureaucratic procedure

had not been enclosed) or that the documentation was faulty (either because it was forged or did not meet the institution's requirements), officials assessed the application negatively. In such cases, applications made no further progress and were temporarily stalled. This state of affairs received the official label *propuesta denegatoria* 'proposed for rejection'. In the province of Barcelona, applications proposed for rejection stayed in this situation for a long time. This state of administrative limbo explains why the waiting time for notification of outcome was longer for unsuccessful than for successful applicants. In fact, all applications registered in Barcelona were not officially rejected, unlike in other provinces (see Chapter 1), until September 2000, six months after the beginning of the campaign.

This long waiting time was allegedly related to uncertainty on the part of the government as to the number of immigrants that they would "have to" regularise by the end of the campaign. In their accounts, bureaucrats highlighted the fact that the Spanish government was under pressure by European institutions to accept a stipulated minimum number of foreigners. If that quota was not reached, initially rejected applications would ultimately have to be accepted, which is in fact what happened during 2001. In the excerpt below, Miquel, one of the officials, explains the situation as follows.

(2)

→	1	*MIQ:	xxx *Espanya està obligada per la Comunitat Europea a*
	2		*legalitzar-ne cent i pico mil no sé quants llavons els que*
	3		*tenen tots els papers són molt poquets.*
		%tra:	xxx Spain is obliged by the European Community to legalise more than a hundred thousand or something like that and there are very few who have their papers in order.
	4	*RES:	xxx.
	5	*MIQ:	*sí la Comunitat Europea ha obligat a Espanya a*
	6		*legalitzar-ne no sé quants.*
		%tra:	yes the European Community has obliged Spain to legalise I don't know how many.
	7	*RES:	*un mínim?*
		%tra:	a minimum?
	8	*MIQ:	*crec que sí.*
		%tra:	I think so.
	9	*RES:	*anda::!*
		%tra:	what a surprise!

→ 10 *MIQ: *però això és un acord intern de la Comunitat Europea*
   11   *perquè estava calculat que si no es legalitzen tots aquests*
   12   *després l'economia no funcionarà el 2026 [?].*
      %tra: but this is an internal agreement of the European Community because it was predicted that if we didn't legalize them the economy wouldn't work in 2026 [?].

   13 *RES: *però això no ha sortit enlloc no?*
      %tra: but this hasn't been published anywhere, has it?

   14 *MIQ: *no això és que això:: ho sap poca gent.*
      %tra: no the thing is very few people know about this.

   15 *MIQ: *total que ara nosaltres sabem que no surten ni borratxos*
   16   *els que tinguin els papers.*
      %tra: in short we know now that the number of eligible applicants is nowhere near the quota.

   17 *RES: *ja.*
      %tra   I see.

→ 18 *MIQ: *tots estan en* propuesta denegatoria *i estem esperant al*
   19   *trenta-u de juliol a veure quants han sortit bé i llavons*
   20   *sabrem falten tants pues allavons tots els que tinguin que*
   21   *comenci el nom per a pues també xxx i direm hasta*
   22   *arribar als que tenim que arribar.*
      %tra: they have all been negatively evaluated and we are waiting to see how many [permits] are granted by July thirty-first to know how many more we need then those [applicants] whose name begins with an "A" we'll also take and we'll continue till we reach the figure we are supposed to reach.

          [...]

→ 23 *MIQ: *+ˆ la Núria no en tenia ni idea al principi i fa cosa d'un*
   24   *mes li van dir a ella algo així i llavons va dir un dia no si*
   25   *al final els agafarem a tots no sé què així -. no però*
   26   *vamos encara no se sap.*
      %tra: Núria (the office manager) didn't have a clue at the beginning. About a month ago she was told and then one day she said in the end we'll take all of them, but the truth is we don't really know yet.

I did not have the chance to compare the information Miquel provided with the views of the office manager or other employees, so I cannot comment on his claims about the procedure the Spanish government allegedly followed to grant legal status to so many illegal aliens. (Miquel's explanation, for example, does not account for why the stalling of applications occurred in Barcelona and not elsewhere.) Nevertheless, Miquel was the most well-informed of all the officials I dealt with and he was often consulted by his workmates on different issues to do with institutional procedures, so his account is of interest as an illustration of how little knowledge institutional representatives had about what was going on.

In the extract, Miquel's words describe a picture in which uncertainty, improvisation and random decision-making define the functioning of the institution. For example, in lines 23–25, he recounts how Núria, the manager, did not know what would happen to rejected applications four months after the start of the campaign. And in lines 20–22, he states that in order to meet the official quota arbitrary criteria would have to be used to decide on entitlement. Beyond the actual veracity of Miquel's claims, this extract shows how officials perceived the context of their work. It was a context in which they perceived that information did not flow freely and where eligibility conditions might change overnight or end up being totally arbitrary. As I shall claim later, it is against this institutional background that certain communicative practices by officials have to be understood. But let us first continue with the detailed examination of the bureaucratic procedure for processing petitions.

Once the first stage was completed, those applications that had received a favourable endorsement were passed on to the police department. The police department's task was to make sure that no mistakes had been made by immigration bureaucrats, that is, essentially to confirm that the documentary evidence provided by immigrants was in order and that the certifications had not been forged. It should be noted, however, that applications were double-checked only after receiving an initial positive ensorsement by immigration officials. In other words, applicants whose request for legalisation was rejected straightaway (on the basis of, for example, having submitted forged documentation) did not get a second chance. This practice indexes the institution's ideological conceptualisation of the social world: though the institution is keen to safeguard itself against clients' cheating practices, it perceives no need to safeguard clients against institutional mistakes. While there, I observed that there were informal channels of communication for sorting out problems in individual applications between immigration officials and police officers, but it is highly revealing that a review of initial rejections was not systematically built into the procedure. (Decisions were only reviewed after immigrants had appealed.) This is particularly worrying if we take into account that it was not experienced civil servants who handled applications but workers on temporary contracts.

At the end of this stage in the application process, if everything was found to be in order, applications were classified into a new bureaucratic category: *propuesta de concesión* 'proposed for approval'. A different police department took then over. Its role was to give the successful applicant a *Número de Identificación de Extranjeros* 'Foreigner Identification Number' (NIE). This is the foreigners' counterpart to the ID number and document each Spanish national has and which is a necessary requirement for all administrative procedures in Spain. A second major task at this stage was to check the applicant's criminal records. Unless records were clean, the permit would not be granted.[9] Example (3) below illustrates how the process could get seriously delayed if there was the slightest suspicion that the applicant had been involved in criminal activities, and even when the information seeker had been found not guilty of criminal charges.

(3)

	1	*RAM:	a ti al final con un poco de suerte te lo van a dar lo que te van
	2		a hacer sudar -. te vas a tener que esperar tela tela y tela.
		%tra:	with a bit of luck they'll give it to you, but they're going to make you sweat -. you will have to wait and wait and wait.
	3	*ENQ:	me peleé con uno éste dice + ...
		%tra	I got in a fight with someone this one says + ...
	4	*RAM:	a mí me da lo mismo lo que hicieras como si le pegases xxx
	5		pero lo que pone en tus papeles es robo con intimidación y
	6		entonces eso se lo tienen que mirar bastante -. yo creo que al
→	7		final te lo van a dar pero te van a hacer esperar tela.
		%tra:	I don't care what you did even if you hit him xxx but what it says in your documents is armed robbery so they have to look at this carefully -. I think in the end they'll give it to you but they'll make you wait and wait.

If the applicant passed this last hurdle successfully, the application for legalisation was officially accepted. The official category appearing on the official's computer screen was *permiso concedido*, literally 'permit granted'. The application then went back to the immigration office, where back-office officials wrote a letter of acceptance which was sent to the applicant's address. Even this was not unproblematic, as immigrants often changed residence but failed to notify the office. In such cases, tracking down the letter could be quite complicated. This new administrative step was recorded in the computer as *notificación de permiso concedido* 'notification of granted permit'. In the letter of notification, the applicant was asked to go back to the office on a specific date so that his/her fingerprints could be taken. This was a necessary step before the permit could be issued. Finally, once an applicant's fingerprints had been taken, the administrative status of his/her application became *citación de entrega de tarjeta* 'request to collect card'.

It took approximately two months before an applicant could pick up his/her work permit from the office, but in the interval, s/he could use the official letter of acceptance sent by the institution to prove legal status for employment purposes. Since at least three weeks elapsed from the moment the permit was granted until the official letter was sent out, it was possible to ask for a provisional letter. This letter was actually a standard form that officials filled out upon request. It contained the applicant's name and newly issued NIE. The institutional name for it was *informe laboral*, literally 'work report', though clients and officials normally referred to it as *informe*. With this provisional *informe*, the applicant was allowed to work legally in Spain.

3. Characterisation of service exchanges

In this section, I shall provide a description of the face-to-face verbal exchanges on which my analysis of bureaucratic practice is based.

One of the striking features of the interactions recorded is that they are very similar as regards theme and structure. There are various reasons for this. First, the office where I conducted my research was specially set up to process applications for legalisation. Thus, all the cases handled had to do with the same bureaucratic procedure. Secondly, even though the information desk provided information on eligibility conditions and required documentation, this information was also available from other sources (the registry, booklets on the legalisation campaign, newspapers, the Internet and staff from other immigration offices). By contrast, details on the progress of already submitted petitions could only be obtained from this particular office. As a result, only those immigrants needing the latter information were prepared to put up with the long queues that formed outside the office every day, while individuals seeking more general information tended to look elsewhere. These two reasons explain thematic similarity. As regards structure, resemblance may be accounted for by the tight control exerted by public officials over discursive production. Finally, the reason for the likeness in officials' information-providing practices can be found in the extreme routinisation of their responses and in the institution's specific information policy.

One structural characteristic of the social interactions that I observed and recorded was their discontinuous nature. By discontinuous I mean that there very frequent moments without verbal participation in these encounters. These moments of discontinuity might be structurally motivated periods of non-speech, as in the case of the "check computer" activity, in which the institutional representative searched the computerised database for information. Other breaks, by contrast, were unrelated to the organisation of the exchange and had to do with the specificity of the setting. For example, the nature of the long queue of people waiting to be served prompted many individuals to approach the counter to try to obtain information without queuing up, although bureaucrats generally refused to serve them. Individual service seekers' moves gave rise to a number of brief exchanges which disrupted the ongoing interaction.

More significant than the discontinuous nature of these social exchanges on an organisational level was their discontinuity on the level of social relationships. I refer to the extent to which the channel of interaction was kept open throughout the exchange, even when nonverbal activities were being carried out. In her analysis of service transactions at a bank, Cook-Gumperz (2000) shows how clerks and customers collaborate in concealing the clerk's movements away from being on a direct body alignment with the customer. This happens when the clerk enters any new deposits or check balances into the computer and is the key to a successful encounter. Social alignment is maintained in the absence of talk and the client does not feel that the clerk has withdrawn from the relationship established. In Cook-Gumperz' view, only when the social channel is kept open can the client go away with the feeling that a truly personal service has been delivered. And customer satisfaction is unquestionably one of the goals of a bank.

There was no sign of that effort in the interactions under analysis. The argument that I shall develop in subsequent chapters is that this was no surprise given the social function of this bureaucracy, which was not to provide a service to immigrant petitioners, but rather to regulate access to Spanish citizenship. The differentiated management of bodily posture that the servers in the bank and the immigration office displayed indexes very clearly the different social goals of the two organisations.

In the immigration office, servers would take advantage of every opportunity to withdraw from any social space of intercourse with their interlocutors. When no talk was being exchanged, the channel was intentionally kept closed. Servers showed no interest in creating a harmonious interactional space with their interlocutors. On the contrary, they endeavoured to keep interaction to a minimum. Talk could only be produced within preestablished social activities, such as those that will be presented in Figure 5. In fact, as mentioned in Chapter

1, my presence around the office gave officials an added and welcome excuse to busy themselves with tasks unrelated to the service exchange.

The following extract (4) illustrates servers' refusal to engage in communication which they did not perceive as "sequentially appropriate" and how hard they tried to discourage enquirers from speaking. In this excerpt, the service seeker, EN1, is a particularly articulate enquirer. Moreover, he is very fluent in Spanish. In turns previous to the excerpt shown here, he tries to establish a friendly relationship with the server by making small talk. He brings up the topic of the server's holidays, as the encounter takes place on the last day of July, and mentions the very hot summer the city is experiencing. The turns presented below take place while Miquel, the official, is waiting for information on the service seeker's application to appear on the computer screen.

(4)

	1	*EN1:	el chico éste www www me parece ## es ésta lo que está
	2		mirando no?
		%tra:	this fellow this www www I think ## is the one you're checking now right?
		%com:	www stands for the name of a person
	3	*MIQ:	sí.
		%tra:	yes.
	4	*EN1:	me parece ya lo tiene concedido no?
		%tra:	I think he's already been granted the permit, hasn't he?
	5	*MIQ:	no lo sé.
		%tra:	I don't know.
→	6	*EN1:	me parece que sí yo ahora lo miraré porque: vino el otro
	7	%tra:	día a preguntar -, y ahora lo que me falta por favor + ... I think so I'll have a look now because he came to ask the other day -, and now what I need please + ...
		@Situation: one of the door staff approaches the counter
→	8	*MIQ:	**Shania Twain**.
	9	*DOO:	qué más.
		%tra:	what's the surname?
	10	*MIQ:	no sabes quién es?
		%tra:	don't you know who she is?
	11	*DOO:	no.

54 *Service activities and bureaucratic procedure*

	12	*MIQ:	es una cantante de country que hace canciones como las de
	13		Mónica Naranjo pero en inglés.
		%tra:	she's a country singer that sings songs similar to those by Mónica Naranjo but in English.

In lines 6–7, it seems that the enquirer is trying to formulate his specific service request ("now what I need please"), although he leaves his utterance unfinished. As becomes apparent later in the interaction, he wants to be given an *informe* letter, that is, a provisional letter certifying he has been granted the permit. Yet this request can only be formulated after the official is certain that the permit has been granted. While Miquel is waiting for the computer to show the information requested, the enquirer produces two turns concerning the application that is being checked (lines 1 and 4). These two turns end in a tag question, which, sequentially, force the official to respond. His rather laconic answers in lines 3 and 5 ("yes", "I don't know") index his unwillingness to get interactionally involved until the status of the enquirer's application has been determined. In line 8 he manifestly disengages himself temporarily from the service exchange by turning around and resuming a previous conversation with one of the door staff (DOO) and myself about a famous pop singer. This has the desired effect of inhibiting the information seeker from pursuing his line of talk.

3.1. Episodes and activities: An overview

The face-to-face exchanges in which officials and immigrants engaged were (at least formally) of a service nature in the sense first posited by Merritt (1976). That is, they involved two clearly defined speaking parties with two a priori complementary goals: one lay party who requested some kind of service (in this case, information) from a professional party who was there to provide it (though the extent to which state officials in this office were there to provide information is arguable and shall be discussed at length in Chapters 3 and 4).

In their formal status as service interactions, these encounters share their basic structural organisation with other types of service exchanges. Their *core* or nuclear activities (Ventola 1987: 119), that is to say, those activities that realise actors' goals, are, logically, the service request and the provision of service. They are always present –even in the most minimal interactions – and can be performed verbally or nonverbally. These activities, in turn, form the nucleus of the two episodes identified, that is, the service request episode and the provision of service episode. I have posited them as a way of showing the two distinct parts in which exchanges are structured. Transition from one part to the other is clearly marked by, among other things, long pauses, different

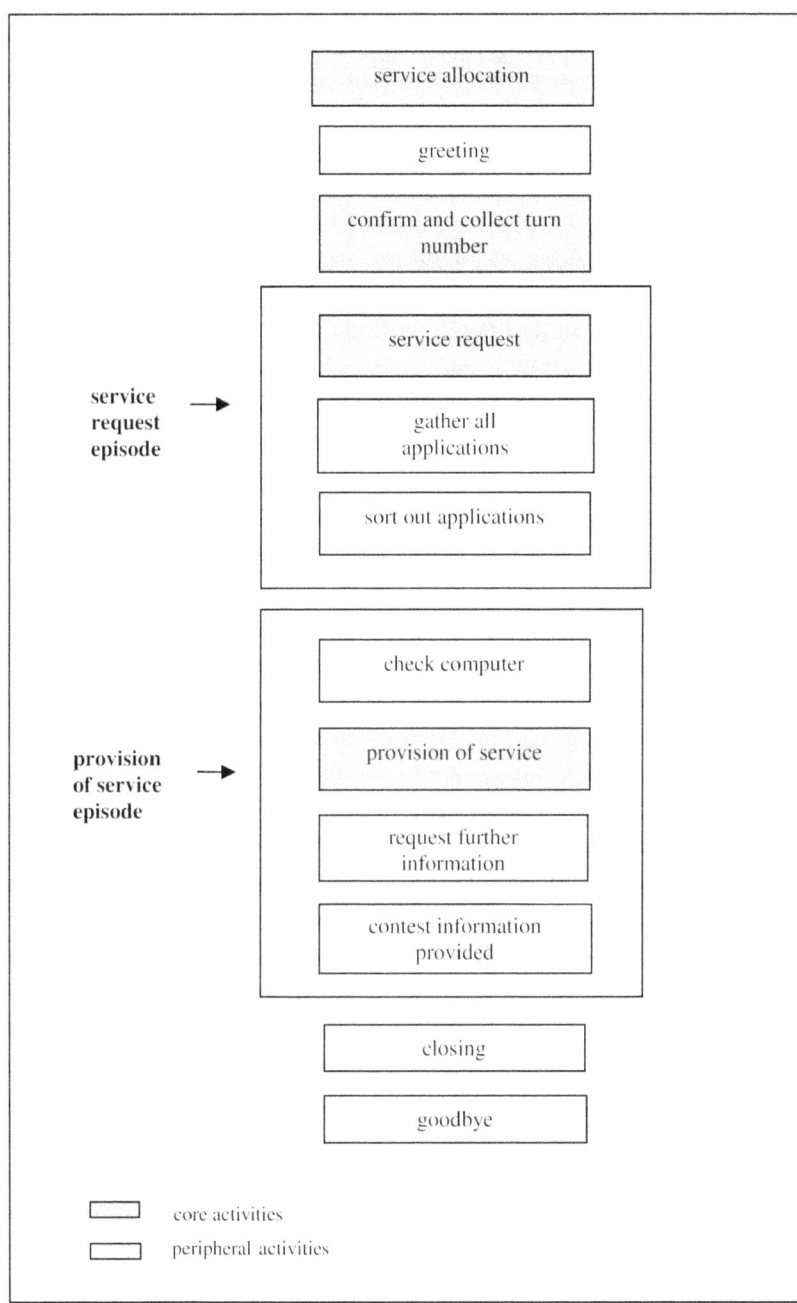

Figure 5. Structural organisation of service interactions

language choices, and most importantly, the bureaucrat's withdrawal from the social space of intercourse. Also, I have used the notion of *episode* to group together activities which are different but nevertheless thematically related to either the demand or the provision of the service. An *activity* is understood as a sequence of moves, either verbal or nonverbal, oriented to the accomplishment of a specific goal. Each activity can span more than one turn and can involve more than one speaker. I have distinguished two types of activities, namely obligatory or *core*, and optional or *peripheral*. The rationale for distinguishing between these two types has to do with whether the absence of an activity is made interactionally relevant or not by speakers.

As Figure 5 shows, though the central activities in the two large episodes are the service request and the provision of service, each episode may also contain other social activities. In the case of the service request, the two additional activities identified (i.e. "gather all applications" and "sort out applications") are employed by the public official to refine the client's request. In the case of the service compliance, the "check computer" activity refers to the server's preparatory actions prior to the provision of service. They involve searching the institution's computerised database for information on a client's application. The social activities "request further information" and "contest information provided" build upon the information supplied by the official in the provision of service turn. Responding to these two activities is part of the official's provision of service moves.

The interactional scheme presented in Figure 5 is not meant to be comprehensive but rather seeks to represent the most frequent social activities undertaken by participants at the immigration office. The most common type of interactions, namely those in which immigrants were informed that they would have to keep on waiting because a final decision on their applications had still not been made, are taken as baseline data for the figure. This explains the presence of activities like "request further information" or "contest information provided". The overall description of the exchanges formulated here is an idealised scheme from which in actual practice social actors sometimes deviated. For example, activities not related to the service nature of the exchanges were sometimes present. Comprehension checks and language negotiation sequences are a case in point. They have not been included in the chart for two reasons: firstly, because of their general conversational nature; secondly, because they could occur at a number of interactional places and are consequently problematic to represent.

3.1.1. Service activities in detail

In the reality of the immigration office, one of the most visible structural features of service interactions was that the "greeting", "closing" and "goodbye" episodes rarely occurred, and the rarest of all was, perhaps surprisingly, the greeting episode. In fact, social intercourse was usually initiated by an applicant's approaching the counter and establishing eye contact with the official. Yet to be "allowed" to do so, the client number had to have appeared on a screen displaying current number served. Officials refused to serve any client who did not have a number or whose number had yet not been called. The standard procedure was for officials to push a button located under the counter indicating their readiness to serve. This caused a buzzer to sound and caused the illuminated number on a large screen to advance. This move, together with the client's reaction, constituted the first activity of the encounter, that is, the allocation of the service.

As greetings were generally absent, the next move usually consisted in the client handing over the application forms whose status s/he wanted to have checked. This constituted the initiation of the service proper, as the mere handing over by the client of his/her application forms worked as a service-prompting move. In the majority of encounters, these three initial moves (allocation of service, greeting and service request) were performed nonverbally. So it often happened that no talk occurred until the official uttered his/her provision of service turn.

Let us examine the opening activities of these encounters by looking at example (5) below. For illustration purposes I have chosen a rather complete exchange, which is nevertheless the exception rather than the rule in this context.

(5)

→ 1   *MIQ: número.
           %tra: number.

    2   *EN1:   0.
           %tra: gives MIQ the number together with one application form

→ 3   *EN1:   mira por favor [=! softly].
           %tra: check it please.

→ 4   *MIQ: vale **only one**?
           %tra: okay only one?

    5   *EN1:   0.
           %act: makes a gesture indicating non-understanding

    6   *MIQ: **only one**?

58 Service activities and bureaucratic procedure

	7	*EN1:	0.
		%act:	indicates one with his finger
	8	*MIQ:	**no more**.
→	9	*EN1:	<u>no</u>.

In this extract, we can observe the obligatory nature of the "confirm and collect turn number" activity. In line 1, the official (Miquel) asks for the number explicitly, as presumably EN1 has not yet handed it over. The fact that this activity appears in the first turn underscores the need for this action to be accomplished before any talk can be exchanged.

In general, after the service request had been formulated (in this example, exceptionally, we have a verbally realised request), the official would try to find out whether the immigrant had only one application to be checked or more. This is what I have called the "gather all applications" activity. The client would then either produce more applications or state that s/he did not have any more. In the example above, this sequence is played out in lines 4–9. The official's need to repeat his initial question may have to do with the client's lack of language competence, but it may also have to do with the unexpected nature of the sequential organisation suggested by the official (providing all applications, and thus all requests, right at the beginning of the exchange).

In the event that the client produced several forms, the public official would only take a maximum of five for checking. Rather than explain this norm, which was not written anywhere and as far as I know established by the front-line staff, the official would often assume the client to know. Therefore, the fact that officials returned some forms to the clients before having them checked puzzled many clients and prompted a number of requests for clarification. Some months later the policy in this regard changed. If applications other than the applicant's own were taken to the office for checking, an authorising document from each of other applicants was required, which made the process of obtaining information even more complicated.

In the encounter below, the official agrees to check only five applications out of the seven the client has brought.

(6)

	1	*ENQ:	0.
		%act:	hands copies of several application forms over to MIQ
→	2	*MIQ	sobran dos -. te quito estos dos?
		%tra:	you've given me two extra -. do you want these two back?

→	3	*MIQ:	**only five.**
	4	*EN1:	**okay.**

@Situation: MIQ checks status of applications

In the next stage, after all the applications had been collected, the official usually examined them in order to find out on which date the applications had been entered in the registry. This is the "sort out applications" stage. This activity was undertaken because it took up to a month for the institution to process newly entered petitions (i.e. creating a new file and subjecting them to a preliminary assessment). If all the applications handed over for checking had been entered long enough previously to have been processed, no verbal turn was uttered by the official. In short, the "sort out applications" sequence was only present when the petitions taken in for checking still remained to be processed.

Apart from clerical officials, *ordenanzas* 'door staff' were also supposed to know how fast applications were being processed. Though the primary function of the door staff was to organise the queues of people waiting, another of their functions was to advise enquirers about whether waiting would be worth their while or not. So, for instance, if they saw that all the applications a given applicant had brought for checking had still not been entered into the institution's database, they would inform this person that no information was available. The problem was that the information door staff had in this regard was not always particularly accurate. Example (7) below illustrates this situation.

(7)

→	1	*DOO:	está hasta el ha: hasta el diez de mayo me parece no?
		%tra:	they've been processed until the: until May tenth I think right?
		[…]	
	2	*MIQ:	hasta el cuatro de mayo sólo.
		%tra:	only until May fourth.
	3	*DOO:	entonces tengo que echar a muchos fuera.
		%tra:	then I'll have to throw a lot out.
		[…]	

60   *Service activities and bureaucratic procedure*

→ 4 *TER: veintidós de mayo no está no hay no está el veintidós de
  5   mayo cinco de mayo no está -. *tindríem que dir-li que el*
  6   *maig no hi és que xxx que no fagin cua.*
     %tra: May twenty second is not available there is May twenty
              second is not available may fifth is not available –. we
              should tell them that May is not available so that they don't
              waste their time queuing up.

     [...]

→ 7 *TER: *però que no fagin cua pobres si és del mes de maig -! # si*
  8   *no hi és per què fan la per què tenen que fer cua!*
     %tra: but they should not be queueing up poor things if their
              applications are from May -! if their applications have not
              been processed yet, what do they have to queue up for?

This extract is part of an interaction recorded around 11:30 a.m. As can be seen in line 1, DOO, the door person, still seems to have doubts as to what to tell information seekers. In fact, it turns out that she has incorrect information (line 2). This means that she has been misinforming clients for a significant part of the morning and that now she will have to ask many of them to leave. One of the officials, in this case Teresa, complains a few turns later that more accurate information ought to be provided to clients (lines 5–8).

If among the applications handed over for checking one or several which had still not been entered into the computer were found, they were returned to the information seeker. This step sometimes required some explaining on the part of the official, as applicants tended to be unclear about the lapse of time that was required between the submission of applications and their bureaucratic processing. In the extract below (8), Miquel sorts out the application forms he has been given (lines 5–7). This example is particularly illuminating because, quite exceptionally, the official produces some explanatory talk to facilitate the enquirer's understanding of what is going on. In lines 11–12, after a question–answer sequence motivated by the information seeker's incomplete understanding of the official's previous turn, the official ventures a prediction as to when details on the enquirer's applications will be available for consultation. Very rarely did state representatives make predictions of this sort.

(8)

  1   *ENQ: 0.
      %act: hands document over to MIQ

  2   *MIQ: sólo uno?
      %tra: only one?

	3	*ENQ:	tres más.
		%tra:	three more.
	4	*MIQ:	dámelos.
		%tra:	give them to me.
	[...]		
→	5	*MIQ:	diecinueve de mayo todavía no está -. once de mayo todavía
	6		no está -. quince de mayo todavía no está -. sólo tenemos
	7		hasta el diez de mayo.
		%tra:	May nineteenth is not available yet -. May eleventh is not available yet -. May fifteenth is not available yet -. information is only available until May tenth.
		%act:	gives application forms back to ENQ
	8	*ENQ:	cuánta mayo?
		%tra:	how many May?
	9	*MIQ:	diez.
		%tra:	tenth.
	10	*ENQ:	diez?
		%tra:	tenth?
→	11	*MIQ:	hoy diez -. la semana que viene seguramente estará pero hoy no.
	12	%tra:	today tenth -. next week it'll probably be available but not today.
	13	*ENQ:	vale.
		%tra:	okay.

The sequence which accomplished the sorting out of applications completed the service request episode. The next activity to be undertaken was already part of the group of moves connected with the provision of the service. This activity, which I have called "check computer", was not verbally realised. It consisted in entering the name and surname of each applicant into the computer. If the data was correct, the applicant's electronic file would be shown on the computer screen. Each new file that was created was allocated a number. Usually, the service provider would write down this file identification number on the application the first time it was taken to the office for checking. The file number and not the applicant's name and surname was then employed in subsequent searches.

When the bureaucratic information on a specific application was available to the official s/he was ready to comply with the service seeker's request. The provision of service activity sometimes also contained one or several non-understanding sequences, comprehension checks, language negotiation episodes and reformulations. Simultaneous to the provision of information details, the immigration official would write the date and the information provided at the top of each application form in an abbreviated manner. After the provision of service turn had taken place, the information seeker might decide that s/he was satisfied with the information s/he had been given, or else that s/he might feel that s/he wanted more specific details. S/he could then initiate a "request further information" activity. The most frequent type of question had to do with how to relate current details with information that the applicant had been told on previous occasions. The objective was to understand whether applications were making progress or not. The typical case was that of applicants who were trying to reconcile the news that an application was *en trámite* 'being processed' with what they had been told previously, namely that the documentary evidence they had furnished to prove arrival in Spain before 1 June 1999 had not been accepted. I shall discuss this issue at length in the following chapter.

After the "request further information" activity, clients might initiate a "contest information provided" sequence. This activity was independent of the previous one. They might cooccur but did not necessarily do so. A contesting sequence might take place right after the official's provision of service turn or after supplementary information had been furnished.

Example (9) below illustrates the different activities making up the provision of service. A few intervening turns between the provision of service and the client's request for further information have been omitted because they were irrelevant to the exchange.

For descriptive purposes, I shall discuss this interaction in some detail. However, I will not dwell on key aspects of the way in which information is provided by officials and contested by clients because this will be the object of study of the following two chapters.

(9)

	1	*MIQ:	a ver él dos y tú tres.
		%tra:	let's see he's got two and you've got three.
	2	*MIQ:	ya está -? no tenéis más?
		%tra:	is that all -? don't you have any more?
	3	*EN1:	no no ya está.
		%tra:	no no that's all.

@Situation: MIQ checks state of applications in computer

→	4	*MIQ:	en trámite tiene que <esperar tres semanas más> [>].
		%tra:	it's being processed you have to wait three more weeks

[…]

→	5	*EN1:	vale quiero preguntar un [/] una cosa # está todo bien o::
	6		<falta> [>] + ...
		%tra:	okay I want to ask some [/] something # is everything alright or is there anything missing?
	7	*MIQ:	<no se sabe> [<] cuando está en trámite quiere decir que
	8		están mirando si los papeles están bien # y todavía no se
	9		sabe si falta o no falta.
		%tra:	<it doesn't say > [<] when it's being processed that means that they are checking if the papers are okay # and we don't known whether anything is missing or not.
	10	*EN1:	señor [?] no no no falta nada no?
		%tra:	sir [?] nothing nothing is missing right?
	11	*MIQ:	no se sabe.
		%tra:	it doesn't say.
	12	*EN1:	<u>ah</u>!
		%tra:	oh!

[…]

@Situation: MIQ continues checking applications

	13	*MIQ:	eh: trámite <tres semanitas> [>].
		%tra:	uh: being processed <just three weeks> [>].
	14	*EN1:	<también igual> [<]?
		%tra:	<same also> [<]?
→	15	*EN1:	ah discúlpeme señor # ah # éste ya pasó cuatro mes xxx
	16		no tengo xxx.
		%tra:	uh sorry sir # uh # four months have elapsed for this one xxx I don't have xxx.
→	17	*MIQ:	el día treinta y treinta y uno de marzo vino muchí::sima
	18		gente y van muy lentos.
		%tra:	on March thirtieth and thirty-first very many people came and applications are being processed slowly.
	19	*EN1:	por qué?
		%tra:	why?
	20	*MIQ:	+ˆ no lo sé -. no lo sé -. en principio está en trámite.
		%tra:	I don't know -. I don't know -. in principle it's being processed.

64 *Service activities and bureaucratic procedure*

→ 21 *EN1:   y otra perso(n)a # y de paso once de abril o siete de abril
  22   # ya ha recibido de una carta de residencia no sé y treinta
  23   y uno de marzo <#> [>] no tengo ayudar.
     %tra: and somebody else # who gave application on April
              eleventh or seventh # has already received a residence
              card I don't know and March thirty first <#> [>] I don't
              have any help.

  24 *MIQ: <ya> [<].
     %tra: <I know> [<].

→ 25 *MIQ: el treinta y el treinta y uno de marzo van muy lentos.
     %tra: those entered on March thirtieth and thirty-first are being
              processed very slowly.

  26 *EN1:   vale muchas gracias señor.
     %tra: okay thank you very much sir

  27 *MIQ: de nada.
     %tra: you're welcome.

The example begins with the typical "gather all applications" activity (lines 1–3). The "sort out applications" activity, which usually comes afterwards, is likely to have been accomplished nonverbally, as there are no verbal traces of it. The official searches the institution's database for information and utters the provision of service turn in line 4.

The information the official provides is actually not very informative. This prompts the client to enquire further in order to establish what really matters to him, that is, whether his application is really making progress or not. The official gives him an uncommitted reply twice – namely, that he cannot tell him because his documents are still being examined. Seeing that his previous strategy did not yield any results, after the official complies with the fourth request, the information seeker utters what could be interpreted as a mild complaint. In response, the official matter-of-factly explains the reasons why it is taking the institution so long to process that specific application. The tone of the complaint becomes more direct when the client counters by undermining the credibility of the official's response. He states that somebody he knows, who entered his application later, has already been granted the permit.

The reason why such inconsistencies in the processing of permits happened was connected with the way work was distributed between the two work shifts. The morning shift was initially put in charge of applications entered between 21 and 31 March, while the afternoon shift took care of applications entered between 1 and 15 April. The second group of applications was processed more quickly, as many more applications were entered during the first ten days of the campaign than afterwards. This was insider information that Miquel was probably not expected to furnish to clients, even more so because it showed that work was not organised in a coherent or efficient manner. It is in the light of these institutional pressures that his response in line 25 has to be understood. He sticks to his institutional role, does not react to the client's appeal and mechanically repeats the simple account he gave in lines 17–18.

Finally, when the interactants wished to bring their service interchange to an end, a closing sequence took place. In the example above, this sequence occurs in line 26. Its function is to close the encounter by acknowledging that the service has been provided ("*vale*" 'okay') and thanking the server for it ("*muchas gracias señor*" 'thank you very much sir'). After the closing sequence, a goodbye sequence might or might not be present. In this case, for example, it does not occur.

As a rule, the closing and goodbye sequences were initiated by the service seekers, as it was up to them to decide whether they were satisfied or not with the outcome of the encounter, or wanted to ask any further questions. Yet when interactional conflict occurred, information providers would sometimes unilaterally decide to bring the exchange to an end in a brusque manner. This is what happens in example (10) below. In this extract, one of the two enquirers at the counter (EN2) is trying to have his application checked (line 4). The problem is that Miquel, the official, is under the impression that they have come to check the status of only one application, that of EN1, and he has already done so. Miquel is annoyed because it seems that, in the "gather all applications" stage, the enquirers stated that they only wanted to have one application checked, as we can see in lines 5 to 7 ("I said one? only one? nobody else? no friend?"). He uses the lexical item *adiós* 'goodbye' to close his reprimanding turn and brings the interaction to an end. This move is further reinforced by his ringing of the buzzer to indicate availability to serve another client. EN1 and EN2 have no other option but to leave the counter.

(10)

    1   *EN1:   uhm maintenant #0_1 esto quel número?
          %tra: uhm now #0_1 this which number?

    2   *MIQ: esto el número del # ordenador.
          %tra: this the number of the # computer.

    3   *EN1:   ah ordenador #0_3 vale [=! soft].
          %tra: uh computer #0_3 okay [=! soft].

	4	*EN2:	entonces yo amigo.
→		%tra:	now I'm his friend.
→	5	*MIQ:	<amigo> [=! shouting] -? te he dicho uno -? uno -? uno
	6		sólo -? <nadie más> [>1] -? no amigo? no nadie? no -.
	7		sólo uno -. pues sólo <uno> [>2] -. adiós.
		%tra:	<friend> [=! shouting] -? I said one -? one -? only one -? <nobody else> [>1] -? no friend? no nobody -? no -. only one -. then only <one> [>2] -. goodbye.
	8	*EN2:	<yo amigo> [<1].
		%tra:	<me friend> [<1].
	9	*EN2:	<vale> [<2].
		%tra:	<okay> [<2].

4. Concluding remarks

This chapter has presented the main features of service communication at the immigration office. I have made an effort to provide clear descriptions and essential elements, while at the same time, pointing out the complexities of depicting talk in any simple manner.

My descriptive account has already foregrounded a few key topics that define the service provided in this office and that will be taken up in the following chapters. I have mentioned, for instance, that discourse is tightly controlled by officials and that talk produced by clients outside appropriate sequential contexts is often ignored. Another important issue I have noted is the fact that there are a few procedural rules governing service communication that all immigrant clients are expected to know and follow. Even though these rules of conduct are taken for granted and not explained anywhere, clients are held accountable for violations and severely reprimanded if they try to subvert them. A third topic that has come up is the routinisation of officials' responses and their general disregard for their interlocutors' difficulties in comprehension.

The detailed description of the bureaucratic procedure I have supplied in this first section has highlighted the bureaucratic embedding of talk. This account of decision-making stages constitutes an exceptional window into the ways in which state bureaucracies work. I have also touched on some of the fundamental ideologies underlying bureaucratic practice. For example, I have suggested that suspicion as the basis for client construal is built into a procedure which establishes that documents submitted by immigrants are double-checked, while there is no such mechanism for ensuring that institutional decisions are reviewed.

Part II

Information as valuable capital

Chapter 3
An illusion of information

1. Introduction

Though the cliché that information is everywhere nowadays may be true, it is no less true that individuals have unequal access to it, a situation that serves to reinforce social inequalities and create new causes of social exclusion. In the immigration office setting, officials' and clients' knowledge of the bureaucratic procedure was highly asymmetrical. That is not surprising if we take into account their different situated roles. However, what is perhaps remarkable is that this imbalance of information and knowledge was in no way redressed by the service communication which ostensibly took place.

Information in this setting was a capital that was fought over. For those who had it, that is, the bureaucrats, information was a capital they could strategically handle to safeguard their own well-being and institutional position. For those who did not have it, that is, the clients, access to information could enhance their understanding of the contexts they inhabited, enable them to adjust their actions to new scenarios, and especially, give them a sense of ontological security. We must not forget that their only way to abandon the marginal social and material circumstances in which they lived was by having their status legalised. Having precise information on what progress their petitions were making was therefore essential.

What makes the study of the processes of information provision particularly interesting is the fact that, as a verbal service, information is demanded, transmitted and obtained through linguistic means. For this reason, the analysis of information can hardly be distinguished from the analysis of the linguistic formulae, strategies and routines that are employed to convey it. In the case of this office, additionally, information was never given in writing; it was exclusively conveyed face-to-face, in and through social interaction. The study of service discourse thus offers insights into the multiple connections that exist between language, information, the exercise of power and control, and the creation or recreation of social exclusion.

When linguistic resources are asymmetrically distributed among participants, as was also the case in this office, minority speakers are clearly at a disadvantage. Their opportunities for discursive participation are structurally constrained, but more importantly, there is the potential for structural linguistic asymmetries to be made to work against the interests of the non-native participant.

In this chapter I discuss the ways in which information was handled by public officials and by the institution for which they worked. I explore a number of issues related with the practices that can be observed in the data. First of all, I assess the informative value of officials' provision of service turns. I then enquire into the origin of the information routines they implemented. I take the position that, in information provision, as in verbal communication, choices are made, and that alternative choices are possible and desirable. Next, I try to assess the role of the institution in defining an information policy for the information desk that ensured that mutual understanding was achieved and that a certain amount of information was provided to all clients. In other words, I ask to what extent there was institutional and individual concern over clients' information needs. In fact, I argue that the information practices described actually worked to reinforce asymmetries of power and knowledge between participants, and that the knowledgeable participants, that is, the officials, managed to exercise a great deal of power over clients by creating a new reality through their systematic use of a fixed set of ostensibly informative terms.

Finally, I examine in detail the change that took place in the office over the months of my presence with regard to information provision. I explore the arguments employed by the institution to justify its new policy and the different ways in which the office bureaucrats positioned themselves with respect to it. I also discuss the effects of this new policy on face-to-face service communication and on the relationships among members of staff.

2. Written vs. oral communication

This study of front-line institutional communication focuses on the verbal mode. The reason is that this was the only mode institutionally sanctioned for clients to obtain specific details on the status of their applications. On the one hand, the institution did not allow applicants to file written requests for information (which would have had to be answered in the same mode). On the other hand, information officials systematically refused to write down their verbal responses, even when explicitly asked to do so by clients with low competence in Spanish or English. This attitude can be observed in the following excerpt.

(11)

    1 *ENQ: tú puede escribe no?
       %tra: you can write, can't you?

→	2	*MIQ:		no no puedo.
		%tra:		no I can't.
	3	*ENQ:		tiene tres semanas.
		%tra:		have three weeks.
	4	*MIQ:		tres semanas.
		%tra:		three weeks.
	5	*ENQ:		ahora no concedido?
		%tra:		now not granted?
	6	*MIQ:		ahora no concedido.
		%tra:		now not granted.
	7	*ENQ:		señor por favor escríbeme yo no lo sé -. pode?
		%tra:		sir write me please I don't know it -. possible?
→	8	*MIQ:		no no puedo.
		%tra:		no I can't
	9	*ENQ:		no sólo escribe por favor.
		%tra:		no only write please.
→	10	*MIQ:		tres semanas -. te acuerdas de eso -? tres semanas tres
	11			semanas tres semanas tres semanas vale?
		%tra:		three weeks -. do you remember that -? three weeks three weeks three weeks three weeks ok?
→	12	*ENQ:		no toda la gente pida yo no sé.
		%tra:		not everybody asks I can't
→	13	*MIQ:		escribe tú.
		%tra:		you write.

Miquel's refusal to write anything is blunt and unmodulated, and his irritation at being asked to do so is evident in lines 10–11. His repetition of the key information "three weeks" four times and without pausing sounds fairly patronising. Note also Miquel's use of the verb "*poder*" 'be allowed to' in this extract. To my knowledge, there was no explicit prohibition that forbade officials to write information down for clients. So why did bureaucrats oppose writing so strongly?

In an informal discussion with me, Miquel justified his attitude by referring to "cheating" practices. He argued that many Chinese immigrants would repeat a particular request while claiming not to know Spanish but then it would turn out they did. (Although he referred explicitly to Chinese clients, I was able to observe that his determination not to use the written channel extended to all client groups.) Another interesting justification he gave was that he found it demeaning for clients to go away with information written on a piece of paper – as if they were dogs, he said, going away with a piece of bread in their mouths.

This points to a number of ideological issues. First, Miquel sees the role of writing as exceptional, even demeaning (!), and as a mode to be used only when the verbal is not possible. He defends the strict separation of modes and does not contemplate the possibility that clients' meaning-making processes might be enhanced by multimodal interaction. Secondly, he identifies immigrants' dishonesty as the reason behind his rejection of writing. Blaming the client is a favourite strategy in this bureaucratic context to justify all sorts of practices, as I will discuss in Chapter 5. This is why I am inclined to think that this is a mere rethorical device used by Miquel which draws on the ideology of mistrust (Sarangi and Slembrouck 1996), deeply rooted in the bureaucratic imagery, rather than the actual reason why Miquel refuses to write down information responses.

I would argue that the real reason for Miquel's refusal to write (which we must not forget is not just individual but institutional) is to protect the institution (and its officials) from criticism, that is, to safeguard institutional interests. The written is not ephemeral – as the verbal is – and written information can be a useful resource for clients to challenge contradictions in information provision. Verbal responses are uncommitted in a way written responses are not.

The link between writing and the possibility of comparing information is demonstrated by Miquel's radically different attitude in the following example. In this case, he does not refuse to write the information he has given the client orally because, as we see, a letter containing the same information has already been sent by the institution.

(12)

	1	*MIQ:	le hemos enviado una carta -, # para que nos traiga el
	2		original de la cartilla del banco vale?
		%tra:	we have sent him a letter -, # for him to come and bring us his bank savings book okay?
	3	*ENQ:	0.
		%act:	by means of gestures asks MIQ to write information overleaf.
→	4	*MIQ:	a ver que te lo escribo.
		%tra:	let me write this for you.
		%act:	writes information
	5	*MIQ:	hoy sale la carta de aquí.
		%tra:	the letter will be sent today.

This example shows that, under certain circumstances, writing is actually allowed. What are these circumstances? The clue is in the different nature of the information given in this example (a request for extra documentation). This is a type of information that, contrary to what happens with specific details on petition status, does not commit the institution to a specific course of action or outcome. If it is not "risky", it can be written.

At the immigration office, enquirers' interest in writing was as intense as officials' rejection of it. Writing was highly valued because it could facilitate the comprehension of the message. The written mode enables the temporal and spatial disembedding of information. Immigrants would be able to draw on the expertise of friends or relatives to make sense of the information they had been furnished. This is what Hussain discusses in lines 5–6 of the following extract of his informal interview with me.

(13)

	1 2	*RES: %tra:	o sea si no hablas español ellos consideran que que es tu problema no? so if you don't speak Spanish they think it's it's your problem right?
	3	*HUS: %tra:	sí. yes
	4	*RES: %tra:	no no se esfuerzan para explicarte + ... they don't make any effort to explain + ...
→	5 6	*HUS: %tra:	no no no porque ellos tienen que escribir hija -. que oye si no sabes -, escribes oye toma llévalo hablalo. no no no because they have to write it dear -. listen if you don't know -, write listen take it talk it over.
	7	*RES: %tra:	pero ellos quieren escribirlo a veces no quieren verdad? but do they want to write it sometimes they don't want right?
→	8	*HUS: %tra:	sí a veces que no quieren. yes sometimes they don't want to.
	9	*RES: %tra:	y por qué no quieren escribirlo? and why do they not want to write?
→	10 11 12	*HUS: %tra:	no sé por qué no -. porque como está cansados -, trabajandos hay mucho trabajo mucha faena trabajadores pocos. I don't know why not -. because as they are tired -, working there is a lot of work a lot of work and few workers.

74 *An illusion of information*

```
        13   *RES:    claro.
                      I see.
→       14   *HUS:    quieres descansado o algo así -. pero no tienes ganas de
        15            trabajo -. puede ser esto también.
             %tra:    you want relax or something like that -. but don't feel like
                      working -. it may also be that.
```

It is interesting how Hussain refers to the institutional order to explain officials' rejection of writing practices (lines 10–12) but then also to individual motivations ("they don't feel like working"). Interestingly, the tension between individual agency and institutional constraints that Hussain so clearly depicts is the crux of many of the arguments discussed in this chapter.

3. Front-line service talk

The insistence on the verbal mode was a source of profound inequalities. Petitioners who were not competent in Spanish, English or French were structurally disadvantaged. It is true that Miquel spoke Arabic and that Juan spoke Russian, but clients rarely found that out because that information was not posted anywhere. Thus, by not allowing the use of writing, many clients were automatically excluded from understanding anything. There were also a few other factors that complicated clients' sense-making processes. They are presented in what follows.

A striking feature of these encounters was that most of them were extremely short, often only consisting of a few turns. The second basic characteristic was that they all sounded very similar. The amount of information that was given and the way information was phrased was often the same. Given both the number of administrative stages that petititions might be at and the diversity of clients' communicative abilities and language proficiency levels, this similarity would seem surprising, not to say unfair. The third feature of bureaucrats' responses was that they were brief. They often only consisted of key words which were repeated over and over, and the information that these words provided was in most cases minimal. If enquirers wanted to know more details, they had to ask for them; these details were never volunteered by bureaucrats. That said, it is also true that, even if requested, certain kinds of insider information were never furnished, as the following chapter will illustrate. This has to do with the gatekeeping nature of the site and the bureaucrats' professional obligation to safeguard institutional interests. Yet it does not undermine my claim that in these exchanges no spaces were opened for immigrants to make sense of what was happening; on the contrary, the interactional onus was placed on them to find out relevant information. I would argue that these service encounters were about staging the pretence of a process of information exchange, but that truthful and meaningful information was hardly ever supplied. This argument will be developed in closer detail later in this chapter. Now let us concentrate on the specific discursive routines officials would employ in their face-to-face service talk.

3.1. *Reporting the initial assessment of petitions*

When their status was queried, the majority of applications were reported as being *en trámite*. When I started visiting the office, this response was meant to indicate that an application had received an initial positive endorsement, that is, that it was at the *fase de instrucción* stage.

If that first assessment was already negative, officials told clients that they had failed to turn in all the necessary documentation (*faltan papeles* 'some papers are missing' were the actual words used). The meaning of that expression was not literal. When documents were said to be "missing", bureaucrats always referred to the fact that the certificates submitted to prove arrival in Spain before 1 June 1999 had not been accepted, either because they did not meet the requirements of the institution or because they were forged. In other words, what was missing was valid evidence to prove period of residence.

Not any document was considered valid proof. As a state institution, this office protected the state's regimes of truth and mistrusted any certificates issued by individuals or private companies, except for those issued by large bureaucratised corporations, like banks. This way an individual having a savings book in his/her name was able to certify that s/he was in Spain when the account was opened, as physical presence at the time of opening is a requirement. Some other examples of valid documents were official certificates of registration with the local municipality, counterfoil slips from the post office, police entry stamps on passport, and in general, any certificate issued by the police or by a medical practitioner but only if s/he worked for the public health system.

If any other kind of documentation was missing, such as a photocopy of the client's passport, the officials would say so explicitly and a letter would be sent to the applicant's home. This means that the fact that part of the documentation submitted had been rejected could only be found out through the sorts of verbal exchanges examined here. In sum, the institution offered clients the possibility of submitting new evidence to prevent a rejection of their petitions

76   *An illusion of information*

but only to those who were astute enough to go and enquire in person. This situation would later change and the possibility of submitting new evidence would disappear, but let us now continue with the description of front-line service talk.

3.1.1. *"Trámite"* and "three weeks"

As I said before, when an application had been positively reviewed, the word *trámite*, a kind of pidgin abbreviation of the Spanish *en trámite*, as a response to clients' information requests was often the only word uttered by officials. No further details were supplied. Another typical feature of information responses was that *trámite* was always produced in Spanish and never translated. There are two issues to be discussed here: first, what the word means in Spanish, and secondly, what immigrant petititioners were able to understand by it.

In Spanish, when a petition is *en trámite,* it means that it is being processed. Although the word *trámite* belongs to general, non-specialised vocabulary, its most common use is in connection with bureaucratic processes. It is thus unlikely that immigrants who were poor speakers of Spanish would have come across this term in ordinary life, unless that is, they had had previous dealings with Spanish bureaucratic organisations. For them, *trámite* might have been as technical a term as any other. However, as I shall discuss later, the fact that *trámite* was always spoken in Spanish may have given the impression to clients that it was a key word that was in fact giving them an insight into the procedure.

One of the officials at the research site, namely Ramon, was more inclined to reduce information to a minimum. Miquel, by contrast, was more willing to offer more details. However, Miquel's turns tended to be more routinised than Ramon's. The excerpt below (14) illustrates Ramon's characteristically laconic information responses.

(14)

→	1	*RAM:	trámite ale.
		%tra:	being processed there you go.
	2	*EN1:	**okay** xxx?
→	3	*RAM:	no -. trámite.
		%tra:	no -. being processed.
	4	*EN1:	falta.
		%tra:	missing.
	5	*RAM:	falta **two weeks**.
		%tra:	missing two weeks.

6   *UUU: #0_4.

7   *RAM: **after two weeks come here**.

As can be seen, Ramon's information responses are, paradoxically, terribly uninformative. In addition, when asked to explain what he means by *trámite*, Ramon simply repeats this key word (line 3) without offering further details. It is the enquirer who has to ask again in line 5. But what this seems to prompt Ramon to do is not to explain better what is being done about the client's application, but rather to confuse the client.

In the cases in which officials did decide to give more details, they would employ the word *trámite* accompanied by a discursive directive of the type described by Agar (1985). By means of this directive, the institutional representative indicated to the immigrant client how to proceed, that is, essentially, when to come back to the office. This was basically the only piece of information that most enquirers were able to comprehend, that is, that they would have to wait.

Interestingly, the amount of time enquirers were requested to wait was always three weeks, regardless of the administrative stage their applications were at. The startling degree of repetition of identical responses attested to the extreme routinisation of service communication and indexed bureaucrats' complete disregard for accuracy. Their frequent and formulaic use of "three weeks" to indicate the period after which an applicant should return to the office was also likely to provoke among enquirers feelings of mistrust towards the institution.

Such directives regarding the next visit could be expressed in Spanish, English or in both languages, one after the other. In fact, a very common practice (although only when the client was South Asian) was for the Spanish word *trámite* to be followed by the "three weeks" directive in English, often without there having been previous interactional evidence that English was the language preferred by the enquirer.

To an outside observer, like myself, the frequent use of "three weeks" echoed a culturally specific way of providing information in which service responses by public representatives tend to be fairly uncommitted. I would like to argue that in their dealings with bureaucracy, Spaniards are well aware that bureaucrats' time predictions are not intended to be taken at face value. In that sense, "three weeks" may be as good a response as any other. Interestingly, this is confirmed by Miquel in backstage informal talk (see lines 1 and 2).

(15)

→   1   *RES: xxx *és per dir algo*.
        %tra: xxx is to say something.

→ 2 *MIQ: *és un temps aproximat.*
%tra: it's an approximate length of time.

3 *RES: *és un temps aproximat.*
%tra: it's an approximate length of time.

4 *MIQ: *sí.*
%tra: yes.

5 *RES: *podria ser un mes.*
%tra: it could well be a month.

6 *MIQ: *sí sí.*
%tra: yes yes.

→ 7 *MIQ: *perquè si els hi dius tres semanes vénen al cap d'una o dos*
8 *si els hi dius un mes vindran demà.*
%tra: because if you tell them three weeks they come after one or two if you tell them a month they will come tomorrow.

Apart from it being a cultural practice, the reasons why Miquel is uncertain as to how long it may take his backstage colleagues to process a given application are to be found in the lack of rational ways of organising work and communication among staff in this office. This idea was already mentioned in Chapter 2 in connection with example (9) and will continue to be discussed in section 6.2 of this chapter. The fact that the institution itself did not seem committed to working efficiently probably discouraged bureaucrats from running the risk of losing face by making time predictions which might not come true.

It is interesting to note also that Miquel's choice of "three weeks" is not random (see lines 7–8). Miquel's motivations seem to be to regulate the frequency of enquirers' visits to the office, in other words, to exert some degree of social control. Officials' routines were shaped by their negative expectations about clients' behavioural patterns, as they assumed that immigrant information seekers would not wait as prescribed. Thus, the value of "three weeks" was the effect it had on the addressee. It is a long enough period of time to space immigrants' visits to the office, but not too long to have the opposite effect.

It must be noted that in officials' information responses, no reference was ever made as to what immigrants could expect at the end of the "three week" period. Implicit in bureaucrats' responses is an assumption of relevance. Sarangi and Slembrouck (1996) claim that one of the features of bureaucratic discourse is that clients are expected to take for granted the truthfulness of what the bureaucrat says. An analysis of my interactional data reveals that bureaucrats' responses were assumed to be not only truthful but also relevant. Even if no mention was made of what changes were expected to occur at the end of three weeks, immigrants were expected to assume that *some* change would take place. That is, the bureaucrats' position of speaking as knowledgeable participants framed talk in such a way that the relevance of their responses was taken for granted. This provides evidence for the claim by Sarangi and Slembrouck that pragmatic investigations of speakers' interpretative processes and the ways in which meanings are constructed in interaction cannot ignore socially informed analyses which take into account the fundamental asymmetries underlying processes of information exchange in bureaucratic settings.

3.1.2. *"Falta"*

If an application had not been successful, it might be in one of two possible conditions: either it was truly being processed (or awaiting processing) or else some of the documentation submitted by clients had not been accepted. As I have noted, this latter possibility was represented in bureaucrats' talk by *"faltan papeles"* or in the immigration office pidgin abbreviated version, simply *"falta"*. The use of this term in the ways that I will explain below is a syntactic and semantic innovation of this setting.

In the immigration office, like *trámite*, *falta* was never translated. The language of the interaction in which it was embedded might be Spanish or English. Its idiosyncratic use is illustrated in such typical sentences uttered by immigrant clients as "any *falta*?" "I don't know who checked it but they tell me that there is *falta*"; "what is the *falta*, sir?" Note that, in all these instances, *falta* functions as a noun. Even though the noun *falta* does exist in Spanish, its meaning is either that of 'shortage' as in the sentence *"hay falta de trabajo"* 'there is a shortage of work' or 'offence, misdemeanour' as in *"cometer una falta leve"* 'to commit a minor offence'. By contrast, in the contexts where it was used at the immigration office, *falta* meant something like 'problem' (as in "any *falta?"*) or it might mean 'something that is missing' (as in "I don't know who checked it but they tell me that there is *falta*").

The use of *falta* was more popular among South Asians than among other ethnic groups. This might be due to the similarity of *falta* to English "faulty". This idiosyncratic use of *falta* was so popular among South Asians that it got extended to non-bureaucratic domains, as I could attest in my informal chats with Hussain.

The following extract (16) provides evidence for my argument about the similarity of *falta* to English "faulty". In line 3, the information seeker utters the English word in a position where *falta* would be the most likely choice.

(16)

	1	*ENQ:	**three weeks?**
	2	*MIQ:	**yes.**
→	3	*ENQ:	uh: **three weeks no fault?**
	4	*ENQ:	<**everything is clear**> [>]?
	5	*MIQ:	<**I don't know**> [<].

North Africans, who, due to geographical and historical proximity, are far more acquainted with the use of Spanish than other migrant groups (except Latin Americans, of course), employed other words like *probas* or *prufas*, probably derived from Spanish *pruebas*, besides *falta*.

One key issue in connection with *falta* is that it was incorporated by officials into their linguistic routines in the same idiosynchratic way in which it was used by clients. They uttered sentences like, "*al principio salía falta, ahora no sale en el ordenador si falta*" 'at first it showed *falta*, now the computer doesn't say if anything is missing'; "*no sé si falta, en trámite no se sabe si falta o no*" 'I don't know if anything is missing, being processed we don't know whether anything is missing or not'. In both these utterances, *falta* is used in non-standard ways, which can be interpreted as a way of facilitating communication with immigrants. However, the analysis of officials' practices reveals that *falta* is in fact a frequent source of miscommunication.

Service talk shows that bureaucrats were aware of the particular way in which immigrants used *falta* and what it meant. In the following extract, for example, Miquel is able to retrieve the "faulty" meaning of *falta* in line 6 (by contrast to the standard meaning that a number "is missing"). Miquel's ability to grasp the intended interpretation of *falta*, aided by the preceding sequential context (he had problems finding the file in the computer and discovered that there was a wrong number), prevents a misunderstanding sequence.

(17)

1	*EN1:	ahora esto ya está señor?
	%tra:	is this now done sir?
2	*MIQ:	sí.
	%tra:	yes.
3	*EN1:	sí falta.
	%tra:	yes fault.

	4	*MIQ:	qué?
		%tra:	what?
→	5	*EN1:	+ˆ uh antes uh antes sí falta la número.
		%tra:	uh before uh before yes faulty the number.
→	6	*MIQ:	había un número mal.
		%tra:	there was a wrong number.
	7	*EN1:	oh vale!
		%tra:	oh okay.

The skill he shows in the above encounter contrasts with other exchanges in which he seems oblivious to the potential for misunderstanding that standard uses of *falta* entail. In Spanish, the verb *faltar* occurs frequently in temporal expressions like *faltan dos semanas* 'there are two more weeks to go'. These sorts of expressions are extremely common in a setting like the immigration office, where clients want to know when a decision will be made. In those temporal contexts, the meaning of *falta* has nothing to do with problem; it only means that enquirers have to wait. As a result, native uses of *falta* create confusion and complicate clients' processes of sense-making. Although Miquel is trying to say that in two weeks' time the permit will be granted, ENQ's attention focuses rapidly on the term *falta* and the bad news this word conveys to him.

(18)

→	1	*MIQ:	está casi concedido pero faltan dos o tres semanas vale?
		%tra:	it's almost granted but there are still two more weeks to go okay?
	2	*UUU:	#0_2.
	3	*MIQ:	entiendes?
		%tra:	understand?
	4	*UUU:	#0_2.
	5	*ENQ:	**what** señor **is the** falta falta?
	6	*MIQ:	no falta # todo bien.
		%tra:	no problem # everything okay.

3.2. Beyond initial assessments

Not all applications were in the initial phases of the administrative procedure; some of them had moved on. However, it was true that, during my time at the immigration office, many of them were stalled in the *propuesta denegatoria* stage and were pending a final decision (see Chapter 2). This explains why so many responses were similar, that is, essentially because many petitions were in precisely the same administrative situation.

Another reason for similarities was the officials' practice of simplifying information as much as possible and providing only key words like *trámite*. But the information they offered was not only minimal; it was also ambiguous and confusing. The reason why I am saying this is because *trámite* was often the only word provided, regardless of the actual stage an application was at. For example, some applications that were actually in *propuesta de concesión*, that is, about to be granted, were also said to be *en trámite*. This practice had the effect of keeping enquirers in the dark about the crucial change that was about to take place in their lives. This can be seen in the encounter below (19), where the enquirer, whose application has actually been approved, is merely advised to wait.

(19)

		1	*AGE:	www.
		2	*MIQ:	www.
→		3	*MIQ:	**wait three more weeks** -,.
		4	*EN1:	**this week** [=! softly]?
		5	*EN2:	**this week** [=! softly].

@Situation: MIQ continues checking

	6	*RES:	*alguns posen una cara de resignació!*
		%tra:	some of them look so resigned!
→	7	*MIQ:	*aquest està en* propuesta de concesión *però si em poso a*
	8		*explicar-ho i no m'entenen* <#> [>] *i em fot una ràbia i* !
		%tra:	this one is about to be granted but if I start explaining and they don't follow and it makes me so angry a::nd!
	9	*RES:	<[=! laughs]> [<].
	10	*MIQ:	*i aquest també* !
		%tra:	and this one the same!
	11	*RES:	+ˆ *això vol dir que d'aquí tres semanes estaran resolts* [?].
		%tra:	this means that in three weeks' time a final decision will have been made.

→   12   *MIQ: *no suposo que ja se'ls ho ha dit perquè ja ho posa.*
         %tra: no I think they have been told already because it says so.

In lines 7 and 8, Miquel justifies his decision not to provide any relevant information by referring to his frustrating communication experiences. It is interesting, however, that he feels the need to account for his uninformative practices to me, indexing that he feels uncomfortable about them. Later on (line 12), he prefers to continue justifying himself rather than respond to the question I have asked.

I should note that the practices I have just described are tendencies rather than absolutes. In some cases, bureaucrats did indeed provide more details. Even here, though, the explanation was perhaps unnecessarily long-winded. The following are some examples of this discursive practice: "This is are the papers okay but you have to wait three more weeks to be accepted # understand?" "*Éste está más que en trámite pero todavía falta una o dos semanas para concedido*" 'This is better than being processed but there is still one or two weeks to go before the permit is granted'; "*aquí parece que todo está bien pero todavía faltan dos o tres semanas hasta que esté concedido*" 'Here it seems like everything is okay but there are still two or three weeks to go before the permit is granted'. Although one would expect to find these more informative explanations reserved for occasions when clients' competence in Spanish or English was high, this was not necessarily the case. Indeed, it often seemed that decisions on the amount of details to be furnished were determined by circumstances (long queue, a previous encounter which had been particularly difficult, etc.) that had nothing to do with enquirers' competence as displayed in situated talk

When the petition had been accepted, applicants were told that their permit had been "*concedido*" 'granted'. Again, this term was almost never translated.

4.   Extreme routinisation, equality and fairness

It is possible to classify, as I have done, information responses into a limited set of categories because of the extreme routinisation to which talk was subjected. Public representatives' discourse was so routinised that at times it seemed to follow a preestablished script. The routinisation of talk standardises responses and homogenises clients, but clients in this context were very heterogeneous. Not only did they come from different sociocultural backgrounds but they also had different linguistic repertoires and language abilities. The equality of treatment that routinisation ostensibly brings about was actually detrimental to them because it failed to recognise the individual needs of a highly diverse clientele.

Following Sarangi and Slembrouck (1996), I understand bureaucracy as a specific set of practices that construe particular types of social events as "bureaucratic". Bureaucracy does not exist independently of the social actors that create and recreate it. It is in and through language practices that bureaucracy comes into being. One such practice is routinisation. From a clients' perspective, routinisation depersonalises the service offered and is usually experienced negatively. However, the notion of routinisation is not always understood in negative terms.

In his seminal work on bureaucracy, Weber (1948) argued that the more "dehumanised" bureaucratic organisations were in their functioning, the more successful they would be in removing from public business all purely personal, emotional, and therefore, non-rational elements. He saw the impersonal nature of bureaucracy as an advantage over local powers which were driven in their actions by arbitrary personal considerations. This functioning principle was the result of the demand for "equality before the law" which lies at the heart of any modern democracy (Weber 1948: 224). Along the same lines, Goffman (1983) claimed that contemporary service transactions proceed under the assumption that all clients will be treated equally. The routinisation of service procedures may be considered an efficient way of ensuring that neutrality of treatment is achieved.

From the perspective of the service provider, routinisation may save effort and provide a sense of security in one's job. This feeling of security is examined by Cook-Gumperz (2000) in interactions between workers and customers at a fast food restaurant. These social exchanges are tightly controlled by a prescribed organisational script and leave little room for improvisation. Yet workers do not experience these scripted exchanges as constraining. For them, they constitute an interactional "safe zone", as they do not have to make judgements about how to relate to each individual customer. These interactions provide structural opportunities for both participant groups to collaborate in the accomplishment of the goals of the exchange.

By contrast, the kinds of routinised practices I focus on in this chapter were not structurally designed to enable the participation of both speaker groups. On the contrary, they were meant to reduce information, and I would even say interaction, to a minimum. Routinisation turned information into a pure formality because it did not take into account clients' possibilities of understanding what was said. Similar information was provided to all service seekers in the corpus, regardless of their linguistic skills. Some of them, as will be seen in the following chapter, were able to mobilise linguistic resources of various kinds to try to go beyond bureaucrats' scripted responses and challenge them. Many others, however, did not possess the linguistic abilities to attempt to uncover relevant details about their applications. Routinisation was disadvantageous for all groups of information seekers, but most especially for those who were least competent in Spanish or English.

The key question that arises then is the extent to which equal treatment guarantees equality of opportunities. The traditional view, held by Weber and Goffman, is that equality of treatment protects individuals from being subject to discriminatory practices. In Chapter 1, I discussed cultural pluralist approaches to diversity which argue instead for an "equality of difference". Along the same lines, Subirats (2002) claims that, in contemporary social life, a non-differentiated treatment of individuals no longer guarantees equality and fairness in the provision of services. In fact, the principle of non-differentiation conflicts with the demands of a new society in which the recognition of difference must be a constitutive element of citizenship. Far from providing equality of treatment, it is by failing to adjust to the different demands of culturally and linguistically diverse interlocutors and by failing to acknowledge the different sets of resources and capitals to which such people have access that institutions exclude certain groups from participation and put them at a disadvantage. This has tangible consequences for their lives.

5. The representation of the bureaucratic procedure

A key issue in the interactions discussed concerns the way in which bureaucrats' knowledge about the procedure gets represented to clients. In the previous sections I discussed how bureaucrats' minimalist information responses could be classified into three categories: *trámite*, *falta* and *concedido*. These response types (except, significantly, *concedido*) did not correspond to the official labels employed by the institution to define the stages that made up the administrative procedure. In fact, some of them, like *trámite,* could be used for a multiplicity of purposes. So where and how did bureaucrats' information practices originate?

5.1. Whose choice?

In his interview with me, Miquel stated that it was the team of information officials at this particular office who decided to replace "obscure" institutional terminology with lay words like *trámite*. It seems that the institution had given no specific instructions to officials as to what type and how much information ought to be provided about the processing of applications. It must be recalled that the four bureaucrats that served clients at this information desk had been hired only recently.

It is astonishing how little training in general the institution offered these inexperienced employees. Miquel recounted that on their first day of work they had been given general information on requirements, deadlines and necessary documentation so that they could answer petitioners' questions. In addition, somebody from the *INEM* (the state employment agency) had lectured them on general issues related to gaze, body posture and "friendly" communication. Among other things, they had been advised to look enquirers in the eye when addressing them (instead of, for example, staring at the computer screen), and employ respectful language. Although important, these were all very general recommendations which did not take into account the sociolinguistic complexity of the institutional site examined. It is also clear that no specific training was provided about issues related with communication in general and communication in intercultural contexts in particular.

The behaviour of this institution indexes two things: firstly, a complete disregard for immigrants' civil rights, among which their right to be treated appropriately, which in this case meant ensuring that they had access to key information, and secondly, a manifest lack of interest in officials' working conditions and practical needs. This generalised institutional indifference towards front-line officials was the context which framed and legitimised bureaucrats' uninformative practices.

5.2. Facilitating understanding

The reasons that Miquel put forward to justify bureaucrats' simplification practices were grounded on the need to facilitate communication. For him, it was a matter of common sense to think that the technical phrases employed by the institution, such as *fase de instrucción* 'preparatory phase' or *propuesta denegatoria* 'proposal for rejection', were beyond the ability of immigrant information seekers to understand. These difficulties arose, in his view, as a result of immigrants' poor command of Spanish, which was the language in which the institution functioned and the only one employed for official terminology. In short, officials allegedly simplified their productions to make them more accessible to their interlocutors.

Interestingly, this same assumption was attested by Sarangi (1996) in the British bureaucratic context. Bureaucrats assumed that clients, as outsiders, did not have the background to interpret "technical responses", and that it was their duty to keep explanations as simple as possible. Yet this conflicted with clients' efforts at understanding the bureaucratic procedure.

By and large, Miquel seemed unaware of the effects of their practices. In fact, in the interview, he did not problematise the ways in which the key isolated words the information team used meant nothing to most of their clients.

Because information is a verbal service, the content of what is said can hardly be distinguished from the way it is said. The linguistic format determines the types of meanings which are conveyed by a given utterance. Yet, from an analytical perspective, it is important to distinguish these two levels of investigation.

When Miquel referred to the linguistic difficulty of technical phases like *fase de instrucción* 'preparatory phase', what he had in mind was the difficulty of decoding the abstract or lexical meaning of this phrase. Not very proficient speakers of Spanish are likely to be unable to do that. However, what we are talking about here goes beyond decoding lexical meaning; it is about providing details that would allow immigrant petitioners to understand what was going on. That means in practical terms giving some indication of what was being done to the applications, who was examining them and how decisive that stage was for the final outcome, and of course saying all that in ways that clients would be able to comprehend.

Because of their insider position, bureaucrats were able to locate each stage within the procedure, assess its significance and make predictions with regard to the final outcome. For example, an application which was in *fase de instrucción* had received an initial positive evaluation which had only to be confirmed by the police. The documentation submitted would be checked again, and if everything was found to be in order and the applicant had a clean criminal record, the permit would be granted. These were the contextual interpretations that the term *fase de instrucción* indexed. This is what clients needed to know and what, in my view, officials ought to have explained.

However, it is true that in general insider knowledge of this sort is usually not made accessible to clients. As Sarangi and Slembrouck (1996: 55) state, "the institution will not provide any information that could be used to the client's advantage". The more information clients have, the higher the likelihood that the institution and its practices will be challenged. So in the institution's view, officials' duty is to provide information to clients, but above all, to protect the institution. Therefore, much of what I discuss here is not specific to this setting, but has to do with how bureaucracies work. By the same token, I do not want to claim that information-providing practices were intentionally more deficient in this office merely because the clients of the service were immigrants. In fact, much of what I observed was terribly familiar from my experience as a citizen in Spain.

In general, Spanish civil servants are characterised by their poor service. In his book on the Spanish public administration, Nieto (1996: 102) states that all citizens have at some point experienced indifferent, arrogant and even humiliating treatment at the hands of a civil servant. The key difference, though, lies in that Spanish or Catalan speakers possess the linguistic resources to demand further details, negotiate mutual understanding, and if necessary, challenge the information given. By contrast, most of the immigrant information seekers in this study lacked the linguistic skills to be able to make sense of the vague and confusing pieces of information they received. In fact, by not allowing clients to understand the situation, these officials were disempowering them; they were making the granting of a work permit seem even more valuable than it was. Much of what happened had to do not just with information processes, but also with giving the appearance that the gate was being kept closed, a gate which would only be opened as a result of clients' having good luck, as Ramon poignantly says in one of the encounters (see extract [63] on page 181).

5.3. Avoiding miscommunication

The issue that I want to address here is the way in which avoiding communication difficulties is presented by bureaucrats as benefitting immigrant service seekers. The motivation for public officials not to use "technical" vocabulary was not to enable information seekers to comprehend their turns, as Miquel claims, but rather to minimise the likelihood of engaging in long miscommunication sequences. Miscommunication is a constant threat to face, since the process of working through understanding problems is highly disruptive of any social interaction (Bremer et al. 1996: 69).

The more words bureaucrats provided, the higher the chances of communication difficulties emerging. The solution is clear: reduce information to the minimum. But who benefits from that? Clearly not immigrants. It must be conceded that, in this setting, engaging in long-winded processes of meaning clarification to ensure mutual understanding would have worked against institutional expediency. As Agar (1985: 157) states, "the time required for such privileged treatment of the client would consume the private profits or public budgets, and the institutional representative would be out of a job". In this office, a large number of information seekers had to be served every day. In addition, as long queues were the most visible feature of the service, they were also the main source of concern for the managerial staff in part because long queues periodically attract media attention[10] and are presented as indicators of poor service and deficient organisation. Managers were interested in having as many immigrants as possible served every day to reduce the long queues. By way of contrast, no interest was shown in the quality of the service provided. The significance of local linguistic practice was neglected. Paradoxically, it is by examining situated talk that we can gain an insight into how and why, far from diminishing, waiting queues only continued to grow longer.

5.4. Constructing an illusion

Here I want to argue that in spite of their emptiness, service providers' routines created the illusion that *some* information was being transmited.

The ecology of terms I have described to enquiries about the status of an application included two possible responses, that is, *trámite* and *falta*. The meaning of one response was defined by reference to the other. Put in other words, although *trámite* was an empty word in terms of conveying news, its status as non-*falta*, that is, as the absence of a negative evaluation, gave it a positive connotation. However, such indirect inferences could only be made by information seekers who were familiar with the whole system of terms, and most of them were not. That implies that the slightly positive information that the term *trámite* conveyed was hardly accessible to clients. And even in those cases in which clients *were* able to infer that everything was going fine, their inferences had the status of a hypothesis, since no explicit reassurance was ever conveyed. In that sense, *falta* was a much more informative term than *trámite,* because immigrants found out something tangible, namely, that their applications were not making progress. If they wanted, they could try to reverse the situation.

In spite of the uninformative nature of officials' responses, an appearance of information was carefully maintained. There are several indices of this. Firstly, a special information service was offered to deal with immigrants' requests. This service was open all day, from 8 a.m. to 10 p.m. Secondly, the fact that officials always employed the same words to refer to petitions and that these terms were systematically produced in Spanish might certainly give the impression, at least to foreigners not proficient in Spanish, that they were being given *some* kind of insider information. The recurrent use of the very term *trámite*, which, as I have noted, might have been unknown to immigrant clients, worked to reinforce that idea. It seems clear then that, rather than for its lexical import, this ever present term was employed for the effect it had on the audience. Hence, its value was not informative but tokenistic. In fact, *trámite* was usually accompanied by the time adverbial "three more weeks". This is essentially the only meaningful piece of information service seekers were provided. Note that when officials were asked to translate *trámite* into English they regularly just translated the temporal directive. This lends support to the notion that the value of the term was purely tokenistic. In sum, the interactional routine of always using *trámite*

90 *An illusion of information*

served to conceal, at least on a formal level, the fact that enquirers were given no information. Thus, the mechanisms whereby information was withheld from enquirers were difficult to expose because of the subtle ways in which they operated.

The formulaic import of *trámite* is illustrated in the following extract, namely (20), taken from the interview with Hussain. He is asked to explain how he interprets the word *trámite*. His illuminating response is contained in lines 10–18.

(20)

| | 1 | *RES: | no xxx a ti cuando vas a la oficina te dicen bueno tus papeles |
| | 2 | %tra: | están en trámite -, qué quiere decir -? qué significa? |

no xxx to you when you go the office they tell you okay your papers are being processed -, what does it mean -? what's the meaning?

	3	*HUS:	qué significas -? cómo trámite no sabes qué significa -? tú no
	4		sabes qué significa trámite?
		%tra:	what you mean -? how don't you know what being processed means -? don't you know what it means?

| | 5 | *RES: | hombre sí lo sé pero quiero saber si tú lo sabes! |
| | | %tra: | well of course I do but I want to know if *you* do! |

| | 6 | *HUS: | en mi idioma -. no que. |
| | | %tra: | in my language -. or what. |

	7	*RES:	no cómo explicas o sea si te dicen trámite tú qué piensas -?
	8		ah bueno # esto está bien está mal tengo que volver o sea
	9		qué es lo que piensas?
		%tra:	no how you would explain that is if they say being processed what do you think -? oh okay it's good it's bad I need to come back in other words what do you think it means?

→	10	*HUS:	no no es depende -. tú tienes que cuando te dicen miran tus
	11		papeles escriben de fecha de hoy -, oye tal fecha que él
	12		vienes para preguntar qué escriben # trámite -.
	13		por ejemplo ellos cuando dicen trámite tú piensas que vale
→	14		muy bien es trámite -. si quieres preguntas qué está mal o
→	15		está bueno trámite o si no falta algo -, tú tienes que
	16		preguntar -. si no -, pues tú sabes tú preguntaste lo que ellos
	17		dicen te dicen oye es trámite viene dentro de un mes para
	18		mirar otra vez xxx.

The representation of the bureaucratic procedure 91

	%tra:	it's not it's it depends -. you have to when they say they look at your papers write today's date -, listen on that day he came to ask what do they write being processed -. for example when they say being processed you think okay fine it's being processed -. if you want you ask it's bad, it's fine being processed or something is missing -, you have to ask otherwise -, you know you asked what they said to you listen it's being processed come back after a month to have it checked again.
19 20	*RES: %tra:	y entonces si tú quieres más información tienes que preguntar no? then if you want more information you have to ask right?
21	*HUS: %tra:	sí . yes.
22	*RES: %tra:	o sea trámite no se sabe -. no tú si está bien o está mal. so being processed one doesn't know -. no you whether it's good or bad.
23	*HUS:	no no no.
24 25 26	*HUS: %tra:	si tú prefieres preguntar si tú no sabes tienes que preguntar más -. si no normalmente te dicen ## toma es trámite viene dentro de un mes. if you prefer to ask if you don't know you have to ask more -. otherwise usually they say ## okay it's being processed come back after a month.
27 28 29	*RES: %tra:	aha -. y a ti te parece bien eso o crees que te deberían dar más información -. o sea porque trámite no es mucha información no? uh huh -. and do you think that is okay or do you think they should give you more information -. I mean because being processed is not a lot of information is it?

→ 30 *HUS: no porque ellos tienen que decirte más -. que oye que tus
    31 papeles está muy bien pero es trámite vale -? espera un par
    32 de mes o un quince días o un mes viene puede ser que te te
    33 dicen algo -. pero no hace falta no falta nada ni una cosas
→ 34 -. pero tus papeles está bueno -. como llevan estos papeles -.
    35 pues esta persona seguro no viene otra vez cuando sólo
    36 dicen ## escriben de fecha vale toma trámite -. pero no

92 *An illusion of information*

37		saben qué es qué trám cómo trámite qué es qué pasa está
38		mal está bueno qué es está bastante oscuro [?] por eso vayan
39		cada vez o quince días otra vez -. qué ya ha acabado trámite
40		o no?
	%tra:	no because they have to tell you more -. listen that your papers are good but it's being processed okay -? wait for a couple of months or fifteen days or a month come back it's possible that they tell you something -. but it's not necessary it's not necessary nothing -. but your papers are good -. like they take these papers with them -. then it's sure this person will not come back when they only say ## write the date okay there you go being processed -. but they don't know what is what pro what being processed what is what's going on it's bad it's good what is it it's pretty dark [?] that's why they go every time or fifteen days again -. has being processed finished or not?

Hussain's words provide evidence for my claim that in these encounters the interactional onus with regard to information is placed on clients. They have to ask for whatever additional details they want to know (see lines 14–16). For enquirers whose competence in Spanish or English is low, this is likely to be an arduous task in the minute-to-minute management of talk. Another element that links up with our previous arguments is that the standard *trámite* response does not guide enquirers towards what really matters to them, that is, whether they will finally be granted a work permit or not. In lines 30–34, Hussain describes the type of information immigrants ought to receive. In his opinion, they need to be reassured that their applications are making progress and that no more documentary evidence is needed.

The indeterminacy of *trámite* baffles clients, frustrates them and creates anxiety (see lines 35–39). This explains why they tended not to wait the amount of time prescribed by officials. Uncertainty about their future led them to seek information more often than necessary, which explains why waiting queues continued to grow rather than diminish. In other words, bureaucrats' information provision practices had the opposite effect of what was intended. Miquel accounts for officials' simplification of their turns as a means to avoid engaging in complex processes of meaning clarification which would work against the institution's need for expediency. Yet, as Hussain points out, the lack of information conveyed by words like *trámite* ended up increasing rather than reducing officials' workload.

5.5. Information and the exercise of power

In the previous section I argued that the routines established by officials not only failed to offer relevant details, but also worked to construct the illusion that some kind of information was being transmitted. In this section I would like to go a step further by arguing that, by employing these practices of information, institutional representatives managed to exert a great deal of power over their clients.

It could be argued that the nature of the power of bureaucrats at the immigration office resided in their ability to conceal information from clients. Yet I wonder to what extent we can claim that they deliberately did this. Remember that in the interview Miquel defended their "simplification" of institutional terms as a way to facilitate clients' understanding of service talk. He seemed genuinely committed to providing information, and except after the institutional change in information policy, he did not deliberately intend to hide details from clients. Throughout my fieldwork, none of the officials investigated claimed to do so (except, as I said, to follow institutional guidelines); but this is another issue. There is a sense, however, in which information was non-deliberately concealed. The question is, is it possible to establish a connection between the non-deliberate concealment of information and bureaucrats' exercise of power and control? The answer is yes, and to explain it, I shall resort to Foucault's and Giddens' understanding of the nature of power.

I have discussed how the bureaucrats' systematic use of a whole set of fixed terms like *trámite* and *falta* created an illusion of information. I want to argue here that it did more than that; that is, that it created a bureaucratic reality that stood for the actual procedure and concealed it. This is where power resides. That is, it resides in the bureaucrats' ability to create new realities and construct "objects of truth". As Foucault argues, "power produces; it produces domains of objects and rituals of truth" (Foucault 1977: 174). Power must not be conceived solely in terms of its repressive capacities. It is also profoundly creative. The power of bureaucrats disguises realities and redefines meanings. One could argue against the idea of considering these bureaucrats "agents of power" by stating that they are largely unaware of the consequences of their acts, in this case, of their language practices. Yet, as Giddens (1979: 92) claims, "the notion of power has no inherent connection with intention or 'will'. For Giddens, "the unintended consequences of action are of central importance to social theory in so far as they are systematically incorporated within the process of reproduction of institutions" (1979: 59).

Unintentionally but also intentionally, the bureaucrats in this study contributed to the maintenance of an unequal social order. Bureaucracies are institutional machineries that work independently of the needs of the individual clients they are supposed to serve. This understanding of bureaucracy is deeply rooted and it is sustained and reproduced in this setting through the way in which information is provided or not provided.

Within a bureaucratic organisation, the role of its representatives is defined by its contradictory goals and tensions. Bureaucrats are caught in a web of pressures. They are expected to perform their job well, while at the same time safeguard institutional interests. They are in a subordinate position with respect to institutional regulations and policies, which they must carry through even if they do not agree with them. Their activities are subject to the workings of organisational power. The metaphor of the web used by Foucault (Gordon 1980) serves to illustrate bureaucrats' position. Power is employed and exercised in a net-like organisation. Accordingly, individuals are not only its inert target, but the elements of its articulation. In that sense, public officials were always in a position of simultaneously undergoing and exercising power. This idea emerges still more clearly in the following section in which a crucial change in the institution's information policy is discussed.

6. A crucial change in information policy

Moments of change in institutional policy enable the visualisation of tensions, require participants to position themselves and facilitate the articulation of discourses. These give us insights into the institution's ideological conceptualisation of the social world.

During my fieldwork at the immigration office, the decision was made to curtail the quantity of information to be given to immigrants. In this section I assess the significance of the new policy in terms of what it unveils about the institution's perception of its social function. Secondly, I examine the discourse produced by the institution to legitimise its decision, as well as the discourses and counterdiscourses produced by institutional representatives to justify or challenge its application.

This analysis of the ways in which the institutional order is entangled in the production of interactional talk is undertaken through the detailed examination of a conversation between two public officials. Each of them has a different view with respect to the policy change mentioned. Analysis of this conversation is of interest because it brings into the open the contradictions with which bureaucrats have to cope. A fundamental tension has arisen between their role as information providers and the pressures of the institution not to disclose certain types of information. And their difficult position is further aggravated by the fact that the officials working the afternoon shift continued to provide to their clients the information that had been forbidden.

6.1. Setting the scene

In June 2000, while I was in the midst of my research, the office manager called a meeting of the information desk staff in which they were instructed that in instances where there were problems involving the evidence submitted to prove arrival by 1 June 1999, information staff was no longer to inform clients that this was the case. This was because when faced with news that submitted documentation was not in order, the reaction of most applicants was quite naturally to try to submit new documentation in hopes of avoiding a definitive rejection. The office manager argued that with the limited human resources available, the office could not handle the extra paperwork generated as a result of providing this specific piece of information. The manager added to her argument that in most cases this paperwork turned out to be a waste of time, as many of the supplementary documents submitted were forged. It was therefore not worth giving service seekers a second chance.

For the implementation of this new policy, the office management made recommendations as to language use in face-to-face communication. It is significant that for once they did focus on language use. The manager advised officials to extend the use of the term *trámite,* which she knew they employed in service communication, to include those applications which were about to be rejected. In other words, all applications which had still not been accepted were to be denoted in *trámite*. Some of them would eventually be accepted, while some others – the vast majority – would finally be rejected. Endorsement by a manager of the use of *trámite* as a means to conceal the fact that relevant details were not provided confirms that this word had acquired a purely formulaic use.

Another of the recommendations made by the manager concerned the way in which officials should account for the change in the information they provided. She advised officials to "stage" the change as resulting from a shift in the amount of information produced by the computer. Relevant details on information seekers' applications could no longer be provided because – supposedly – they were not available to officials. The blame was to be placed on the machine or on the back office, to which access was denied.[11] Immigrants were thus left in a powerless position. The official to whom they had access could not be held accountable (because s/he allegedly had no information) while at the same time they did not have access to anyone that could.

6.2. Accepting managerial authority

In his analysis of administrative behaviour, Simon (1957) examines the issue of managerial authority in organisations. He defines authority as "the power to make decisions which guide the actions of another. The superior frames and transmits decisions with the expectation that they will be accepted by the subordinate" (1957: 125). What happens is that the subordinate holds in abeyance his own critical faculties for choosing between alternatives. In other words, individual choice is suspended in favour of coordinated behaviour, which is essential for administrative activity to be efficient.

The different factors that may induce acceptance of authority are, among others, purpose and economic security. Employees will be more willing to accept managerial decisions when they sympathise with the purpose to be achieved and when they believe that the decision made will be effective in achieving it. This confidence may be based less on the knowledge of the correctness of the decision than on faith in the ability of those who made it. The effectiveness of the second factor mentioned, namely, economic security, is undoubtedly more transparent. As Simon (1957: 133) remarks, "obedience may be the price of retaining the position, securing a higher salary or other advantages". He also admits that the fact that many organisations tolerate a great deal of insubordination without dismissal diminishes the effectiveness of these sanctions as a means for securing authority.

Focusing on institutional settings, Agar (1985) emphasises the systemic nature of institutional discourse. He describes institutions as "discourse ecologies", where individual agency gets blurred away in favour of an analysis based on the conceptualisation of speakers as social actors who are socially and institutionally constrained in terms of what they want or are able to say or do. To illustrate his point, Agar argues that there is very little room left for public officials to act outside the prescribed order of things. Even if they wanted to hand control over to the client, they could not afford to do so. They would run the risk of being accused of "disloyalty" or, as he puts it, of misusing public funds, and would face dismissal. If that is added to "a recent institutional representative history of unemployment in a glutted labour market" (Agar 1985: 157), the threat to their well-being becomes even more acute.

Returning to the immigration office, the two factors mentioned by Simon, namely, purpose and economic security, had an obvious bearing on the bureaucrats' reactions towards the change. In order to examine that bearing a detailed analysis of the institutional order is required. The institution investigated was defined by numerous contradictions. Institutionalised sloppiness and a lack of managerial accountability led to an irrational division of work between shifts which caused significant delays in the processing of applications, constantly changing practices for processing paperwork, difficult communication between information desk and the back office, lack of managerial control over officials' work and so on. Decisions seemed to be made ad hoc and there existed no sense of collective responsibility.

The following extracts show the bureaucrats' negative perception of the institutional order in which their work was embedded. Extract (21) alludes to the fact that the administrative processing of applications did not seem to follow rational criteria ("everything is possible!"). Extract (22) describes managers' lack of interest in what was going on in the office. And example (23) gives us insights into how changing criteria for processing paperwork had a restrictive effect on the amount of information provided to service seekers.

(21)

	1	*TER:	*escolta Ramon pot ser que un del dia vint i tres de març*
	2		*estigui en instrucció -? fase d'instrucció* ?
		%tra:	listen Ramon can one [application] from March twenty-third still be in preparatory -? preparatory phase?
→	3	*RAM:	*bue:no: -! de tots colors* !
	4	%tra:	everything is possible!

(22)

	1	*RES:	*i els jefes no li diuen res* ?
		%tra:	and how come the managers don't tell him off?
→	2	*MIQ:	*els jefes no s'enteren del que passa aquí* !
		%tra:	the managers have no idea what's going on here!

(23)

→	1	*MIQ:	*és que durant una època no sé per què als que ja es veia*
	2		*que:* [/-] *si estan els papers bé es posa* en trámite *si no es*
	3		*posa lo altre -. doncs va haver-hi una època que quan veien*
	4		*que estaven bé ja posaven directament* propuesta de
	5		concesión.
		%tra:	there was a time when I don't know why those [applications] which seemed [/-] if the papers are fine they write being processed, otherwise they write the other thing -. so there was a time when if everything seemed fine they wrote proposal for approval straight away.
	6	*RES:	<u>ah</u>!

98 *An illusion of information*

→	7	*MIQ:	*i llavors # hi ha uns expedients d'aquests que són realment*
	8		*els que estan en* propuesta de concesión *i falten dos o tres*
	9		*setmanes i n'hi ha d'altres que tarden més -. llavors ells*
	10		*diuen pues a mi m'ho vas dir* !
		%tra:	so there are some of these files which are really about to be accepted in two or three weeks but there are some others which take longer -. then they say you told me!
	11	*MIQ:	*o sigui que el millor és no dir-los-ho.*
		%tra:	which means the best thing is not to tell them.

In this last encounter, Miquel describes how he is challenged by service seekers because of organisational changes in the way applications are processed (see lines 7–10). The front-line bureaucrats were suffering the consequences of erratic management practices in the form of protests, challenges, and threats to face by service seekers. The organisational context outlined did not induce "acceptance of authority", in Simon's terms. Obviously, no causal relationship can be established, since different officials may have had different perceptions of the situation and may have attached importance to different elements of the contextual background. Yet it is likely that some of the factors mentioned above explain the sceptical attitude some officials like Juan and Teresa showed towards the change in the information policy examined in this section.

Economic security is the second factor Simon highlights in relation to acceptance of authority. All the officials working at the information office had been hired on twelve-month contracts. Before taking up this job they had all been unemployed. Like the institutional representative described by Agar, Miquel and Ramon had a long history of temporary job contracts and were anxious to hold down a permanent post.[12] Both had university degrees in the field of humanities which did not seem to open up many professional opportunities for them. In a conversation with me, Miquel mentioned a couple of times that he hoped to pursue a career in the civil service. Work stability seemed to be a lasting source of worry for him. An example of this constant preoccupation with his job is an email message sent to me on 4 December 2000 in response to a question I had asked about how to translate certain words from the tapes which were in Arabic. An English translation of Miquel's message is provided below. (The original in Catalan is given in a footnote.)

(24)

> Hello before the holiday, maqbul and mahfuz with long u mean granted and rejected. That thing you mention that Ramon and myself used to say I don't have a clue what it is. Ramon is on holidays, so we cannot ask him until next week. I have no idea what bilifits means, tarabya could be Arabic (arabiya), and as for

bakawuab, I don't know either. Baka on its own means it's missing, but I have no idea what wuab means. If you don't bring it here it's impossible to know, but it will have to be after the holiday. *By the way here we are all really scared because they want to sack us all because they say there is no more work to be done and we are all pretty upset.*[13] (italics added)

After answering my questions, he immediately raises the topic of his uncertain job situation (in italics). Note that his choice of words ("really scared" and "pretty upset") tinges the message with an air of drama, which certainly indicates the importance he attaches to his work situation. In the informal interview we had almost a year later, the first thing he told me was that he and Juan were now out of work, while Ramon and Teresa, who had been reported for their rudeness by service seekers twice, continued to work for the immigration services. He felt frustrated and completely let down by the institution.[14]

I do not propose to claim that economic considerations alone serve to explain Miquel's attitude with regard to the managerial decision discussed here and set him apart from his other colleagues. In fact, economic factors are only one part of the complex set of interlocking contextual conditions that inform, yet cannot be mapped onto, participants' behavioural patterns.

6.3. Justifying individual positions

In this section I explore how bureaucrats as social actors made sense of the new policy they had to implement and how they positioned themselves vis-à-vis the managerial decision. I do this through a detailed examination of an interaction involving Miquel, Teresa and myself. It was motivated by a provision of service turn carried out by Teresa that was considered inappropriate by Miquel. Miquel, who was at the time engaged in a different interaction, reacted by admonishing his colleague. A fairly heated argument between the two then erupted. Miquel and Teresa put forward their divergent views on the institutional policy change and the various reasons that justified their respective attitudes and actions. Some of their reasons echoed the arguments given by the institution to justify this policy change; others were related to their own practical experience; still others had to do with an expressed concern for immigrants' well-being or for their chances of active participation in the procedure. In the foreground was the fact that the new policy was undermining the logic of their work and thus their own sense of self-esteem.

(25)

→	1	*TER:	está igual -. faltan faltan papeles -. # faltan papeles -. ## faltan
	2		papeles.
		%tra:	nothing has changed -. papers are missing missing -. # papers are missing -. ## papers are missing.
		%com:	TER is engaged in a different encounter.
→	3	*MIQ:	Teresa, *estan* en trámite *tots*.
		%tra:	Teresa, they are all being processed.
→	4	*TER:	están en trámite -. trámite.
		%tra:	they are being processed -. process.
	5	*UUU:	#0_2.
→	6	*MIQ:	*no ho podem dir*.
		%tra:	we are not allowed to say that.
	7	*TER:	xxx.
	8	*MIQ:	o del.
		%tra:	or from.
→	9	*TER:	*però és que els de la tarda sí que ho diuen ara* !
		%tra:	but our colleagues in the afternoon they are saying it now!
→	10	*MIQ:	*ja però però la Núria* <*la Núria*> [>] # *la Núria no ens ho va*
	11		*deixar dir a nosaltres* !
		%tra:	I know but Núria <Núria> [>] # Núria did not allow us to say that !
	12	*TER:	<*ara al revés*> [<]!
		%tra:	<now it's the opposite> [<]!
→	13	*TER:	*però que si estan en* en trámite *estaran sempre* !
		%tra:	but if they are being processed they will always be!
	14	*MIQ:	*ja* !
		%tra:	I know!
	15	*TER:	*no cal mirar-ho ja* !
		%tra:	there is no need for us to check them!
	16	*MIQ:	en tres semanes.
		%tra:	in three weeks' time.
	17	*TER:	*ja no cal mirar-ho* !
		%tra:	there is no need!
	18	*MIQ:	*a vegades*.
		%tra:	sometimes.

A crucial change in information policy 101

→ 19 *TER: +ˆ *a veure si està en fase vuitanta tres no canviarà mai* !
      %tra: listen if they are in phase eighty-three their status will never change!

→ 20 *MIQ: *a lo millor han portat papers perquè com algú els ho diu* !
      %tra: perhaps they have handed in more papers because somebody tells them to!

[…]

21 *TER: *és que amb tots és això -. si mires els expedients -, els que estan*
22   *en fase vuitanta tres -, <quan estan xxx> [>].*
      %tra: it is the same for all of them -. if you look at the files -, those which are in phase eighty-three -, <when they are xxx> [>].

23 *MIQ: <trámite> [<].
      %tra: <being processed> [<].

24 *RES: xxx.

25 *TER: <no si no xxx> [>].
      <well if they aren't> [>].

26 *ENQ: <puedo preguntar> [<] esto -? ## éste cómo alguien que
27   presente del tre:s de marzo -, # uh qué pasa trámite qué?
      %tra: <can I ask> [<] this -? ## this how somebody who submits on March third-, # uh what happens being processed what?

28 *RES: <xxx> [>].

29 *MIQ: <ni idea -. trámite> [<].
      %tra: <no idea -. being processed> [<].

30 *TER: *clar jo suposo que fins que no: # no <arribi una ordre> [>1] de*
31   *Madrid o lo que sigui xxx <desfavorables> [>2] favorables*
32   *perquè els hi falta <en principi> [>3] els hi falta algo -. # si*
33   *estan denegats és perquè els hi falta algo però clar no els hi*
34   *podem dir que: # que estan denegats perquè encara no xxx vale*
35   +/.
      %tra: of course I guess that until we # <get an order> [>1] from Madrid or whatever xxx <negative ones> [>2] negative ones because it's missing <in principle > [>3] something is missing -. # if they are turned down it is because something is missing but of course we cannot tell them that their applications have been rejected because they are still xxx right +/.
      %add: RES

36 *ENQ: <hay falta: -? papeles> [<1]?
      %tra: <anything missing: -? papers> [<1]?

| | 37 | *MIQ: | <no sa::le si hay falta [=! impatient tone]> [<2].
| | | %tra: | <it doesn't not show if anything is missing [=! impatient tone]> [<2].
| | 38 | *MIQ: | <aquí sólo sale trámite -,> [<3].
| | | %tra: | <the only thing it shows is trámite - ,> [<3].

@Situation: MIQ checks status of following application

| | 39 | *RES: | +ˆ xxx és un cacau això.
| | | %tra: | this is a mess.
| | 40 | *TER: | és un cacau.
| | | | it's a mess.
| | 41 | *UUU: | #0_3.
| → | 42 | *TER: | perquè perquè xxx si els hi dius que falten papers com a mínim
| | 43 | | que portin algo si poden !
| | | %tra: | because because xxx if you tell them that they need more papers at least they can hand in something!
| → | 44 | *MIQ: | la versió de la Núria és que no se'ls hi pot dir perquè si ja ho
| | 45 | | tenen ho han tingut que portar.
| | | %tra: | Núria's version is that we are not allowed to tell them because if they had anything they should have provided it.
| | | %com: | Núria is the name of the office manager
| | 46 | *TER: | per què -? per què ?
| | | %tra: | why -? why?
| → | 47 | *MIQ: | que si ho tenien -, ho tenien que haver portat quan van portar
| | 48 | | els papers.
| | | %tra: | if they had it -, they should have provided it when they submitted their papers.
| | 49 | *TER: | sí però llavors.
| | | %tra: | yes but then.
| → | 50 | *MIQ: | si no el que fan és fer-ho fals.
| | | %tra: | otherwise what they do is provide forged documents
| | 51 | *TER: | fals?
| | | %tra: | forged?
| → | 52 | *MIQ: | és pitjor per a ells perquè la policia els detindrà.
| | | %tra: | it's worse for them because the police will arrest them.

	53	*TER:	*sí no això també la veritat és que sí -. perquè clar d'alguna*
	54		*manera o altra intentaran aconseguir el que sigui per # per*
	55		*treure-ho.*
		%tra:	yes well in fact that's also true -. because of course some way or other they will try whatever they can to get it.
		%act:	moves towards counter to serve client
	56	*TER:	*sí que de vegades no saps què és millor.*
		%tra:	yes at times you don't know what's best.
→	57	*MIQ:	*però jo ja li he dit tres vegades a la Núria que els de la tarda ho*
	58		*diuen -, i es queda <u>ah</u> !*
		%tra:	but I've told Núria three times that our colleagues in the afternoon tell them -. and she goes oh!
	59	*TER:	*és que abans nosaltres ho dèiem.*
		%tra:	'cause we used to tell them.
	60	*MIQ:	*ja ja.*
		%tra:	yeah I know.
	61	*TER:	*i ara és al revés -. o sigui que no ho entenc.*
		%tra:	and now it's the opposite -. so I don't understand.

At the beginning of the excerpt, Teresa is telling her interlocutor that his application is not making progress because he cannot prove that he fulfils one of the eligibility criteria established by the government. Before the service seeker is able to respond, Miquel chips in. He corrects his colleague's words, reminding her that the appropriate response to give is that applications are *en trámite*. His use of the quantifier *tots* 'all' is significant. Strictly speaking, it is not literally accurate to say that all applications are in *trámite*. Miquel knows as well as Teresa does that a number of permits have already been granted. Rather, the use of *tots* points at the blurring of previous informative distinctions, that is, it indexes the new binary mode of thinking established by the institution's new policy, whereby any application that has yet not been accepted is categorised as being in process.

What Teresa does immediately after being corrected is striking. She retraces her words and gives the client a completely different version of the status of his application (see line 4). The service seeker thus receives completely different information in two consecutive turns. As a result, the bureaucrat projects an image of arbitrariness which contradicts the essence of bureaucratic practice as defined by Weber (1948), that is, rationality and fairness of treatment.

Teresa's discursive behaviour is illuminating in terms of how she perceives and constructs the space of social relationships in which these service interactions are embedded. One way of interpreting Teresa's behaviour is to claim that she disregards her addressee's ability to spot and bring her inconsistencies into the open, either because she takes the latter to be slow-witted or because she thinks he lacks the linguistic resources to understand what is going on. Another interpretation would be that Teresa conceives of their role relationship as being clearly asymmetrical. The implications are that, even if the service seeker is able to identify the contradiction, Teresa will not be challenged - as she has the position of strength - or if she is challenged, she will feel no obligation whatsoever to render her actions accountable to such an interlocutor. Whatever the case, Teresa constructs her interlocutor's potential for action as severely restricted.

When Miquel reminds his colleague in line 6 that they have been forbidden to say that new documents are needed for enquirers' applications, Teresa retorts by exposing the blatant inconsistency of the situation. Even though they have been forbidden to give that particular item of information to enquirers, she points out, their colleagues working in the afternoon have ignored the order and continue to provide it (line 9). The arguments Teresa uses to support her subversion of managerial authority have to do with the lack of a clear, unified policy. This is connected to Simon's notion of "purpose" as a key factor in inducing acceptance of authority. If measures are not taken to guarantee that policies are carried out by all bureaucrats, acceptance of authority becomes almost a matter of good will. This is especially true of the policy change at the immigration office because it affects the very essence of bureaucrats' jobs. Their task is to provide information, but at the same time the institution is asking them to conceal key details. This raises the question of what is left for them to do.

The policy change thus embodied an attack on bureaucrats' understanding of their work as meaningful and worthwhile. If public officials could no longer advise information seekers to provide new documentary evidence, their applications would not make any progress (see line 19)[15] and the bureaucrats' professional activity would become meaningless. This is precisely the point Teresa makes in lines 13–19. A few turns later (lines 42–43), she continues to show her disapproval. On this occasion, the reasons she provides have to do with immigrants' opportunities for participation. By providing precise details, immigrants are given the opportunity to change the course of events. In brief, Teresa's arguments show a mixture of concern about her own situated social role on the one hand and her clients chances of success on the other. Her main argument, though, and the one she puts forward first, has to do with the very definition of her professional role as an information provider. Her worries about immigrants' opportunities for action become an argument to challenge the institutional framing of the situation insofar as they work to lend support to Teresa's positioning against the new information policy.

A crucial change in information policy 105

Worried as he is with presenting "a unified front", Miquel uses a variety of strategies to counter his colleague's criticisms. In lines 10–11, for example, he responds to Teresa's accusation that managerial recommendations are being flouted by the behaviour of afternoon officials by appealing to the authority of the manager. Miquel is, in Simon's terms, suspending his own critical faculties for choosing between alternatives. Implicit in Miquel's words is the idea that it is not up to Teresa and himself to make judgements on the appropriateness of the institutional decision and that they should adopt the recommended mode of behaviour. Miquel is then confronted with a new argument by Teresa: if the possibility is not left open for enquirers to file additional documentation, the situation becomes nonsensical. There is no longer any need for service seekers to queue up or for bureaucrats to continue checking the status of immigrants' applications. This argument constitutes an attack on the very essence of the public officials' work, and consequently, on their sense of self-esteem. In response, Miquel needs to find arguments to keep on justifying his professional adherence to the new policy. The speaking voice is that of the professional whose sense of self-respect is being questioned. Miquel's reasons move down to the terrain of everyday reality. He states that the possibility of there being changes in the status of applications is real because "somebody" keeps telling service seekers that they need to submit new documentary evidence (line 20). This line of argumentation is twisted indeed: he is implying that it is only because of the existence of subversive practices among bureaucrats that their work as information providers makes sense.

Another of Miquel's arguments to justify his position in relation to this matter is presented in lines 44–45. Miquel carefully phrases it as the voice of the institution: *"la versió de la Núria és ..."* 'Núria's version is that ...'. This turn allows us an insight into the discourse produced by the institution to legitimise its new policy: all supplementary evidence should have been provided when applications were first submitted, that is, clients should get their documents straight from the beginning. (From the clients' perspective, this was a less than reasonable proposition if we take into account that details of the types of documents accepted by the institution to prove arrival in Spain by 1 June 1999 were not contained in the information booklet distributed by the government.) Of course, this is only the argument rationalised by the institution to back up its policy, but even as a mere argument it is patently weak. In defending the institution, Miquel needs a better argument. Consistent with what was commonly claimed in discourse among immigration office staff, Miquel argues that what most applicants do after being told that their documentary evidence is not valid is forge new documents (see line 50). Whatever effort is made to process new paperwork will thus be useless anyway. This, he implies, is what justifies the decision to prevent more paperwork from being filed.

At this point, these officials' concerns about service seekers' well-being surface once again. In line 52, Miquel claims that it is in the clients' own interest that they not be told that their documentary evidence has not been accepted, because if they submit forged documents, the police will arrest them. Miquel's words echo and respond to Teresa's previous concerns about clients' opportunities for action (see lines 42–43). As with Teresa previously, however, Miquel appears to use the safeguarding of service seekers' interests as only a secondary argument to lend support to his main position.

Miquel eventually manages to convince his colleague that not giving detailed information is best. However, to show personal alignment with his colleague, Miquel does accept some of Teresa's arguments. He raises again the issue of the two work shifts' inconsistent information provision practices (see lines 57–58) and underlines the fact that he has told his superior on three occasions but has not got a clear response. Miquel's words evidence the lack of managerial responsibility over the collective image of the institution. It was precisely this type of attitude that was working to undermine employees' trust in their managers' ability to organise their work efficiently.

In the interaction above, Miquel used the institution's argument that all certificates should have been submitted by applicants when petitions were first filed, but carefully framed it as "institutional discourse". However, as excerpt (26) shows, the reasons Miquel used to convince his colleague were not necessarily arguments he himself adhered to. His attitude needs to be understood with reference to his being a social actor whose actions were constrained by his position in the institutional structure.

(26)

		1	*MIQ:	*que li faltaven tots els papers que no tenia res i com que no*
		2		*tenia peles segons ell si tenia peles li donarien falsos però*
		3		*com no en té que vol que ho borrem.*
			%tra:	that he was lacking all the papers that he did not have anything and that as he did not have any money according to him if he had money he would get forged papers but since he does not have any he wants us to erase it [his file].
→		4	*RES:	*si hagués estat aquí realment tindria papers no ?*
			%tra:	if he had really been here he would have papers [documentary evidence] wouldn't he?
→		5	*MIQ:	*ja bueno hi ha molta gent que no eh -? però + . . .*
			%tra:	well there are many people who don't, but + . . .

6   *RES: *bueno ja però* + ...
    %tra: yes well but + ...

This exchange is a backstage discussion between Miquel and myself about a rather tense encounter the state official had engaged in. In the first three lines he explains to me the client's situation, which has to do with not having valid certificates to prove length of residence in the country. When I use the same argument that is put forward by the institution to justify the policy change, Miquel admits that the institutional argument is tenuous, since in fact many applicants do not have documents to show they meet the government's eligibility requirements.

The above example illustrates the need for researchers to be cautious in making claims about opportunities for individual agency in institutional settings. As has been remarked, the arguments Miquel offers in his social role as a public bureaucrat do not harmonise with his individual views on the matter. Participants' interactional contributions in institutional settings have to be understood as shaped by their social positioning in the complex web of interest and pressures which make up the institutional order. Researchers need to analyse these institutional conditions in detail to be able to comprehend the constraints framing institutional talk. Yet this does not imply that talk is totally determined by contextual considerations. Social subjects have their own understandings of the institutional scene and it is in relation to these subjective, individual perceptions that discourse occurs and social actions are shaped.

6.4. *Team work and the lack of a unified front*

In the previous section it was shown that acceptance of authority could not be taken for granted. Some public bureaucrats, such as Miquel, decided to go along with the institution's new information policy, while others, such as Teresa, were reluctant to implement the changes. This results in a considerable degree of tension among workmates and had a clear impact on an interactional level. Officials may have had different reasons for acting as they did, but what was significant was the fact that the non-implementation of the new institutional guidelines by some of the office staff was tolerated by the institution. In his study of Spanish bureaucracy, Nieto (1996) argues that, in Spain, no one is ever held accountable for the malfunctioning of a public service. It is a system where, in cases of conflict, the solutions adopted try to ensure the least possible "disturbance" for institutional actors, even when this is at the expense of institutional efficiency. The policy change analysed here is a case in point. To prevent new certificates from piling up, certain information was no longer to be provided. The devastating consequences that decision had, mostly for clients but also for bureaucrats, did not seem to be taken into consideration.

Nieto refers to the set of habitual institutional practices in Spain as the "environmental niche" in which the work of civil servants is embedded and to which they adjust. A good civil servant is someone who complies with institutional guidelines but does not trouble managers with the practicalities of his/her work. Nieto's comments are relevant here. Spanish civil servants tend to work in isolation and independent of their colleagues' actions. The notion of "team", referred to below, is largely nonexistent in Spanish bureaucratic contexts. And yet bureaucrats' actions are consequential for their colleagues' work and the image of the institution. When the information provided by the institution is not consistent, clients are given arguments to challenge officials' words. This is especially the case when the information provided is not favourable to their interests.

These situations are profoundly face-threatening. They represent a personal attack on institutional representatives' image of fair and honest individuals. More importantly, they affect clients' perception of the treatment they receive. It is in these types of situations that feelings of discrimination originate. As Goffman (1983) points out, "equality of treatment" is a perceptual achievement in interaction rather than an objectively identifiable feature. As soon as immigrants have the impression that they are deliberately being confused, the public institution loses credibility.

Employees in an organisation have been described by Goffman (1959) as members of a "team" engaged in staging a "show". He refers to them as "performers" in that they work to sustain a given definition of the situation. In Goffman's words, they maintain a "line" before an "audience" (i.e. service seekers).

The metaphor of the "show" is particularly useful to understand what went on in this immigration office. The change in the institution's information policy had to be staged with care by officials. The same information as previously was available to them, but fewer relevant details were to be provided to immigrants. As Goffman (1959: 83) points out, public representatives must be cautious "not to give the show away". It is essential that officials keep a unified front, since otherwise public disagreement among members of the team may embarrass "the reality sponsored by the team" (1959: 86). A unified front is a means of self-protection. If all members of the team stage the same representation of reality, it is less likely that officials will be challenged on an individual basis.

Example (27) shows the extent to which Miquel resents his colleagues' "disloyal" behaviour. In the extract, he remarks on the fact that his interlocutor has been given more information than prescribed (lines 4–5). That is, the applicant has been told twice by some other member or members of the office staff that he needs to submit new documentary evidence to prevent the rejection of his application. This is precisely the information that the institution does not want officials to reveal. Miquel knows that the enquirer has been given it twice because, as noted Chapter 2, it is common practice for officials to write the response provided to enquirers at the top of application forms every time they were taken in for consultation.

(27)

| | 1 | *MIQ: | espera. |
| | | %tra: | wait. |

| | 2 | *MIQ: | sólo traes uno eh? |
| | | %tra: | you only bring one right? |

| | 3 | *ENQ: | uh huh. |

@Situation: MIQ checks status of ENQ's application in computer

→	4	*MIQ:	*a aquest li han dit dos vegades que li falten # això vol dir*
	5		*que falten i això vol dir que falten.*
		%tra:	this one has been told twice that things are missing # this means it's missing and this means it's missing.

| | 6 | *RES: | *i no ha portat res més?* |
| | | %tra: | and has he not brought anything else? |

| → | 7 | *MIQ: | *si li apunten això vol dir que el qui l'hi apunta l'hi diu.* |
| | | %tra: | if they write that it means that the person who writes it also tells him. |

→	8	*MIQ:	todavía está en trámite -. no se sabe si:: has traído más
	9		papeles tú o no?
		%tra:	it's still being processed -. we don't know if:: [-/] have you handed in more papers or not?
		%add:	ENQ

| | 10 | *ENQ: | sí. |
| | | %tra: | yes. |

| | 11 | *MIQ: | pues todavía tienes que esperarte. |
| | | %tra: | then you still have to wait. |

	12	*MIQ:	del seis de junio -, falta un mes por lo menos.
		%tra:	from June sixth -, one more month to go at least.
		%com:	ENQ gives him a form which MIQ looks at.

In this exchange, it is interesting to examine Miquel's provision of service turn (lines 8–9). The background context discussed above influences the way in which

110   *An illusion of information*

the official shapes his turn. He starts off by providing the official "line" ("*todavía está en trámite -. no se sabe si::*" 'it's still being processed -. we don't know if::'). Then, suddenly, he stops and goes off on a completely different track ("*has traído más papeles tú o no?*" 'have you handed in more papers or not?'). Miquel acknowledges that the enquirer has been asked to submit new evidence. Exceptionally, Miquel's response is not routinised but shaped in response to the contextual information that he has. Miquel does not stage his show because he knows that the show has already been given away. Interestingly, this results in a more "interactive" exchange. The enquirer is given not the confusing standard information, but rather details that are relevant to his particular case. This example has shown how the lack of a unified front can be quite consequential for the quality of service provided. On that occasion, although quite exceptionally, it worked to the enquirer's benefit.

The following excerpt (28) shows how the lack of a unified team can also create tension in face-to-face interaction and among co-workers. This excerpt contains Miquel's backstage comments about a rather strenuous service interaction he has just been involved in.

(28)

→	1	*MIQ:	*segons ell havia vingut avui amb els papers que no estaven*
→	2		*escrits ni res i li hem dit que li faltaven papers i nosaltres no*
→	3		*ho podem dir encara que el senyor que se senta aquí ho diu*
→	4		*a mi m'ho han prohibit hem de dir que està en tràmit pos ell*
	5		*deia que em falten papers i jo pos aquí no posa quins papers*
	6		*falten i jo jo no sé per què aquí no està i ell pos aquest matí*
	7		*m'han dit que me'n faltaven llavons jo li he dit xxx i diu ahir*
	8		*vaig portar més papers i ens els va portar ahir dic si ens els*
	9		*portes ahir t'has d'esperar un mes a que estiguin introduïts i*
	10		*volia veure el seu expedient.*
		%tra:	according to him he came today with his papers which weren't written or anything and we told him that papers were missing and we cannot say that although the gentleman that sits here does so I have been fobidden to say it we have to say that it's being processed but he was saying that I am lacking more papers and I was saying here it doesn't say which papers are missing and I go I don't know because it's not in here and he goes this morning I was told that I was lacking papers then I said xxx and he goes yesterday I handed in more papers so he handed them in yesterday I go if you handed them in yesterday you have to wait for a month before they are processed and he wanted to see his file.

Miquel is concerned not to give the show away to such an extent that on some occasions he even avoids using the official term *propuesta denegatoria* in front of me. He treats it as a taboo term, either because he fears that he may be overheard by members of the public, or because he tries to erase its very existence by denying it discursive reality. This linguistic practice is illustrated by example (29) below.

(29)

	1	*MIQ:	*pues primer es miren si estan bé i s'introdueix i es posa* en
→	2		trámite *o es posa lo altre que també vol dir* trámite *per a ells*
→	3		*saps lo que et vull dir* ?
		%tra:	so first we check whether they are okay and we enter [the information] and we write being processed or the other thing that also means being processed for them do you know what I am talking about?
	4	*RES:	fase de instrucción o +...
		%tra:	preparatory phase or + ...
	5	*MIQ:	<o denegatoria> [>].
		%tra:	<or rejection> [>].
→	6	*RES:	<propuesta denegatoria> [<]?
		%tra:	<proposed for rejection> [<]?

7. Concluding remarks

In this chapter I have shown how decisions made at an interactional level are not neutral but have intended and unintended consequences for clients. The analysis has shown that the clients' right to accurate and truthful information was systematically neglected. In fact, no spaces were opened for them to be able to make sense of what was going on in this state agency. These exchanges reproduce the systematic exclusion of immigrants in the social arena; they also bear witness to the neglect for equality in the provision of service that would seriously accommodate immigrants' heterogeneity. Instead, officials uniformised information and tried to put these petitioners off interacting with them.

At the immigration office, clients were supplied minimal and often also ambiguous responses which fell short of satisfying their most elementary information needs. At no time was insider bureaucratic knowledge made available to them; on the contrary, officials' routines worked to construct an illusion of information which in fact allowed clients limited access to the workings of the organisation and enabled the exercise of institutional control.

I have discussed the role that participants' unequal access to key linguistic resources played in shaping talk at the site. I have argued that the officials' minimal responses emerged as a result of their problematisation of clients' linguistic competences. But, besides Spanish, only global languages like English or French enjoyed wide currency in this setting. The existence of a number of service providers who were competent in other languages, like Arabic or Russian, was not publicised in any way.

Even though officials were aware of clients' limited linguistic abilities, that did not lead them to problematise the way in which information was withheld from them. I argue that that was because immigrants' right to accurate information conflicted with officials' need to protect the institution and with their role in staging the gatekeeping nature – both real and symbolic – of this agency.

Bureaucrats minimised interaction with immigrant clients as a way of saving time and effort. This was accomplished through the routinised provision of single key words. Comprehension was prevented by insisting on information being furnished face-to-face and by resisting other forms of communication; it was also hindered by placing the onus of deciphering scripted responses on immigrant clients.

Another element that I have explored in this chapter is the multiple ways in which the institutional order can be entangled with the production of situated face-to-face communication, and how the link between these two levels is multidimensional. At this office, officials' information routines were not dictated by the institution; in fact, they had a highly individual component. Yet they took the form they did, to a large extent, because of institutionalised disinterest in service communication. The routinisation of the officials' responses, together with the institution's lack of investment in providing a good service, favoured and I would even say legitimised officials' uninformative behaviour. By way of contrast, when the institution needed to implement a restrictive policy of information, it instructed officials on how to go about doing it. Obedience to managerial authority, however, could not be taken for granted, as we have seen how different officials adopted fairly divergent attitudes and practices in relation to that policy change.

Finally, I have examined the contradictions and the tensions that emerged among members of staff as a result of institutional disorganisation. The absence of a "unified front" invalidated the efforts made by the institution to prevent the submission of piles of new documents. Individual bureaucrats, as social actors, were expected to adhere to the new institutional policy of withholding information, but because of immigrants' challenging moves, in actual social interaction they devised ways of maintaining individual face while detaching themselves from the institutional role they were expected to enact. How they accomplised this is described in the following chapter.

Chapter 4
Strategies of information management

1. Introduction

In this chapter I examine how service talk unfolded at the immigration office; how vital information was taken at face value or challenged; how inconsistencies in information provision were brought into the open; and how speakers did all that in the minute-to-minute unfolding of situated verbal action. I undertake a detailed analysis of the microstrategies that each group of social actors deployed to pursue their specific interactional agendas.

This chapter supplements the analysis provided in the previous one and helps construct the complete picture of information exchange in this setting. Here I focus not on individual responses, but on longer pieces of discourse. In particular, I examine the provision of service episode to understand what could be negotiated and what could not. In Chapter 3, I undertook a critique of officials' information-providing routines, but I said little about how migrants reacted to officials' talk. In this chapter, I examine interactional practice in detail to provide an account of the discursive strategies migrant information seekers put into play to go beyond their interlocutors' uninformative mode.

Admittedly, the type of client behaviour I present here was not necessarily typical. The majority of migrants were only able to merely acknowledge the information supplied and go away puzzled and frustrated. Yet it is interesting to see how those who attempted to contest the service did so, what interactional resources they drew on, and with what effects. That will lead me to argue that there exists a more profound level than that of information responses at which bureaucratic control is exerted; in fact, information control is structurally built into the workings of bureaucratic agencies. Bureaucratic practices are by definition constrained, controlled and exclusionary (of the public, that is). In this particular agency, additionally, bureaucratic control and constraint became foregrounded by the institution's decision to conceal relevant information details from petitioners. That policy change, unfair and unwarranted as it was, acts in this context as a magnifying glass; it enables us to make a precise observation of the actors' discursive tactics to retain or gain control of the interactional mode. In particular, it allows for the detailed examination of these bureaucrats' subtle management of role and identity to keep professional and individual face while trying not to disclose relevant institutional knowledge.

116 *Strategies of information management*

This chapter is divided into two parts. The first focuses on the analysis of how this group of institutional actors managed the tensions and contradictions of their work and with what consequences for their clients. The second illustrates clients' attempts to achieve meaningful communication and what their outcomes were.

2. Handling clients' challenging moves

At the immigration office, officials systematically thwarted all attempts by enquirers to find out more and more concrete details regarding the progress of their applications. In this section I want illustrate not only some of the interactional strategies officials used to handle enquirers' challenging moves but also the ways in which they managed the tensions between the demands of the institutional and interactional orders. The examples presented are intended to be not fixed stereotypical representations of behaviour, but rather the means to discuss some of the conspicuous and inconspicuous discursive procedures public officials put into play at this site.

Most of the examples in this section involve one of the officials in particular, namely Miquel, because he was the one who bore the burden of information provision in this office (the other being Juan, the official who refused to be recorded). Miquel was also the best informed of the information desk staff and a sort of leader among the four members of the desk staff. Teresa was mostly in charge of receiving new documents for files and Ramon's work varied from sometimes providing information to standing in for Teresa when she was away. (Because of the controlling nature of Ramon's behaviour, it is dealt with in a specific section of the following chapter.)

2.1. Coping with contradictions

The work of the bureaucrats in this office was defined by the numerous contradictions and tensions they had to manage. The most fundamental contradiction was linked to their official function as information suppliers and the ways in which that was understood differently by their clients and the institution.

For clients, officials were the means of communicating with the institution. It was to officials that questions were asked and that complaints and pleas were made. Everything clients wanted to know, they had to find out through interacting with bureaucrats. But for clients, officials were not just vehicles of information; they also were the institution's representatives. It was through them that immigrants might glean an insight into the procedure in general and into the progress of their applications in particular. These officials were the clients' guides through the legalisation process; they were, essentially, their only window into the institutional world. For the institution, by contrast, a member of staff was someone who was responsible for containing the public, someone who was smart enough to answer individual queries while at the same time not disclosing any real details of the procedure. In sum, someone who was in charge of keeping the door closed.

In this office, those rules of role enactment existed nowhere in writing, but rather formed part of the bureaucrats' socialisation process. The minimal information responses they themselves devised to avoid meeting enquirers' need for relevant information while keeping up the appearance that information was being given is an index of how quickly these new members of staff became socialised into acting institutionally.

But because all these processes took place interactionally, we must not forget the interpersonal dimension of talk and discursive behaviour. This is what Goffman (1983: 8) argues when he claims that, because a great deal of the work of organisations is done face-to-face, it is "vulnerable to face-to-face effects". In his view, "insofar as agents of social organisations of any scale, from states to households, can be persuaded, cajoled, flattered, intimidated, or otherwise influenced by effects only achievable in face-to-face dealings, then here, too, the interaction order bluntly impinges on macroscopic entities".

The tension between the institutional and individual side of these bureaucrats' work became foregrounded when the new information policy was implemented. As individuals, these officials did not want to be accused of giving untruthful details or being downright liars. In fact, as noted in Chapter 3, they were quite concerned to make sense, both personally and collectively, of the new scenario created. They needed to find a way of keeping individual and professional face in their one-to-one interactions with clients, while at the same time behaving in institutionally appropriate ways.

The difficulty of that task was aggravated by the fact that the details officials were asked to conceal appeared before them on the computer screen every time an application was checked. On a practical level, that meant that these officials were constantly reminded of how untruthful they were actually being to clients. I have discussed how this made some of them particularly uncomfortable.

The lack of a unified front among staff in the office, which worked to give the bureaucrats' game away, complicated things even more. The most tangible consequences of the lack of a unified front were that officials found themselves often confronted by clients on account of the contradictory information the office had supplied. Officials responded to such challenges either by ignoring them or by underscoring their individual dimension. But even this latter option ran counter to their institutional position.

In the following two sections, I will first focus on how officials went about providing more details on the status of petitions. Secondly, I will look at how they coped with challenges to the way their work was organised at this office, and in particular, how they accounted for those aspects that affected the efficient processing of petitions.

2.2. Providing further information

The prompt most frequently employed by clients to request further information was "Any *falta?*". By it, clients essentially sought to be reassured that their case was making progress.

Bureaucrats reacted to that question (which they could not now answer truthfully) by saying that they did not know, either because petitions were still being reviewed or because the computer did not give them that information. Although identical in practical content, these two different answers had different interactional and interpersonal implications, and were therefore employed in response to different sequential, interactional and interpersonal contexts.

2.2.1. Teaching clients what *trámite* means

One frequent discursive routine used by desk staff, especially by Miquel, was not only to deny having the means to answer the question of whether any *faltas* had been found with regard to an application, but actually to teach enquirers why that was the case. This is illustrated below in an interaction where Miquel responds to a client's request for more concrete details by saying that the review of the client's petition has not been completed.

(30)

        1   *MIQ: en trámite -. tres semanas más.
            %tra: being processed -. three more weeks.

        2   *UUU: #0_2.5.

→   3   *MIQ: entiendes?
            %tra: do you understand?

        4   *ENQ: 0.
            %act: nods

            @Situation: MIQ continues checking status of rest of applications

	5	*ENQ:	**any** falta -? falta -? <u>no</u>?
→		%tra:	anything missing -? missing -? no?
→	6	*MIQ:	en trámite: **we are looking if it is all right or don't -. we**
	7		**don't know**.
		%tra:	in proce:ss we are looking if it is all right or don't -. we don't know.
	8	*ENQ:	<**okay**> [?].
	9	*UUU:	#0_55.
	10	*MIQ:	trámite -,.
		%tra:	being processed -,.

@Situation: MIQ continues checking applications

	11	*MIQ:	en trámite.
		%tra:	being processed
	12	*MIQ:	0.
		%tra:	rings buzzer to serve following enquirer

The characteristic discursive routine I mention above is prompted by the client's question in line 5. Miquel does not simply provide a yes or no answer. He actually recycles the word *trámite* and provides an institutional definition for it ("*en trámite:* we are looking if it is alright or don't"). The striking feature of Miquel's turn is that its sequentially most relevant part, that is, the stretch of talk that actually responds to the client's question ("we don't know") is not produced straightaway but comes at the end of his turn. The fact that he chooses such a marked structuring of his interactional contribution is significant. I would like to argue that the first part of Miquel's response functions as a kind of "teaching line". This hypothesis is borne out by the prosodic and intonational features of the turn, such as the lengthening of the final vowel *e* in *trámite*, the lack of pausing after this phrase, and the rising intonation that is maintained throughout.

Providing a definition of *trámite* as if wanting to instruct his interlocutor is one of Miquel's habitual linguistic practices. Interestingly, in some interactions – as in (31) below – he actually employs the verb phrase *quiere decir* 'means', thus reinforcing the didactic effect.

(31)

	1	*EN1:	vale quiero preguntar un una cosa # está todo bien o::
	2		<falta> [>] +...
		%tra:	okay I want to ask som something # is everything okay or is there something missing

	3	*MIQ:	<no se sabe> [<] cuando está en trámite quiere decir que
→	4		están mirando si los papeles están bien # y todavía no se
	5		sabe si falta o no falta.
		%tra:	<we don't know> [<] when it's being processed that means that they are checking if the papers are okay # and we don't know whether anything is missing or not.

Going back to excerpt (30), I have remarked that the official's teaching line occupies a prominent position. Explaining the meaning of *trámite* seems to be more important for the official than fulfilling the requirements of the adjacency pair, that is, answering his interlocutor's question. What does this marked construction of his turn tell us about how he interprets that question?

It could be argued that Miquel's insistence on defining what *trámite* means derives from a desire to provide a good service, that is, to make his interlocutors understand the procedural import of the term. However, Miquel and other officials offer "lessons" of this sort only in very specific sequential contexts, namely, after questions containing the term *falta*. I would suggest that the reason for the peculiar shape the bureaucrat's turn takes has to be found in the institutional order framing these interactions. Indeed, the word *falta* echoes a particular practice of information provision that the institution's new policy is now intent on eliminating. As was shown in Chapter 3, this specific official (Miquel) feels uneasy about having to tell all applicants that their petitions are being processed *(trámite)*, but sees it as his duty to implement the new policy. Immigrants' use of the word *falta*, however, works to foreground rather than background (as is Miquel's objective) the institution's change in information provision. Clients' mentioning of *falta* has the effect of recontextualising (Auer and di Luzio 1992) the exchanges where it is produced. *Falta* highlights that these are not isolated interactions between strangers, but links in a chain of interactional events. *Falta* works as a contextualisation device (Gumperz 1982a), indexing that the contextual background that is brought to bear in the understanding of talk is not just the immediate sequential or interactional context but the whole trajectory (Giddens 1984) of information practices in the office. This recontextualisation of interactions has the effect of bringing into the open inconsistencies and contradictions in the information being supplied and this makes Miquel particularly uncomfortable.

In the previous chapter we saw that Miquel displayed a policing attitude towards his colleagues' practices of information provision. He sought to make sure that all office staff endorsed the same definition of reality. In the new reality brought about by the policy change, the term *falta* did not exist any more. Miquel was concerned with removing all traces of *falta* from the talk that occurred in the office, either in face-to-face service communication with immigrants or in his own backstage comments addressed to me, as I illustrated in Chapter 3. To achieve this goal, Miquel had to make sure that service seekers understood the new institutional meaning of *trámite,* which was now used in a narrowly defined way as the absence of a final decision on the application.

In extract (30) we can see observe how, like a teacher who is trying to make his pupils reason, the official provides the general frame first, that is, the institutional definition of the word, and then presents his actual response as deriving logically from it. He tries to illustrate step-by-step the reasoning procedure behind his response ("we don't know"), in the hope that enquirers' will stop asking about the existence of *faltas*. In fact, on several occasions, Miquel actually told me that he interpreted enquirers' questions on the issue of *falta* as deriving from their being accustomed to officials' previous information provision practices and not being aquainted with the new terminology. He thought that by teaching clients that *trámite* meant their documents were still being checked, they would stop asking about *faltas.*

I would argue that Miquel's interpretation of this state of affairs was highly questionable because it missed an important point. In the real life world of his interlocutors, *falta* signified an opportunity for action (a way of retaining agency, as Jacquemet [2005] puts it), whereas *trámite* embodied an enforced passive stance. Miquel was bringing an institutional frame to bear in that he was interpreting the situation in institutional terms, that is, as a matter of changing interactional routines; yet for the enquirer it was probably his relation with the real world that mattered.

Example (30) could also be understood as an attempt by the service seeker to question, albeit in a mitigated way, the information presented to him. Indeed, speakers' turns are multidimensional; they usually have multiple layers of meaning and may function to simultaneously accomplish different goals. In the previous example, providing a definition of *trámite* is also operational to Miquel in terms of the tension he has to manage between projecting a positive self-image while at the same time having to withhold information from his interlocutors. Miquel's teaching utterance contextualises his claim that they do not know if problems have been found with the client's application and functions as a justification for his uncommitted response.

2.2.2. Redefining role-identity

At other times, similar client requests for further details were responded to in a rather different way. On those occasions, officials stated that they did not know whether a given petition for legal status had been positively reviewed because the computer did not provide that piece of information. This response type indexes bureaucrats' attempts at achieving some degree of individual detachment from the workings of the institutional order. Bureaucrats' favourite coping strategy is based on a redefinition of their professional role and of their relationship with the institution they work for. They do not want to be seen as "institutional spokespeople" but as mere "mouthpieces" (Thomas 1986).

Hall, Sarangi and Slembrouck (1999) argue that it is not possible to define social roles, such as professional occupation, unproblematically. Rather, it is necessary to examine how sets of expectations associated with specific roles are subject to a process of differentiation in situated institutional talk. To capture the ways in which social actors actively manipulate and negotiate social role expectations to present themselves in a specific light, Hall et al. put forward the concept of *role-identity*. Roles are viewed as non-static and as a resource that speakers draw upon to create a particular identity for themselves in local face-to-face interaction. Role-identities constitute the background against which speakers' actions and moves have to be interpreted and from which they derive their meaning.

Of the various social activities that made up their institutional role as information providers, officials at the immigration office strategically chose one and ignored the others. Thus, they presented themselves as mere "computer checkers". Checking the computer to find out about the status of clients' applications was one of the central activities of their professional routines. As insiders to the institution, however, it was expected that they would be able not only to find out relevant details of clients' applications, but also to make sense of them, account for the presence or absence of certain responses, and explain what the consequence of a certain processing status might be. Yet all these abilities were denied by their construction of their professional identity. They could not account for anything because "they only saw what was in the computer". They constructed themselves as mere transmitters of information and denied having access to any type of insider knowledge. When they presented themselves as mere "computer checkers", officials no longer felt that they were acting as representatives of the institution. They worked for the institution but they did not behave as its face, as real mediators between clients and the institutional realm. On the contrary, their strategic role-identity foregrounded their powerlessness and subordinate position within the institutional hierarchy. As Jacquemet (2005) also observes, by alluding to a superior authority (in this case the computer) institutional representatives minimize responsibility for their own responses.

The extract below (32) illustrates how these bureaucrats strategically use their new professional identity to avoid providing truthful information.

(32)

	1	*EN1:	éste no falta no?
		%tra:	this one no missing [papers] no?
→	2	*RAM:	trámite **I don't kna** [//] **know** -. **computer when is i:n**
	3		**paper in** trámite # <u>eh</u>: **don't say it** # falta o: # o no falta.

The official (in this case Ramon) does not answer the client's question. In fact, he refuses to be the recipient of such a question on the basis of his not having access to the information requested.

At other times, this strategic presentation of self as a mere computer checker is also employed to account for divergent information responses among staff members.

(33)

	1	*MIQ:	trámite.
		%tra:	being processed.
	2	*EN1:	xxx eh: diferente de xxx **somebody telling that** falta xxx.
		%tra:	xxx eh: different from xxx somebody telling that missing xxx.
→	3	*MIQ:	**I don't know** -. **here is** trámite **only**.

In line 3, the official justifies his giving the client information at variance with what the client has been told previously by emphasising that he does not have access to other details. In example (34) below, the bureaucrat even claims to be transmitting information without changing it in any way. If the computer shows that the application is in *trámite*, that is exactly what he tells enquirers. His final "*yo!*" 'me!', accompanied by a shrugging of his shoulders, marks his desire for detachment from the institution. He makes it clear that he does not want to be held accountable, as he is only a mere "computer checker". This is of course not true, but little can be said or done by clients when bureaucrats claim not to know more.

(34)

1	*ENQ:	cuánto tiempo yo sólo espera -? # cuánto tiempo?
	%tra:	how much time I only wait -? # how much time?
2	*MIQ:	tres semanas.
	%tra:	three weeks.
3	*ENQ:	eso siempre tres.
	%tra:	that always three.

124 *Strategies of information management*

		4	*ENQ:	por favor esto escribe tres **week** cuatro vez -. # siempre ##
		5		trámite.
			%tra:	please this write three weeks four times -. # always ## process.
→		6	*MIQ:	yo sólo sé lo que pone aquí -. si aquí pone trámite -, trámite -.
		7		yo!
			%tra:	I only know what it says here -. if here it says being processed -, then being processed -. me!
			%act:	shrugs his shoulders

The local role-identity sponsored by bureaucrats is only very rarely contested. The following example (35) illustrates how this might be done. The enquirer is a young Moroccan woman who wants to find out whether her new documentation has been accepted.

(35)

		1	*MIQ:	ya ya aquí pone que todavía no lo han puesto aquí -. yo te
→		2		digo lo que sale en el ordenador.
			%tra:	yeah yeah here it says that they haven't noted it on your file -. I'm telling you what it says in the computer.
		3	*ENQ:	dónde dónde puedo: dónde haces esto?
			%tra:	where where ca:n I where is this done?
		4	*MIQ:	esto lo hacen aquí pero cuando está esto puesto.
			%tra:	this is done here but when this is examined.
→		5	*ENQ:	tengo que preguntar gente que trabaja con esto no aquí.
			%tra:	I have to ask people who work with this not here.
→		6	*MIQ:	gente que trabaja con esto no habla con la gente -. aquí estoy
		7		yo para informarte -. aquí sale que todavía está en trámite y
		8		que tienes que esperarte tres semanas más.
			%tra:	people who work with this don't talk to people -. I'm here to inform you -. here it says that your papers are still being processed and that you have to wait three weeks.

Previous in this exchange, the two speakers had argued about whether the enquirer's new evidence should already have been examined or not. Now the official tries to bring the argument to an end by stating that, according to the computer, the documents have not been processed yet, and that this is the only piece of information he can give her (lines 1–2). What is significant in this interaction is the enquirer's reaction to the official's strategic construction of himself. She rejects Miquel – in his role as "computer checker" – as a valid interlocutor.

Yet she is not allowed to go beyond the constraining institutional order, as defined by him (see lines 6–8). He asserts that he is her only possible interlocutor, and repeats the same information he provided in line 1. His turn contains no traces of face-redressive strategies. The turn construction units are short, unmodulated statements. The language is blunt ("*aquí estoy yo para informarte*" 'I'm here to inform you'; "*tienes que esperarte tres semanas*" 'you have to wait three weeks'). The enquirer's attempts at finding a way round the official's uncooperative behaviour are thwarted immediately. The official uses his situational powers to discourage the enquirer's attempts at negotiating interactional and institutional orders that would allow her space for more active participation.

2.2.3. Wavering between institutional and individual positions

In the transcripts, one interesting feature of officials' productions is their fluctuating use of personal pronouns. The ambivalent ways in which these officials position themselves with respect to the institution, that is, either as representatives or as mere mouthpieces, is indexed by their vacillating use of the personal pronouns *I*, *we* or *they*. Sometimes, an inclusive *we* is used, as in (36) below (line 5).

(36)

    1   *MIQ: en trámite -. tres semanas más -. **three more weeks**.
          %tra: being processed -. three more weeks -. three more weeks.

    2   *ENQ: **three weeks**?

    3   *MIQ: **yes**.

    4   *ENQ: **okay** ODER <u>uh</u> +...
          %tra: okay or <u>uh</u>

→   5   *MIQ: **we are looking if it is alright or don't -. we don't know yet**.

    6   *ENQ: **yes**

    7   *MIQ: +ˆ **you have to wait three weeks**.

Here, through the use of inclusive *we*, Miquel constructs himself as a full-fledged institutional representative. At other times, first person *I* is contrasted with third person *they*, as in (37).

(37)

	1	*MIQ:	éste es en trámite.
		%tra:	this one is being processed.
	2	*MIQ:	www.
	3	*RES:	www.
	4	*ENQ:	perdón **document** [?].
		%tra:	sorry document [?].
	5	*MIQ:	yes.
	6	*ENQ:	**what adjustments [?] do they find?**
→	7	*MIQ:	**I don't know -. in the computer in** trámite # **they are**
	8		**looking if the papers are good or don't -,.**
	9	*ENQ:	yes.
→	10	*MIQ:	**and we don't know yet.**

In line 7, the institution is presented not as a unitary whole but as separate entities with an independent way of functioning. It must be said that the latter depiction is actually closer to real institutional arrangements than the former. However, the appearance of a "fragmentary" institutional order may give enquirers arguments for contesting officials' responses and their status as valid interlocutors (as was seen in extract [35] above). This may explain why, two turns later (line 10), Miquel goes back to his inclusive institutional *we*.

2.3. Accounting for organisational arrangements

Officials at the immigration office systematically refused to explain to clients anything regarding the organisation of work in the office and the processing of paperwork. Some complaints by clients were responded to candidly, as when officials stated that applications entered on the first two days of the campaign were being processed very slowly due to the large number of them (see example [9] presented in Chapter 2). At other times, a simple agreement token *yes*, as if accepting the current state of affairs, accompanied by a shrug was the only response given. Sometimes clients' complaints were rejected through the imposition of an institutional rather than a personal framing of the situation. For example, an enquirer's assessment of the time elapsed since submission as excessive is rejected by the official in example (44), which I shall analyse in detail in section 3.4 below. On this occasion, the enquirer's complaint was brushed off because, from an institutional viewpoint, other applications were making even less progress, and thus, this particular case could not be considered especially problematic. Finally, bureaucrats' strategies to face up to clients' complaints sometimes even consisted in blaming clients themselves for the alleged unfavourable treatment received from the institution (38), and if necessary, threatening them (39).

(38)

> 24 *MIQ: de aquí te dijeron tres sema:nas <y> [>] ha pasado una!
> %tra: they told you to wait for three weeks <and> [>] only one has elapsed!

In this encounter, Miquel blames the client for not waiting the prescribed length of time before coming back to the office.

(39)

> 33 *MIQ: a ver tú has traído todos los papeles que tenías cuando
> 34 presentas esto -? pues ya está -! si falta no puedes hacer nada
> 35 si traes algo falso no te lo van a dar jamás.
> %tra: let's see did you bring all the papers that you had when you submitted this? then that's it! if something is missing there is nothing you can do if you bring something forged they will never give it to you.

The intended effect of Miquel's turn above is to put an end to the enquirer's challenging moves rather than to make real predictions about the future. Examining documents is not part of front-line officials' work. So many actors intervene in the process of assessing applications that making predictions of this sort is rather futile. In this instance, however, the official's goal was only partially achieved, as the enquirer tried to pursue his agenda for a few more turns before bringing the exchange to an end.

3. Clients' strategies of contestation

Different immigrant service seekers displayed different modes of reacting interactionally to the information presented, depending on a number of factors. One of them was command of the linguistic codes they were able to employ in communicating with information providers, in particular, Spanish or English, but to some extent also French. Sometimes, however, other factors might also come into play, such as culturally defined forms of talk and behaviour in encounters of this sort, and specific perceptions of how appropriate or beneficial it might be to request further details, contest the information presented, and so on. Although the cultural dimension of clients' behaviour might open interesting avenues for investigation (along the lines, for example, of the work presented in Gumperz and Roberts 1991), it is beyond the goals of this study to undertake systematic comparisons of that type.

Immigrants' reactions as displayed in situated talk can be classified into two groups. Either they took the information they were furnished at face value, which is what happened in the majority of cases, or they sought to probe further. The fact that they acknowledged the information obtained but did not inquire further does not necessarily imply that they were satisfied with it. As I mentioned above, other considerations might have played an important role in inhibiting certain types of challenging behaviour. The precise role of these factors could have been investigated by means of follow-up interviews, which, because of the nature of the site, could only be carried out to a limited extent. So, in my analysis here, I shall focus not on the investigation of psychological and perceptual processes but on clients' displayed strategies for handling information.

One of these strategies consisted in asking for linguistic help. Clients sometimes felt uncertain about their ability to comprehend what officials were telling them. In that case, they often asked a fellow countryman to engage in service interaction instead of or together with them. These language "helpers" were often fellow petitioners from the same ethnic community who could speak some Spanish. They might be friends or simply acquaintances who had offered to help in exchange for having their own applications checked simultaneously. In this way, skilled speakers were able to use their language abilities to jump the very long queue of people waiting for information. But, because responses were in general so minimal, such helpers could actually do very little to improve their compatriots' understanding of the situation. At most, they helped their fellow countrymen comprehend that their applications were in *trámite*, and that they would have to wait for three more weeks. Usually, they did not engage in long information-seeking sequences or challenge the little information their acquaintances were given.

Another related strategy that I observed on one occasion was to ask an interpreter who worked for the police and who was in charge of distributing permit cards for help. The fact that the interpreter was connected with the legalisation process but did not work for the immigration services made her intervention less controversial than if it had been a member of the information team trying to act "uninstitutionally" by helping a client. Although the interpreter's behaviour was commented on by one of the information officials, it was understood as being motivated by the clients' insistence. In spite of his efforts, the client did not end up receiving more accurate information, but just the institutional line that his application was still being checked. At this point, the same desk official remarked to me that the client may have imagined he would receive more information if he had this kind of "institutional support", but that that was not the case because he gave the same information to everyone whether client or client's representative. It is interesting to note that the official emphasised his rational and objective mode of proceeding as if wanting to dispel suspicions of differential treatment. This links up with my claim in the previous chapter that these bureaucrats were little aware of the fact that they were creating exclusion precisely by treating all clients equally and not opening spaces for the least competent in Spanish, English or French to be able to understand talk addressed to them.

The importance of clients' strategies of contestation lay therefore in their potential (more symbolic than real) for reframing the interactions presented in counterhegemonic ways. As I discussed in Chapter 3, bureaucrats' default mode of conduct was hegemonic, that is, it tended toward the reproduction of unequal power relations in society. Immigrants' contesting moves, by contrast, were aimed at achieving social spaces of participation and inclusion. They attempted to reduce asymmetries of knowledge by finding opportunities for the negotiation of meaningful understandings and they tried to balance out asymmetries of power by having their most elementary civil rights respected. Even if these attempts were not successful in these local encounters, they can be considered "a kind of swimming upstream against the prevailing currents of history", in Erickson's metaphor (2001: 164). In the following sections I will explore how that "swimming upstream" was discursively undertaken by clients and what effects it had in terms of allowing clients access to information.

3.1. From indirect challenges to the use of key insider knowledge

Migrants' strategies for obtaining truthful information were at times fairly unexpected. The creativity of social actors and their potential for subverting the established order must not be underestimated, even in spaces as closely regimented as this office. The excerpt below is an interesting example of the ways in which practices of control may engender creative strategies of subversion. At the immigration office, some petitioners learned that it was advantageous to make copies of their stamped application forms before the first time they had them checked, that is, before a file number was written on them. That way they could have their applications checked as many times as they wanted since without a registration number on the forms, officials could assume that the status of an application had not yet been checked. Clients could then confront officials if they were given contradictory details as illustrated in lines 5–7 below.

(40)

→	1	*MIQ:	*es fan fotocòpies sense el número i quan els hi posem el*
	2		*número et porten la que no té el número no sé per què*
	3		*te'l fan tornar a buscar.*
		%tra:	they make photocopies [of the application] without the number and then when we write down the number they bring the one that does not have the number I don't know why and they make you check it again.
		%add:	RES
	4	*RAM:	*això és una cabronada !*
		%tra:	that is a dirty trick!
→	5	*MIQ:	*ja m'ho han fet vàrios i després els hi dius el número i et*
	6		*treuen l'altre si però si aquest dia em vas dir això i dius*
	7		*# i per què no m'ho deies -? s'ho guarden!*
		%tra:	several of them have played it on me then you tell them the number and they take out the other one and say but the other day you told me that and you go # well why didn't you tell me -? -. they keep it to themselves!

Nonetheless, this was not the most frequent way of trying to obtain further information. The most common approach consisted in the use of the *any falta?* phrase. This expression could index two rather different contextual scenarios. Sometimes it was just a formulaic request for detail learned from friends, relatives or acquaintances and sometimes it was an authentic response obtained from the office previously in the light of which clients were trying to understand the new information they were being given. In many cases, it was difficult to say which of these two scenarios was being indexed. When that occurred, bureaucrats tended to simply provide the standard teaching line. It is interesting to see, however, that bureaucrats responded differently whenever it became clear that *falta* foregrounded the fact that divergent and often contradictory information was being furnished by the same office. This is what happens in the interaction below.

This interaction involves Miquel and a middle-aged North African enquirer. It unfolds mostly in Spanish, although the information seeker codeswitches into French in his final turns.

(41)

	1	*MIQ:	en trámite.
		%tra:	being processed.
→	2	*ENQ:	trámite ahora?
		%tra:	being processed now?
	3	*MIQ:	todavía tiene que esperar tres semanas más.
		%tra:	you still have to wait for three more weeks.
	4	*ENQ:	<u>eh</u> no fal [/] no falta?
		%tra:	uh no nothing missing?
→	5	*MIQ:	no sale -. sale en trámite -. trámite están mirando si está
	6		todo bien o si no # vale?
		%tra:	it doesn't say -. it only says it's being processed -. being processed they are seeing if everything is okay or not # okay?
	7	*ENQ:	trámite?
		%tra:	being processed?
	8	*MIQ:	sí.
		%tra:	yes.
	9	*UUU:	#0_21.
	10	*ENQ:	trámite -. <u>vuelga</u>: <u>vuelga</u> # <u>vuelgue</u> vuega # <u>volve</u> volver.
		%tra:	being processed -. coom coom came cam com come back.
	11	*MIQ:	volver -. tres semanas.
		%tra:	come back -, three weeks.
	12	*ENQ:	tres semanas otra -. # tres semanas otra.
		%tra:	three weeks other -. # three weeks other.
	13	*MIQ:	0.
		%act:	nods.
→	14	*ENQ:	gracias -. uh no sabe esto: `qu'est-ce que c'est` esto -. no sabe.
	15	%tra:	thanks -. uh doesn't know thi::s what is this -. doesn't know.
	16	*MIQ:	no sé.
		%tra:	I don't know.
→	17	*ENQ:	+ˆ `mais si` -. esto ef # ef <u>uh</u>: ocho tres.
		%tra:	yes you do -. this ef # ef uh eight three.
	18	*MIQ:	quién te lo ha escrito?
		%tra:	who wrote this?

132   *Strategies of information management*

→
	19	*ENQ:	aquí.
		%tra:	here.
	20	*MIQ:	yo no.
		%tra:	not me.
	21	*ENQ:	esto número esto # expediente.
		%tra:	this number this # file.
	22	*MIQ:	el número de expediente del ordenador.
		%tra:	the number of the file in the computer.
	23	*ENQ:	muchas gracias (a)diós.
		%tra:	many thanks bye.

A variety of strategies are mobilised by the enquirer to try to obtain more information than what he is offered. After Miquel provides the formula *"en trámite"* in line 1, the enquirer introduces already a first element of challenge. The use of the temporal adverbial *ahora* 'now' in *"trámite ahora?"* underscores the enquirer's awareness of changes in the information furnished. Implicit is the expectation of some kind of account of why the information he is provided with now is at variance with the information he was given in the past.

Miquel does not pick up on the enquirer's implied request. Instead, he responds by providing the usual routinised directive requesting his interlocutor to wait for three more weeks (line 3). He is trying to avoid having to account for the institution's changing information practices. However, through the use of the adverbial *todavía* 'still', Miquel does acknowledge the other implicit idea in the enquirer's turn, namely, that the enquirer has been awaiting a final decision for a long while.

The enquirer does not give up in his attempt to elicit more details. In line 4, he produces the usual *no falta?* question. His previous *"ahora"* 'now' constructed an interpretive frame in which *falta* is not just an information strategy but also a way of asking bureaucrats to account for the mismatch in the information provided and of challenging it.

These considerations lead Miquel to produce a more elaborate response than we saw in extract (30) previously. On this occasion, he says *"no sale -. sale en trámite -. trámite están mirando si está todo bien o si no # vale?"* 'it doesn't say -. it only says it's being processed-. being processed they are seeing if everything is okay or not # okay?'. Note that this response is carefully framed within Miquel's computer checker identity, distanced from the workings of the institution. The positioning of the key utterance *no sale* 'it doesn't say' at the beginning of the turn shows that he had indeed interpreted the enquirer's question as a challenge to the office's information policy. By emphasising that he does not have access to that information, Miquel preempts an accusation of institutionalised variability of responses at best and of individual secretiveness at worst. However, the absence of a clear response by Miquel generates a number of implicatures that derive from his turn.

To begin with, the fact that the information as to whether problems have been found with the enquirer's application is not available does not preclude the existence of such problems. Secondly, the official cannot tell the enquirer whether everything is okay because that information is not available. The implicature is that someone – the back office, for instance – may have been manipulating the computerised database so that certain details do not become known. The institutional representative is, in very subtle ways, conveying a lot of information, information that he is supposed to conceal. In a display of discursive "acrobatics", he outlines a possible scenario in which the responses clients are "allowed" to be given cannot be mapped on to the real status of their applications (it may be the case that there is a *falta* but front-line officials allegedly do not know).

Many questions arise from an examination of Miquel's turn. What is the usefulness of adding layers of meaning and complexity to his talk? Are the above implicatures likely to be grasped by his interlocutor? Indeed, there is no evidence in the interaction that the client reacts to them. What seems clear is that in a context where clients' may have trouble understanding due to their limited linguistic competences, the twisted way in which Miquel presents the information is likely to further complicate their comprehension process. Yet Miquel's practices have to be understood against the background of the multiple contradictions informing his talk and the tension he has to manage between his individual treatment of clients and the institutional constraints that impinge on service provision.

Now let us examine the enquirer's behaviour. In lines 7, 10 and 12, he repeats key pieces of information already supplied with final rising intonation. These utterances allow him time to think and could provide sequential opportunities for the official to add extra information. Nevertheless, this does not happen.

Then, in lines 14 and 15, the encounter takes an unexpected turn. The enquirer asks what an abbreviation that is written on his application ("F83") means. In fact, F83 stands for *fase ochenta y tres* 'phase eighty-three', one of the technical names used by the institution for the *propuesta denegatoria* 'proposed for rejection' stage. The fact that the enquirer had F83 written on his application confirms that in the past he was told that his application was not moving forward and explains the relevance of his initial *ahora* in indexing his awareness of a substantial contradiction in the information he has received at different times. The enquirer probably knows that F83 is connected with negative reviews of applications. This is thus a final attempt to confront the official. If Miquel responds to his question, and explains what F83 means, he will have to account for why information has changed. The official thus denies being familiar with this term (line 16). The enquirer cannot believe his answer and insists, this time making his question more explicit. The official then resorts to a different strategy. He detaches himself from the institutional team. He is ready to be held accountable for his individual actions only. Within that frame, he refuses to respond to the enquirer's question on account of his not having written the "problematic" piece of information. Finally, the enquirer gives up. He asks an irrelevant question, probably to alleviate the tension created by his previous interventions, and decides to bring the interaction to a close.

In this exchange, the enquirer has used a variety of implicit and explicit strategies to fight for his right to truthful information and has attempted to deroutinise the process of information exchange by trying to go beyond the strict limits imposed by the institutional party. But to no avail. The official does not seem ready to let his institutional position be jeopardised by his acting uninstitutionally. He has claimed institutional ignorance and has avoided picking up on enquirer's implied challenges as strategies to save his individual and institutional position.

3.2. Open challenges

Other service seekers are more successul in articulating their attempts at exposing the inconsistencies in the way the organisation relates to its clients. The enquirer in the extract (42) below, for example, challenges the public official openly.

(42)

	1	*MIQ:	trámite.
		%tra:	being processed.
→	2	*EN1:	xxx eh: diferente de xxx **somebody telling that** falta xxx.
		%tra:	xxx eh: different from xxx somebody telling that missing xxx.
→	3	*MIQ:	**I don't know -. here is** trámite **only.**
	4	*EN1:	uh huh # **and then yesterday** # **I come and give the falta**
	5		xxx.
	6	*MIQ:	**yesterday**?
	7	*EN1:	**and then you say that** trámite.
	8	*MIQ:	**yes.**

→	9	*EN1:	+ˆ **I not understand what is the problem -. this is my**
	10		**passport.**
→	11	*MIQ:	**if you give more things yesterday you have to wait three**
	12		**<four> [>] weeks we have this with the things of**
	13		**yesterday**.
	14	*EN1:	<okay okay> [<].
	15	*EN1:	pero **yesterday give a man filling** [?] **computer.**
→	16	*MIQ:	**yes the computer is not changed.**
→	17	*EN1:	**is it possible to check** xxx **file to what is the** falta.
	18	*MIQ:	**if you give us yesterday you have to wait one month more**
	19		**to have this in the computer.**
	20	*EN1:	**about** eh **falta.**
→	21	*MIQ:	**I don't know.**
→	22	*EN1:	**two day ago my friend** www **take this here and** eh: **I don't**
	23		**know who checked it but** xxx **tell me that** xxx **there is**
	24		falta.
→	25	*MIQ:	**if you have bring us papers yesterday we don't have your**
	26		**papers with this you have to wait one month.**
	27	*EN1:	**thank you**.

The enquirer's strategy begins already in line 2, where he calls attention to the fact that information is now different from what he was given previously. Confronted with this inconsistency, Miquel adopts a mouthpiece role and avows lack of knowledge (line 3). The enquirer goes on to provide more details about his actions, which turn out to be highly useful for the service provider. The enquirer's turns in lines 2, 4–5 and 7 belong together in that they constitute the service seeker's contextual explanation of his query. This can be seen in the way the turns are syntactically constructed –note that both lines 4–5 and 6 are introduced by means of the phrase "and then" indicating that more details on some previous narrative are going to be provided. Furthermore, the enquirer ignores Miquel's question "yesterday?" in line 6, which shows that this is not his interactional priority at the moment.

The enquirer thus sketches a very clear account: he was told that new evidence for his file was needed, he had taken it on the previous day and that now he is being told that his application is being processed. He expresses his bafflement and his lack of understanding. Now, as would be expected, Miquel dodges accounting

136 *Strategies of information management*

for the inconsistencies in the information the enquirer claims to have received. Instead, he pursues the theme of the new evidence provided on the previous day (lines 11 to 13) because that is the only piece of information he can actually disclose.

As the interaction progresses, it becomes clear that the client wants to know what exactly the problem was with the documentary evidence he first submitted, and whether his new certificates will be accepted. As a front-line bureaucrat, it is not part of Miquel's duties to check petitioners' files. (Only very occasionally did I observe any desk officials go to the back office and come back with clients' files for consultation.) This is one of the reasons why Miquel cannot tell the immigrant what the *falta* was. The other reason, of course, has to do with the fact that *faltas* are supposed not to exist and therefore they cannot be discussed.

From an outsider's perspective, the official's talk seems totally confusing. On the one hand, he claims not to know anything about the *falta* issue, yet on the other, he admits that the office is taking in more documents for processing (lines 18–19). Along the same lines, he constructs his role in the office as that of a mere "computer checker", and yet he knows that it takes his back-office colleagues up to a month to process new evidence. Miquel's position does not stand up to logical examination. The minute-to-minute working of the interaction, however, does not allow participants such detailed analyses of each other's arguments. Another example of the slippery ground on which Miquel stands is what he says in line 16, where he states that nothing has been changed in the computer. In retrospect, this would give the enquirer more resources to challenge the "reality sponsored by the team". If nothing has changed, one wonders why information is so blatantly different.

In fact, two different issues are mixed up in this exchange. One has to do with information being contradictory and the other one is linked to the bureaucratic processing of new certificates. Miquel is being truthful in connection with the second one (it takes up to a month for certificates to be processed by the back office) but not quite so in connection with the first one. But because in both cases the response is the same, that is, that no information is available and because no account is given, the message that gets transmitted is that it is not possible for clients, even those who are as skilful as this one, to go beyond standard responses that say virtually nothing.

In this excerpt, there is a total lack of alignment between the public bureaucrat and the service seeker. Each speaker is pursuing his own agenda; at no point do these different agendas converge. One could argue that these interlocutors' positions cannot be reconciled, and that Miquel, as a social actor –and not as an individual speaker– could not act differently. However, what needs to be underscored is a more profound dimension of institutional practice which keeps clients in the dark, conceals key information from them and neglects their right to respectful and democratic forms of service.

On a discursive level, the fundamental asymmetry in participant rights and obligations is indexed by participants' different pragmatic behaviour. As has been shown, the institutional representative can afford to repeatedly not provide relevant responses to enquirer's questions because he knows that he will not be challenged for it. Indeed, as Sarangi and Slembrouck (1996) argue, clients of bureaucratic organisations are often afraid of stating their rights because they feel that may jeopardise their cases.

3.3. *Offering solutions*

Most of the clients' discursive procedures for getting truthful information are based on exposing the information service and its numerous contradictions. In the previous examples I discussed how unsuccessful those efforts generally were. In (43) below I illustrate a different strategy, which consists in presenting oneself as a *professional* client (Sarangi and Slembrouck 1996; Sarangi 1998) and offering solutions to speed up the decision-making process. On this occasion, the enquirer's application has been positively evaluated by the back office and has been transferred to the police department for further examination, but as usual, all this does not get transmitted to the client.

(43)

	1	*MIQ:	en trámite -. **three more weeks**.
		%tra:	being processed -. three more weeks.
	2	*ENQ:	cuántos?
		%tra:	how many?
	3	*MIQ:	<tres semanas más> [>].
		%tra:	<three more weeks> [>].
	4	*ENQ	<cuántos días> [<]?
		%tra::	<how many days> [<]?
→	5	*ENQ:	tres semanas -? mira esto: # primero primero día presenta # y
	6		cuándo <cuándo vas venir> [>].
		%tra:	three weeks -? look at thi:s # first first day I submit # and when <when you are going to come> [>].
→	7	*MIQ:	<primer día> [<]?
		%tra:	<first day> [<]?

	8	*MIQ:	sí sí primer día.
		%tra:	yes yes first day.
→	9	*ENQ:	que tengo tengo una pregunta -. qué ahí tiene problemas o
	10		qué -? no sé.
		%tra:	I have I have a question -. what there does it have problems or what -? I don't know.
→	11	*MIQ:	no salen que haya problemas eh -? parece que está todo bien -.
	12		tienes que esperar.
		%tra:	it [the computer] doesn't show any problems right -? it seems like everything is okay -. you have to wait.
→	13	*ENQ:	porque mi amigo todo amigo Bangladesh # presenta -, todo
	14		concedido para mí esperar.
		%tra:	because my friends all friends Bangladesh # they submitted -, all granted and I have to wait.
	15	*MIQ:	tres semanas.
		%tra:	three weeks.
→	16	*ENQ:	ahí tienes algún problema eh de de:.
		%tra:	there you have any problems uh of o:f .
→	17	*MIQ:	+ˆ no sale que haya ningún problema.
		%tra:	it doesn't show any problems.
	18	*RES:	*està en instrucció no?*
		%tra:	it's still in preparatory [phase] right?
		%add:	MIQ
	19	*MIQ:	*està en instrucció sí sí.*
		%tra:	it's in preparatory [phase] yes yes.
→	20	*ENQ:	que hay mucha mucha tempo y + ...
		%tra:	there has been a long time and + ...
→	21	*MIQ:	sí pero.
		%tra:	yes but.
		%act:	shrugs his shoulders.
→	22	*ENQ:	cuando tienes ahí tienes problema -, cuando quieres una
	23		abogado -, si que ahí tiene problema tú quieres abogado o
	24		qué -? antes cuando viene dice que: tengo una expulsión.
		%tra:	if you have there you have a problem -, if you want a lawyer -, if there is a problem there you want a lawyer or what -? before when I came they said I have a deportation order.

25	*MIQ:	la expulsión no es problema -. aquí todo el mundo no tiene
26		papeles -. hay muchos que tienen expulsión porque no tienen
27		papeles -, por eso estás aquí.
	%tra:	the deportation order is not a problem -. here everybody doesn't have papers -. there are many that have deportation orders because they don't have [legal] papers -, that is why you are here.
28	*ENQ:	pero yo xxx.
	%tra:	but I xxx.
29	*MIQ:	no hay problemas hay que esperar tres semanas.
	%tra:	there are no problems you have to wait three weeks.
30	*ENQ:	tres semanas?
	%tra:	three weeks?
31	*ENQ:	este papele no?
	%tra:	this paper no?
32	*MIQ:	éste no es de aquí -. éste es de la oficina central.
	%tra:	this one is not from here -. this is from the central immigration offices.

Although the client's command of Spanish is relatively good, he is not told that his application is undergoing a second review process and that the first one was already positive. He is given the routinised "wait for three weeks" response. This annoys the enquirer. In line 5, he begins to challenge the institutional procedure. He employs his first remarks to set the scene and construct himself as a conscientious enquirer. He does that by stressing that he submitted his application on the first day. Significantly, the bureaucrat's first reaction is one of mistrust (line 7). This is another example of how clients' talk comes constantly under scrutiny at this site.

The enquirer interrupts his talk and resumes it in line 9 by asking whether there are any problems with his application. The relevance of this question is established by his previous framing of the scene: it has been three months since he submitted his application. The immigration official responds that everything seems in order, but that the client has to keep on waiting. The official expects his interlocutor to accept the truthfulness of his response and sees no need to provide any further explanation. The enquirer is clearly denied an understanding of the situation; he is asked to simply have faith in the official's words (lines 11–12).

Seeing that he cannot unearth further details, the enquirer tries another strategy. This consists in comparing the slow progress of his application with the assertion that all his fellow countrymen have already been awarded a work permit. Implicit in his turn is his dissatisfaction with the official's previous response. He expects a more precise account, but the official repeats the *"tres semanas"* 'three weeks' formula. The enquirer is still not satisfied. Not only does he not understand the institution's erratic practices for processing paperwork, but he is not allowed to do so by not being given any sort of account.

He persists in asking whether there are any problems (line 16) and repeats his complaint that a long time has elapsed since submission (line 20). The official agrees with him and shrugs his shoulders, indexing that there is nothing he can do to accelerate the process. It is true that there is no coherent account he can provide of why this particular file has been delayed, as he does not have access to that information, but as we have noted above, he could be more explicit as to the specific stage this application is at.

Because the routinised answers to his information requests have not brought any reassurances, the client now he decides to adopt a more active role in the exchange. He turns into a professional client in that he suggests causes for the delay (his deportation order) and possible solutions (a lawyer). His earlier construction as an informed service seeker is ratified here. Nevertheless, the official rejects the enquirer's reading of the situation and insists that there are no problems with his petition (line 29).

This extract illustrates how, in spite of all the enquirer's efforts and the variety of strategies he deploys in an attempt to find out more details, he cannot manage to go beyond the information he already had at the outset, that is, basically no information. In this case, lack of competence in the language of interaction is not an obstacle, as the client is perfectly able to conduct a bureaucratic interaction of this sort in Spanish. This interaction clearly shows that beyond scripted responses, obscure as they may be, there lies a more profound dimension of bureaucratic control. Access to institutional knowledge is tightly controlled here by these state officials whose behaviour seems to be shaped by a combination of the desire not to act uninstitutionally on the one hand and the will to avoid putting their own interactional position at risk on the other. This behaviour is framed and to some extent also legitimised by the institution's widespread lack of interest in front-line service communication.

3.4. Trying to change footing

The final example in this section (44) illustrates, once again, how clients, despite their linguistic difficulties, may fight fiercely for relevant information. The enquirer in this example displays the use of an array of strategies, which, as might be expected, do not get him very far. Some of the strategies he uses, such as asking the same questions repeatedly, voicing his mistrust, complaining about the malfunctioning of the organisation and exposing discrepancies between old and new information, we have already examined elsewhere. All of them are related to the enactment of the social role of client of a bureaucratic organisation. What is interesting about this encounter is that, at one point, the service seeker steps out of character and attempts to change the footing of the interaction by moving from an institutional to a personal mode of talk. However, the service provider refuses to align himself with the new frame suggested and the enquirer's efforts consequently fail.

(44)

→   1 *MIQ: está casi concedido pero faltan dos o tres semanas vale?
           %tra: this one is almost granted but there are still two or three weeks to go okay?

  2 *UUU: #0_2.

  3 *MIQ: entiendes?
      %tra: do you understand?

  4 *UUU: #0_2.

→   5 *ENQ: **what señor is the falta falta?**
      %tra: what sir is the missing missing [paper]?

→   6 *MIQ: no falta # todo bien.
      %tra: no missing [paper] # everything is okay.

  7 *ENQ: todo bien?
      %tra: everything okay?

  8 *MIQ: dos o tres semanas y estará bien.
      %tra: two or three weeks and it'll be okay.

  9 *UUU: #0_4.

10 *MIQ: en qué hablas?
      %tra: what do you speak?

11 *UUU: #0_1.

12 *MIQ: **do you speak English?**

13 *ENQ: **I speak English.**

14 *MIQ: **it's alright you only have to wait two or three more weeks**
15   **but the papers are alright -. okay?**

→ 16 *ENQ: xxx concedido uh xxx **passport**.
   %tra: xxx granted uh xxx passport?

17 *MIQ: **yes but now it's okay -. okay -, but not** concedido **-. wait**
18   **two or three weeks but okay**.

19 *RAM: **not** concedido [=! shouting].
   %com: speaker puts on an english accent when uttering the word
         "concedido".

→ 20 *ENQ: xxx **they tell me okay you: come in uh next** <**uh** xxx> [>].

21 *RAM   <*ja se n'ha anat*
22   > [<] *aquell del Pakistan -? aquell de* <*barba -? li haguéssim*
23   *pogut preguntar com es diu això en el en el urdu*> [>] -. ##
24   nos hubiéramos enterado todos un poco más.
   %tra: <is he gone> [<] that one from Pakistan -? the one with a
          beard -? we could have asked him how you say that in the
          the urdu> [>] -. ## we would all have understood a little
          bit more.

25 *MIQ: <**yes but now # it's still have to wait two weeks okay**> [<]?

→ 26 *ENQ: **please** [?] **explain if anything is** falta uh.

27 *MIQ: +ˆ **now** no falta no falta.

28 *UUU: xxx.

29 *ENQ: **last month having any things for** falta uh **give the** falta
30   **papers yeah -? and** uh **next two weeks** uh **to get to get the**
31   **paper** <**to get** falta **get** falta> [>].

32 *MIQ: <**yes but it's not okay it's not okay it's not okay**> [<] **wait**
33   **two weeks**.

→ 34 *ENQ: **this** tramit **is not okay -. my paper is not okay what can** + ...

→ 35 *MIQ: **okay but** falta **two weeks**.

36 *ENQ: **more** [?] **two weeks**?

37 *MIQ: **yes**.

→ 38 *ENQ: **very long time # very lo:ng time**.

→ 39 *MIQ: **very long time**?

→ 40 *ENQ: **my paper is** <**April**> [>].

	41	*MIQ:	<April> [<] there is people from twenty-one of
→	42		Merch not okay -. you are very fast -. # you're very lucky
	43		-. it's okay only have to wait -. that's it -. wait.
→	44	*ENQ:	perhaps you could xxx uh.
	45	*MIQ:	+ˆ when it's okay we send you a letter okay?
	46	*ENQ:	I bring that letter here on Friday two June # my falta isn't
	47		xxx?
	48	*MIQ:	no this is okay now.
	49	*ENQ:	+ˆ okay xxx.
	50	*MIQ:	after two or three weeks we send a letter to you -. if you
	51		want come here in three weeks but we send a letter.
	52	*ENQ:	will you send a letter my house uh address?
	53	*MIQ:	yes this address.
→	54	*ENQ:	this address -. but I I don't give give me in in informe
	55		letter.
	56	*MIQ:	no -. i::s it's not informe -. you have to say concedido
	57	*ENQ:	<papers concedido> [>].
	58	*MIQ:	not concedido.
→	59	*ENQ:	not concedido what falta?
	60	*MIQ:	in two weeks concedido -. # in two or three weeks there is
	61		concedido.
	62	*ENQ:	they told me uh concedido.
	63	*MIQ:	if you want come after three weeks come here # if not we
	64		send you a letter.
	65	*ENQ:	later I come here my papers next week okay here xxx
	66		papers.
	67	*MIQ:	+ˆ next week no in two or three weeks.
→	68	*ENQ:	need [?] letter [=! softly] <need the letter> [>].
	69	*MIQ:	<in two or three weeks> [>] here
	70		concedido.
	71	*ENQ:	concedido wait [?] uh +/.
	72	*MIQ:	+ˆ now no now no.

144 *Strategies of information management*

```
         73  *ENQ:   what xxx # next two weeks?
         74  *MIQ:   yes it's almost concedido.
    →    75  *ENQ:   almost xxx you know you know very it's very big problem no
             76              concedido you know.
         77  *MIQ:   +ˆ yes yes.
             %act:   rings buzzer indicating he is ready to serve another enquirer
    →    78  *ENQ:   it's very big problem.
             %act    hands MIQ another application form
         79  *MIQ:   what is this paper -? you only one paper -. you say only
             80              one paper -, only one paper.
         81  *ENQ:   see this [=! begging tone].
         82  *MIQ:   no no only one paper.
         83  *ENQ:   see this.
         84  *MIQ:   you have more than this?
         85  *ENQ:   no this only.
```

The service seeker's knowledge of Spanish seems limited to a few pivot words like *falta, trámite, concedido,* and *informe,* which, as we have discussed, index the bureaucratic procedure at the immigration office. Although the client does not show a fluent command of English, this does not seem to constitute a barrier for him to adopt a remarkably active role in the encounter. He questions, contests and challenges the official's words throughout the interaction. All his turns from line 5 onwards are oriented to the achievement of his goal, which as becomes clear in lines 54 and 68, is to obtain an *informe laboral*. This is the provisional certificate issued by desk staff once the permit is granted and before the official letter of acceptance is sent out by the back office. With the *informe laboral,* the foreigner can be legally employed. So it is important to obtain this certificate now, because the official letter may take up to a month to arrive at the applicant's address.

At the administrative stage where this client's file now finds itself, his criminal records have been screened by the police. Everything has been found in order and the application has been sent back to the office for administrative processing. It is in the hands of the back-office staff, who are in charge of entering information on the "accepted" status of applications into the computer and preparing the official letters of acceptance. The enquirer's application is probably just waiting to be processed. Nevertheless, as in the previous example, none of this information is conveyed to him. He is only told that everything is okay, and that he has to wait. Also as in previous examples, the exact meaning of having to wait is not made clear. After all, being told to wait is not taken as a good signal by enquirers, as it is almost always equated with problems with the processing of the applications. Yet this perception does not seem to be taken into account by officials.

The client's questioning turns are triggered by a mixture of mistrust towards the institution and a lack of understanding of the situation. The bureaucrat's unfortunate choice of words (more precisely, the use of *falta* in line 1) compounds the speakers' lack of interactional synchrony. The client's fears that something has gone wrong are reinforced by the fact that the previous week he was told that he could go and collect the *informe laboral* in a week's time (see line 20), and now he is told this is not yet possible. This is yet one more instance of how the lack of a common information policy for the office is confusing for clients, undermines the credibility of the institution and endangers the interactional face of individual bureaucrats.

Let us now focus our analysis on lines 38 to 43 and the sequence contained between lines 68 and 78. In line 38, after establishing that he has to wait for two more weeks, the enquirer states that this is a "very long time # very long time". The pragmatic function of this turn is ambiguous. It can be interpreted as a mild complaint on the slow working of the institution or as a personal appeal to the official. In the second case, the enquirer would be trying to evoke pity from the institutional representative with a view to obtaining a more favourable treatment. The response he obtains in lines 41–43 is revealing. Whether the client is complaining or appealing to the official's feelings, it is clear that he assesses time from a personal reference point. The official rejects the enquirer's personal assessment of the situation and imposes an institutional framing of it. He seems to take the enquirer's turn as a complaint. According to the official, there is no reason for the enquirer to complain, as his application is being processed faster than others that were submitted earlier. The bureaucratic frame legitimises the official's outright dismissal of his interlocutor's words. His talk is aggressive and the tone of his voice rises. His turn is made up of short, unmodulated statements, intensifiers ("very fast, very lucky"), and imperatives ("that's it -. wait"). No facework is attempted; there is no space for negotiation. In his following turn (line 44), the enquirer seems to try to formulate a request, but he is interrupted by the official. In an impatient manner, the official states that the enquirer will be sent a letter when the permit is granted. The latter perseveres in trying to get a more informative response. Finally, in lines 54–55 he reveals that his goal is to obtain the "*informe* letter". In response, the official tries to explain why he cannot be given the certificate, but he seems unable to go beyond stating that the enquirer has to return to the office in two weeks' time.

In line 68, the enquirer decides to produce his first personal appeal: "need letter need the letter". He attempts to change the footing of the interaction by stepping out of his situated role as the client of a bureaucratic organisation to position himself as an individual for whom the *informe* certificate is vital. In so doing, he suggests a more symmetrical social relationship in which the official is positioned as an individual person who can understand and even identify with the enquirer's worries. However, he elicits no reaction on the part of the official, as his talk overlaps with the last part of the enquirer's turn. The enquirer tries again a few turns later (lines 75–76), but the institutional representative does not want to align himself with the new footing suggested. He simply produces an agreement token, which is quickly repeated. The latching of his turn with the enquirer's previous turn, together with his quick repetition of the agreement token and his nonverbal behaviour (ringing the buzzer to serve another enquirer) indicate that he does not want to pursue this interaction any further. The enquirer's final attempt (line 78) is again not responded to by the official, as his attention is now focused on the new application his interlocutor has produced.

To sum up, all the strategies employed by the service seeker to attempt to go beyond the tight control of information imposed by the institutional representative fail, because the limits of what is negotiable are established beforehand. Information exchange is not a dynamic process. Public officials' contributions sound like written lines that are repeated independent of the service seeker and of his/her efforts at making sense of the bureaucratic frame. Clients' attempts at deroutinising, that is, *debureaucratising* (Sarangi and Slembrouck 1996) officials' talk are not allowed to succeed. Immigrants are just told to wait and go back to the office as prescribed. What is significant is that this happens no matter what the real status of applications, that is, even if there is no need to control information because what is to be conveyed is not bad but good news.

4. Concluding remarks

In this chapter and the previous one I have painted a picture of information provision in this office; I have discussed various dimensions of the gatekeeping nature of the process. The most obvious one is related to the tangible outcome of the process (being given or denied legal entry into an industrialised society). The second gatekeeping dimension, and one which I have discussed in detail here, is linked to the fact that the bureaucratic procedure is presented as so obscure that, beyond entitlement, being allowed through the gate appears like a question of magic or good luck. Much of what happened in this office had little to do with information or the actual administrative procedure but rather involved giving the appearance that the gate was being kept closed. These interactions were empty of meaning but heavily controlled in interpersonal terms. This is related to the third gatekeeping dimension, which is connected with the need for petitioners to display forms of conduct which can be officially sanctioned by state representatives. This is discussed at greater length in Chapters 5 and 6.

The data shown in this chapter has demonstrated how immigrant clients deployed a variety of techniques to unearth relevant details on individual applications. They ranged from indirect means of information gathering – like taking up bureaucrats' words so that sequential opportunities were provided for officials to expand on previous answers, asking for the meaning of institutional abreviations or alluding to the office's changing information practices – to rather direct challenges – like exposing the inconsistencies in the information provided or openly declaring lack of understanding. When all that failed, enquirers might voice direct complaints, make personal appeals or even offer "professional" solutions to bureaucrats. However, no matter how creative their strategies were, enquirers systematically failed to negotiate a more symmetrical stance with bureaucrats, a stance that would enable them to comprehend the hows, whens and whys of the bureaucracy they had to deal with. Enquirers' local attempts at going beyond bureaucrats' "scripted" behaviour were, for the most part, unsuccessful.

In the minute-to-minute unfolding of interactions, public officials at the site had to deal with the many contradictions inherent in their situated social position. They needed to safeguard institutional interests by not revealing key knowledge about the procedure and complying with policies and regulations, but as individual speakers, they were subject to the pressures of face-to-face interaction. Depending on the demands of the sequential context, they wavered between personal and institutional framings of behaviour. When the team was challenged, they underscored their individual dimension; when a personal mode of talk was suggested, they stressed their institutional identity. They wanted to avoid interpersonal alignment with enquirers, but at the same time they were concerned with doing facework and maintaining a positive face for themselves as professionals and as individual speakers engaged in situated verbal action.

Finally, the pragmatic analysis of speakers' contributions shows that participants' interactional rights and obligations in such contexts are constructed as unequal. Bureaucrats can afford not to pick up on implied requests and they can refuse to answer specific questions without being held accountable for it. Moreover, they can strategically manipulate the definition of their own professional role to serve local needs. By contrast, enquirers' moves are scrutinised.

They are held accountable for inconsistencies in their reports and for whatever action they perform which seems to subvert a strictly defined moral order. The following chapters present a detailed analysis of the ways in which bureaucrats monitor the observance of that moral order and of how they closely regiment the social, interactional and linguistic spaces of the office.

Part III

Regimented spaces

Chapter 5
The scrutinisation of behaviour

1. Introduction

I have noted that one of the defining paradoxes of the bureaucratic office examined is that, despite its being an information service, information was hard to come by. This is because access to crucial institutional knowledge was closely controlled by members of staff. As would be expected, though, the exercise of control was not confined to information management, but was part and parcel of the ways in which immigration officials constructed their professional identities and performed their situated roles. The fact that control was so characteristic of the talk observed is not surprising given the socioinstitutional context. Indeed, bureaucracies are powerful instruments of social control; they regulate the organisation of social life and the distribution of individuals' rights and obligations (Sarangi and Slembrouck 1996). State bureaucracies are, in fact, one of the fundamental means whereby governments exert their power and control over the population. In the sphere of foreign immigration, in particular, the degree of social control which is in the hands of national governments is not negligible.Through the implementation of specific laws, governments decide who is legally accepted into a country, on what conditions and for how long a time.

In this chapter I will show how the public officials studied took on board the socially regulatory function of the bureaucracy they were working for and charged their talk and discursive demeanour with a spirit of close regulation and control. They aimed at normativising all forms of client conduct in a space that they considered to be essentially theirs. They took advantage of whatever instances they could observe of immigrant clients failing to abide by the office's "norms" to expose the latter's behaviour and treat it as fundamentally subversive. In service buraucracies, instances of negative categorisation of clients due to non-observance of the rules get tied up and reinforce the ideological constructions of clienthood based on suspicion and mistrust (Sarangi and Slembrouck 1996), which shape many of the formal and informal procedures public institutions put in place to deal with the public.

At the immigration office, the processes of singling out clients for inappropriate behaviour were more or less frequent and/or intense depending on the individual bureaucrat observed but, most significantly, were always grounded on the exploitation of the linguistic asymmetries between interlocutors.

The present chapter concentrates on three features of bureaucrats' discursive behaviour and productions, namely, the regulation of time and space, the management of interactions' sequential organisation, and finally, the manipulation of register choice and pragmatic expectations. For all three features, I shall discuss the purposes they served and the effects they had.

2. The wish for absolute control

The discursive behaviour of public officials at the site was defined by their wish to control whatever went on in the office. That implied, essentially, the close surveillance of enquirers' behaviour and the will to discipline clients in ways which are reminiscent of traditional practices in educational establishments (Collins 1987; Alcalá 2006). As I shall be discussing in ensuing paragraphs, the officials' desire for control extended to a number of different aspects of their interlocutors' conduct, from the use of public space to the regulation of petitioners' frequency of visits to the office.

Officials wanted to be in control, but above all, they wanted to feel they were in control. Any action by enquirers that was perceived as a threat to the officials' prerogative to determine what was appropriate conduct at the site was severely reprimanded.

This section is divided into two parts. In the first part, I examine those features of officials' discursive behaviour that index the structure of domination which informed their practices and which they routinely implemented. In particular, I focus on their efforts at controlling the use of time and space in the office, but also on the many instances in which they passed explicit judgement on their interlocutors' behaviour and imbued their talk with a disciplinary dimension. These examples construct officials as self-selected keepers of a strict social and moral order to which clients systematically fail to adjust. In the second part, I look at how bureaucrats' controlling efforts extended to the ways in which they organised service provision and to the interactional unfolding of their verbal exchanges with clients.

2.1. Regulating time and space, and defining norms of appropriate conduct

One of the most salient features of the officials' controlling actions at the office was their strict management of public space. The clients' movements in the office were controlled at all times. This control was exerted primarily by door staff, but also by information desk officials. The door staff was in charge of regulating the order of clients waiting to be attended. For example, they sought to prevent service seekers who had not taken a turn number from jumping the queue. Clients were only allowed into the office proper when they were about to be served. Once inside, they were requested to sit on a bench (see the general floor plan in Figure 2 [Chapter 1, section 6]) until their turn number was called.

In spite of all these attempts at regulating who moved where, deviations from the prescribed norms of conduct frequently occurred. Enquirers whose number had not yet been called might approach the counter for a variety of reasons. This would infuriate officials, who would shout frequent unmodulated commands and prohibitions. Eventually, commands would turn into downright threats. Threatening immigrants with calling the police reveals the extent to which these officials, more than just providing information, were acting as representatives of the state. As such, they had the power to call upon the use of the state's coercive instruments to carry out their regulatory functions.

The following excerpt (45) shows how one of the desk officials tries, verbally, to exert control over his interlocutors' management of public space. In this brief exchange, he attempts twice to regulate the movements of clients in the office.

(45)

	1	*MIQ:	0.
		%act:	rings buzzer to serve following enquirer.
	2	*MIQ:	sesenta tú tienes el sesenta?
			sixty do you have number sixty?
	3	*MIQ:	0.
		%tra:	rings buzzer again.
	4	*MIQ:	sesenta y uno!
		%tra:	sixty-one!
	5	*MIQ:	espera # tú tienes el sesenta y uno?
		%tra:	wait # do you have sixty-one?
→	6	*MIQ:	pues esperaos allá hasta que salga el sesenta y dos.
		%tra:	so wait there until sixty-two is called.
	7	*ENQ:	0.
		%act:	hands document over to MIQ.
	8	*MIQ:	sólo uno?
		%tra:	only one?
	9	*ENQ:	tres más.
		%tra:	three more.

	10	*MIQ:	dámelos.
		%tra:	give them to me.
→	11	*MIQ:	aquí no puedes estar -. tú no tienes número -, fuera de aquí.
		%tra:	you cannot be here -. you don't have a number -. get out of here.
		%add:	MEM
	12	*MEM:	<éste xxx número yo soy con él> [?].
		%tra:	<this xxx number I am with him> [?].
→	13	*MIQ:	no estás con él -. ## no estás con él -, ## fuera.
		%tra:	you're not with him -. you're not with him -. out.
		%add:	MEM
	14	*MIQ:	diecinueve de mayo todavía no está -. once de mayo todavía
	15		no está -. quince de mayo todavía no está -. sólo tenemos
	16		hasta el diez de mayo.
		%tra:	May nineteenth is not yet ready -. May eleventh not yet ready -. May fifteenth not ready yet -. we only have until May tenth.

The exchange begins with a turn allocation sequence. The official, Miquel, tries to determine who is to be served (line 2). He assumes it is the turn of a pair of individuals waiting by the counter, but his guess is proven wrong. When he finds out, he not only tells them to move away from the counter, but also indicates by means of the adverbial "*allá*" 'there' where exactly they must wait ("*pues esperaos allá hasta que salga el sesenta y dos*" 'so wait there until sixty-two is called').

Then, while Miquel is in the process of serving his next client (the real number 61), a member of the public (MEM) approaches the counter. In line 11, Miquel tells this person in a fairly direct fashion that he cannot stand by the counter because he does not have a number. When this individual tries to justify his presence by claiming that he is accompanying somebody, the bureaucrat rejects his justification bluntly. It is interesting to observe that the official dismisses not just the functionality of the enquirer's account as justification of his presence by the counter, but also the enquirer's actual presentation of reality ("*no estás con él*" 'you are not with him').

Miquel's insistence on this person's not having a number is related to another of the reasons why door staff and officials had such a great investment in controlling immigrants' movements in the office: to prevent them from jumping the queue. Institutional staff most apparent objective in doing so was to preserve the rights of those information seekers who had spent long hours queuing up. But jumping the queue was also an act of subversion of their strict regimentation of the office's social order. The following extract (46) contains the discursive justification Miquel provides to an alleged offender for not serving him.

(46)

1	*MIQ:	esta gente está aquí esperando en la calle desde las tres de la mañana para que le miremos y está haciendo cola en el sol y tú acabas de llegar y no tienes número -. no te lo voy a mirar.
	%tra:	these people have been here waiting in the street since three o'clock in the morning to have [their applications] checked and they have been queuing up in the sun and you've just arrived and don't have a number -. I'm not going to check [your file].

One of the most noteworthy features of Miquel's explanation is the way in which he constructs himself as the keeper of a moral order. Indeed, he phrases his turn in such a manner that the moral "meanness" of his offending interlocutor is made to stand out. This is achieved by highlighting the harshness of the circumstances surrounding other enquirers' waiting conditions through skilful dramatic strokes: "*desde las tres de la mañana*" 'since three o'clock in the morning' and "*haciendo cola en el sol*" 'queuing up in the sun'.

But not only do public officials closely monitor the use clients make of public space; they also attempt to normativise a number of aspects of their interlocutors' behaviour according to their own self-defined assessment of appropriate conduct in this social setting. Sometimes, as some of the examples will illustrate, officials' self-defined norms of conduct even refer to facets of clients' behaviour and actions that go quite beyond their situated social role as information seekers.

Below I provide two extracts that exemplify this phenomenon. In one of them (47), the enquirer is asked to account for his absent-mindedness, as his number has already been called. Implicit in the official's question ("*dónde estabas?*" 'where were you') is the dual assumption that the enquirer's behaviour has violated what would be the expected appropriate conduct in this setting, namely, that enquirers are attentive to numbers called, and also, that the official has the prerogative to hold him accountable for it. In the subsequent example (48), the official, in this case Ramon, even feels licensed to criticise the propriety of his interlocutor's dress. Striking as his comment may seem, it is interesting to see how it actually reproduces long-standing social ideologies of discipline and order. Managing one's body properly has always been a major aspect of disciplining in institutions committed to that purpose, like, for example, schools (Collins 1987).

156 *The scrutinisation of behaviour*

(47)

    1   *MIQ: hola.
          %tra: hello.

    2   *ENQ: hola.
          %tra: hello.

    3   *MIQ: número?
          %tra: number?

    4   *ENQ: veinticinco.
          %tra: twenty-five.

→   5   *MIQ: dónde estabas?
          %tra: where were you?

        *ENQ: eh ech eso: chaval lo que dice # no sé +...
        %tra: uh ech that mate what he says # I don't know + ...

        *MIQ: espera.
        %tra: wait.

(48)

    1   *RAM: y cuando vuelvas dentro de dos semanas trae el pasaporte sí y una camiseta con mangas también.
          %tra: and when you come back in two weeks' time bring your passport and a shirt with sleeves.

Apart from behaviour, actions and even dress, bureaucrats' controlling moves also aimed to regiment enquirers' use of time. I already noted in Chapter 3 that bureaucrats' information practices involved attempts to regulate the frequency of clients' visits to the office by means of appending the infamous "three weeks" temporal adverbial to most of their service responses. Officials' concern with the regulation of time had to do with worries about their own well-being, since clients' repeated visits to the office added to the already large number of people they had to serve every day.

To prevent enquirers from not following their recommendations about waiting times, officials would use different strategies. Sometimes they uttered verbal prohibitions, as in example (49) below ("you can't come until you get the letter"), or, if there was evidence of unlawful conduct, they might decide to reprimand enquirers severely, as in (50).

The wish for absolute control 157

(49)	1 2	*MIQ: %tra:	en tres semanas te enviaremos una carta para que vengas con las fotos a poner las huellas. in three weeks' time we'll send you a letter so that you come with your photographs to have your fingerprints taken.
	3	*EN2: %tra:	carta [?]. letter [?].
	4	*MIQ: %tra:	tres semanas. three weeks.
	5	*EN1: %tra:	tres fotos no? three photographs right?
→	6 7	*MIQ: %tra:	sí lo pone en la carta que recibirá -. hasta que no tenga la carta no puede venir. yes it's in the letter that you'll receive -. you can't come until you get the letter.
(50) →	1 2 3	*MIQ: %tra: %add:	*aquest és del cinc de maig -. va vindre el dia vint i dos -, li vam dir que s'esperés tres semanes -, i el vint i vuit torna a estar aquí.* this one is from May fifth -. he came on the twenty-second -, we told him to wait for three weeks -, and on the twenty-eighth he is back here again. RES
→	4 5	*MIQ: %tra:	en trámite -. <**three more weeks -. three weeks -. three -. no one -. no two -. <three**> [>]> [=!shouting]. being processed -. <**three more weeks -. three weeks -. three -. no one -. no two -.<three**> [>]> [=!shouting].
	6	*ENQ:	<okay> [<] o o okay <two> [?].

This example is particularly valuable because, in lines 1–2, we are allowed an insight into why the official (Miquel) reacts as he does. Indeed, Miquel offers a backstage comment (addressed to the researcher) in which he underscores the fact that the enquirer has subverted the established social order by contravening Miquel's directive. (It must be recalled that officials knew when an application had been checked last because they wrote that information on applications every time they checked them.) The frontstage consequences of the enquirer's subversive conduct can clearly be seen in lines 4–5, in which Miquel shouts at the enquirer that he must wait for three weeks and "not just one or two" before coming back to the office. It must be noted that Miquel's allusion to the enquirer's inappropriate behaviour is only indirect, as Miquel gives no explanation as to why he is so annoyed. It is likely that as a consequence, the enquirer

158 *The scrutinisation of behaviour*

does not understand why Miquel reacts that way and that he perceives Miquel's aggressive interactional conduct as rather gratuitous.

In one of my informal interviews with him, Hussain also commented on how much this practice of returning to the office too soon irritated public officials. In the extract below (51), we see how Hussain distances himself from this type of client behaviour and explains how, contrary to what other immigrants do, he always waits longer than he is told (line 8). He constructs himself as a knowledgeable participant who knows the rules of appropriate conduct at this site.

(51)

	1	*RES:	o sea las veces que has ido allí a la oficina uh cómo cómo
	2		explicarías la experiencia de ir allí -. o sea es un es algo
	3		difícil es difícil hablar con esa gente -, es fácil o sea +...
		%tra:	in other words when you've been to the office uh how would you explain your experience -. is it something difficult is it difficult talking to those people -, it's easy or +...
→	4	*HUS:	no es para mí no es difícil porque yo como sabía un poquito
	5	%tra:	a mí me dicen una vez cuando yo me fue me dicen oye #
	6		trámite está bien -. me vienes dentro de un mes -. yo no
→	7		vayas dentro de un mes -. yo me vayas un mes y medio -.
	8		por ejemplo yo siempre llegas tarde no pierdes el tiempo.
			it's not for me it's not difficult because since I knew a little bit they told me once when I went they told me # listen being processed it's okay -. you come back in a month's time .- I did not go after a month -. I went after a month and a half -. for example I always arrive late I don't waste my time.
	9	*RES:	[=! laughs].
→	10	*HUS:	porque yo sí sabes como gente vayas cada semana cada
→	11		quince días -, molestan así -. por ejemplo una persona te
	12		dice de oficina -,.
		%tra:	because I do know like people who go every week every fifteen days -, they annoy them -. for example somebody from the office says to you-,.
	13	*RES:	sí.
		%tra:	yes.
	14	*HUS:	oye tú tienes venir # venir dentro de un mes.
		%tra:	listen you have to come back # come back after a month.

	15	*RES:	sí.
		%tra:	yes.
→	16	*HUS:	pero tú vayas dentro de una semana qué te dicen otra vez
→	17		oye vayas otra dentro de un mes por mejor.
		%tra:	but you go back a week later what do they tell you again listen come back after a month better.
	18	*RES:	y tú crees que se enfadan si ellos ven que has ido dentro de
	19		una semana?
		%tra:	and do you think they get angry if they see that you're back within a week?
	20	*HUS:	sí sí.
		%tra:	yes yes.
	21	*RES:	se enfadan.
		%tra:	they get angry.
	22	*HUS:	sí enfadan por .
		%tra:	yes get angry for.
	23	*RES:	+ˆ pues es mejor hacer <lo que te dicen> [>].
		%tra:	so it's better to do <as they say> [>].
	24	*HUS:	<es mejor si haces lo que te dicen> [<].
		%tra:	<it's better if you do as they say> [<].
	25	*HUS:	oye esperamos un poco días más -. porque si tú no vayas tú
	26		no pierdes -. ## por ejemplo tus papeles si salen -, sale
	27		este mes el próximo mes -, cuando tú vayas ellos ya te
	28		dicen oye ya tal día está concedido -. ya sabes.
		%tra:	listen let's wait some more days -. because if you don't go you don't lose -. ## for example your papers are granted -. they are granted this month the following month -, when you go they tell you listen on that day [the permit] will be granted -. you already know.
	29	*RES:	sí sí.
		%tra:	yes yes.
→	30	*HUS:	pues no hace falta que vayas cada semana -. que si vayas
→	31		pero bastantes veces no sale papeles -. no es seguro que si
→	32		vayas muchísimas veces te dan el papeles.
		%tra:	so there is no need for you to go every week -. if you go many times you won't get your papers -. it's not certain that if you go very many times you'll get your papers.

160 *The scrutinisation of behaviour*

	33	*RES:	ah no!
		%tra:	yeah no!
	34	*HUS:	porque gentes piensas -,.
		%tra:	because people think -,.
	35	*RES:	sí.
		%tra:	yes.
	36	*HUS:	como hay muchas gentes que no saben -. gente piensan
	37		cuando vayas cada días -, cada semanas -, ellos molestan él
	38		dicen él pobre viene cada semana puede ser -. porque ellos
→	39		no saben -. qué cómo sale éstas quién hace concedido quién
	40		hace denegados ellos no saben.
		%tra:	since there are many people who don't know -. people think if you go every day -, every week -, they annoy [them] he says poor thing he comes every week maybe -. because they don't know -. what how [permit] is granted who makes granting who makes rejection they don't know.
	41	*RES:	aha.
		%tra:	uh huh.
	42	*HUS:	bastantes -. ahora cuando como una persona si sabe -, él no
	43		vayas bastantes él va dice vale ya va dentro de un mes
	44		quince días.
		%tra:	many -. now when somebody knows -. he does not go many [times] he goes he says okay then he goes back after a month or fifteen days.

Hussain knows exactly how to proceed at the office. When I ask him whether he has ever found communication with immigration officials difficult (lines 1–3), he responds that he has not, because he knows "a little bit". It is interesting that the little knowledge he refers to is not linguistic, as we might expect, but behavioural. For him, communicating with bureaucrats is not difficult because he knows how to proceed. Thus, if he is told to wait for a month, he is aware that that time reference is not meant to be taken literally. Hussain also shows a clear understanding of who and when decisions are made. He knows that frontstage officials do not assess client applications (lines 39–40), and that it is therefore no use trying to elicit pity from them (lines 37–38), or enquiring too often.

Hussain constructs himself as a knowledgeable client and an institutionally appropriate one in that he does not bother officials with "inappropriate" forms of behaviour. He is careful to distinguish himself from the image of the helpless foreigner who is either cheated by mafias or queues up outside the immigration office for hours on end driven by groundless rumours. Hussain's identity as a settled migrant is constructed on the basis of his knowledge of bureaucracies but also on his self-presentation as a busy man. Interestingly, that same feature was also used to by another client in a service interaction at the office (contained in extract [69] of the following chapter). In that instance, the service seeker, who was very fluent in Spanish, provided the same "busy" categorisation of himself after attempts to make small talk with the office employees. He also made use of Catalan, which had great symbolic capital (Bourdieu 1991) in this particular research site because, as I shall argue in Chapter 6, it functioned as the *we-code*. We can therefore claim that being a busy person was one of the features that worked to construct the integrated foreigner identity that both Hussain and this other client were aspiring to.

Types of client behaviour which were perceived by bureaucrats as being "unlawful" in that they subvert the closely regimented social sphere of this office were often responded to by means of threats of police action. This can be seen in excerpt (52) below.

(52)

    1   *RES: *on està -? li han canviat el +...*
          %tra: where is he -? have they swapped the +...

    2   *RAM: +ˆ *aquest sí -. han canviat el número o algo així -.* mira verás
    3   %tra: uno **ready** uno te ha toca(d)o!
                  +ˆ this one yes -. they have swapped numbers or something like that -. look one ready one your turn!

    4   *MIQ: *aquest portava un paper d'un pakistaní* +/.
          %tra: this one had an application by a Pakistani +/.

→   5   *RAM: +ˆ *aquest ha canviat el número a un no sé qui i ara li he*
     6   %tra: *perdut l'altre -.* y está ya medio ficha(d)o!
                  +ˆ this one has swapped numbers with I don't know who and now I have lost his other one and he is halfway to getting himself a police record!

In this encounter, there seems to have been some confusion as regards clients' turn numbers. In lines 5 and 6, Ramon explains that some enquirers have swapped numbers. The perceived "subversive" nature of this action is highlighted in line 6 when, after explaining to Miquel what has happened, Ramon concludes by stating that the client almost got himself a police record as a result of his actions. This is, of course, a symbolic threat, as no real action is or will be taken by officials. It is also in line with Sarangi and Slembrouck's (1996: 59) claim that implicit in bureaucratic procedures (and, in this case, also talk) there is a strong disciplinary dimension. Another interesting feature of Ramon's turn is language choice. The official employs Catalan to answer my question, and then switches over to Spanish to utter his threat, which is clearly meant to be understood by the client or else it might lose its threatening potential. The symbolic and instrumental use of language choice to delimit different social spaces of verbal intercourse is explored in detail in Chapter 6.

Thus, resorting to threats of police action was the ultimate means whereby discipline was enforced and power exercised at the immigration office. The police played a very visible role in ensuring law and order in the office. Policemen guarded the door at all times and kept a permanent eye on the queue. Threats of future police action could also be invoked to prevent enquirers from submitting forged documentary evidence (see extract below). The effectiveness of the threat lay in the exploitation of immigrants' fears of deportation.

(53)

```
1   *RAM:  esto esto esto está toca(d)o -. # esto está manipulado -. este
2          ocho no es éste -. # esto si te lo cojo va a ir a la policía -. #
3          este ocho no es este ocho.
    %tra:  this this this is changed -. # this has been messed with -. this
           eight is not like this one -. # this if I take it it'll go to the
           police -. # this eight is not like this other eight.
```

The significant role, both real and potential, played by the police in this office is not surprising, given that the immigration office embodies the regulatory function of the state in its rawest form; that is, it had the power to decide who could gain access to citizenship, both on a legal and on a symbolic level. When the multiple mechanisms for the regulation of social conduct fail, the state has the prerogative to resort to the most primitive form of the exercise of power, that is, to physical violence (see extract [68] in this chapter for a clear allusion to physical force). As Gramsci (1971) and Foucault argued (Smart 1983; Rabinow and Rose 2003), the exercise of state power cannot be understood without the use of means of coercion side-by-side with mechanisms of disciplining founded on consent. Both forms of power were visible in the daily practices of service provision deployed by state representatives in this office.

Such importance was attached by staff to closely monitoring and controlling clients' behaviour that failure to do so by some officials became a source of irritation for their workmates. Example (54) below illustrates this attitude.

(54)

	1	*EN2:	sí perdón quiero preguntar por qué dice xxx.
		%tra:	excuse me I want to ask why you say xxx.
→	2	*MIQ:	es él.
		%tra:	it's him.
	3	*EN2:	sí sí yo sabe # pero uh por qué dice **this** papel es en en trámite
	4		xxx.
		%tra:	yes yes I know # but uh why do you say this paper is being processed xxx.
	5	*MIQ:	qué?
		%tra:	what?
	6	*EN2:	en trámite que se dice para todos # en trámite para:: <# tres
	7		semanas> [>].
		%tra:	being processed what is said for everybody # being processed fo::r <# three weeks> [>].
	8	*MIQ:	<si están en
	9		trámite> [<] en tres semanas como <mínimo> [>] es para ver
	10		si ya está cambiado o no.
		%tra:	<if they are being processed> [<] in three weeks at least is to see whether it has changed or not.
	11	*EN2:	<para qué> [<]?
		%tra:	<what for> [<]?
→	12	*TER:	pero tú dónde estás allí o aquí?
		%tra:	but where are you here or there?
		%add:	EN2
→	13	*TER:	claro si le estoy atendiendo yo Miquel es que!
		%tra:	of course because I am attending him Miquel come on!
	14	*MIQ:	*però em diu que em vol fer una pregunta i m'ha preguntat que*
	15		*per què quan dic* en *trámite dic* tres *semanas.*
		%tra:	but he says he wants to ask me a question and he has asked me why when I say being processed I say three weeks.
→	16	*TER:	pero tú estás aquí o estás allí?
		%tra:	but are you here or there?
		%add:	EN2
	17	*EN2:	no (a)quí.
		%tra:	no here.

164　*The scrutinisation of behaviour*

→　18　*TER:　pues vigila el bolso de tu:: <#> [>] de la señora si no + ...
　　　　%tra:　　then keep an eye on you:r <#> [>] on the lady's handbag or + ...
　　19　*EN2:　　　　　　　　　<señora> [<].
　　　　%tra:　　　　　　　　　<wife's> [<].

The service seeker in this stretch of interaction was previously being served by the official called Teresa. In the course of their interaction, Teresa needs to move away from the counter for some reason. The client takes advantage of this situation to try to obtain more information from another official, namely Miquel (this is where the excerpt presented here starts). When Teresa comes back and finds them interacting, she gets rather upset. She interrupts them by means of a question addressed to the service seeker asking him to decide which official he is being served by (line 12).[16] Her next utterance is addressed to her colleague Miquel. She blames him for the enquirer's disorderly conduct (line 13). Her use of the final tag "*es que*" 'come on' indexes that she expected her colleague to know better. Miquel retorts to her implicit accusations of unprofessional conduct by appealing to his discursive obligations (lines 14–15). He has been asked a question and has the civil obligation to respond. Teresa's accusations then grow weaker. She asks the service seeker the same question as previously and he responds again by stating that she is still his service provider (line 17). Since it becomes apparent that the enquirer has not attempted to engage in any type of "unlicensed" activities, Teresa tries to identify some other aspect of his conduct that may be subject to criticism. She directs her attention to a handbag that is on the counter and uses the enquirer's "carelessness" to continue exposing the client's inappropriate behaviour (line 18).

2.2. *Managing interactional organisation*

At the office, officials' attempts at managing service interactions one-sidedly were perhaps the key feature that shaped interactional organisation. Interestingly, this same need and practice was observed by Jacquemet in registration interviews for asylum seekers (2005).

　　I mentioned in Chapter 2 that all the interactions in the corpus have a very similar structure and that few departures from this pattern are found. One of the main reasons is that officials exert tight control over the unfolding of exchanges. They routinely implemented a specific sequencing of interactional episodes, which, in some aspects, might differ from enquirers' expectations. These expectations are based on stored knowledge in the form of cognitive schemata acquired through engagement in similar type of social activities. The extent to which officials were aware of how the specific sequential organisation imposed diverged from enquirers' background knowledge is arguable.

In service exchanges, it is common practice for service requests to be made one at a time (see Ventola 1987). Once the first request has been complied with, a second request is made, and so on. By contrast, in the social setting examined, enquirers were expected to make all their requests at the beginning of the exchange. It was explained in Chapter 2 that immigrants' handing over of applications to bureaucrats was interpreted as a nonverbal service request. These nonverbal moves prompted officials to start searching for the information required in the institution's database. Thus, asking immigrants to submit all the applications they had brought at the beginning of the exchange amounted to forcing them to produce all their service requests in one go. Once applications were handed over, the official counted how many there were and started checking them one by one. Note that responses were not provided all in one go, but rather immediately after the administrative situation of each application had been determined.

Officials justified their practice of collecting all applications at the outset by stating that it was a way to prevent enquirers from cheating. They claimed that some enquirers would approach the counter when an acquaintance was being served and pass their applications on to the acquaintance surreptitiously to have them checked at the last minute. They perceived this mode of conduct as unacceptable in that it represented a symbolic subversion of their desire for absolute control over what was happening. Unless the symbolic dimension is brought into the explanation, it is difficult to understand how this practice could be seen as different from giving one's application to an acquaintance for checking right before this person was to be served.

More significant in terms of its consequences is the fact that officials were oblivious of the unexpected nature of this sequential organisation. Research has shown that the less competent in the language of interaction a speaker is, the more s/he will rely on global and general contextual features typical of encounters of the same sort (Bremer et al. 1996). When a sequential organisation which contravenes speakers' expectations is established – especially if it is not metadiscursively explained or marked as exceptional in any way – participants may be at a loss to understand what is going on. Enquirers are likely to go away feeling they have been treated in an arbitrary and/or unfair manner. This works against the image of rationality and objectivity a state organisation like this one ought to project. The fact that the reasons which explain public officials' behaviour are obscure to enquirers makes the institution lose credibility. The wider the perception that the institution is engaging in dubious practices, the more legitimate the "subversive" enquirer attitudes public representatives want to do away with may become.

The following extract (55) contains participants' metadiscursive comments on the sequential development of the interaction. The enquirer's turns give us insights into the organisational structure he assumes (see line 4). It becomes evident that this organisation is radically different from the officials' desired conversational unfolding. As can be seen in line 5, it is the official who determines how to proceed. His unmodulated speech leaves no doubt as to who – in his perception – should be calling the shots. Especially worth noting is his use of the "*tienes que*" 'have to' verbal structure indicating obligation, and the conditional sentence "*si no me lo das ahora no te lo miro*" 'if you don't give it to me now I won't check it', whereby he states very plainly what the significant consequences will be of enquirer's non-compliance. This strategy is effective in ensuring obedience in that the consequences envisaged would clearly go against the interests of the enquirer, who is there precisely to have his application checked. Subordination to the official's dominant position is thus guaranteed.

(55)

		*MIQ:	sólo traes uno?
		%tra:	do you have only one?
	2	*ENQ:	sí:: só sólo tengo esa [=! surprised tone] !
		%tra:	we:ll I on only have that one [=! surprised tone] !
	3	*MIQ:	vale no si traes de algún amigo -, o de + ...
		%tra:	okay I thought maybe you had one from a friend -, or + ...
→	4	*ENQ:	ah ah no sí sí sí pero euh después se mira no +/?
		%tra:	oh oh yes yes but euh they are checked afterwards right+/?
→	5	*MIQ:	+ˆ sí pero tienes que dármelos ahora -. si no me lo das ahora
	6		no te lo miro.
		%tra:	+ˆ yes but you have to give them to me now -. if you don't give it to me now I won't check it.
	7	*ENQ:	vale.
		%tra:	alright.

This extract shows that clients' responses must be handled with caution in interaction. I am referring to the turn in line 2, where the enquirer responds in the positive to the question of whether he has only one application for checking. He interprets the official's question in line 1 as referring to him as an individual applicant. That is why he reacts in a surprised manner. The enquirer's response indexes the extent to which Miquel's framing of the encounter comes as unexpected to his interlocutor. It also shows how carefully affirmative responses such as the one in line 2 have to be handled in interaction. They cannot be taken at face value. In this example, the enquirer is skilful enough to use prosodic means like intonation to convey subtle nuances of meaning. It is his tone of surprise that forces the official to make the interpretive framing of his question more explicit in line 3. The mismatch in participants' schemata is then brought into the open and clarified. Less skilful enquirers might be left wondering why they were shouted at and severely reprimanded by their interlocutors. Something akin to this hypothetical scenario is what happens in the following extract (56).

(56)

      1   *ENQ: hola buenas.
            %tra: hi morning.

      2   *MIQ: hola:.
            %tra: hello:.

      3   *ENQ: 0.
            %act: hands application form over to MIQ

→   4   *MIQ: sólo traes uno?
            %tra: you only have one?

      5   *UUU: #0_1.

→   6   *MIQ: no traes de nadie más?
            %tra: you don't have anyone else's?

           @Situation: MIQ checks status of ENQ's application in computer

      7   *MIQ: en trámite -. tienes que [=! quick] **you have to wait three**
      8   **more weeks**.
            %tra: being processed -. you have to [=! quick] you have to wait three more weeks.

      9   *MIQ: entiendes?
            %tra: do you understand?

    10   *UUU: #0_1.

    11   *ENQ: qué: **three week**?
            %tra: what three week?

    12   *MIQ: **yes**.

    13   *ENQ: **wait**.

	14	*UUU:	#0_3.
	15	*ENQ:	mucho **wait**.
		%tra:	a lot of wait.
	16	*MIQ:	qué?
		%tra:	what?
	17	*ENQ:	**three week** muchos sí.
		%tra:	**three week** many yes.
	18	*MIQ:	muchos!
		%tra:	many!
	19	*UUU:	#0_3.
	20	*ENQ:	pero otro:s # <u>uh</u> no problemo?
		%tra:	but othe:rs # uh no problem?
	21	*MIQ:	no lo sé -. # **they are looking for** [//] **i:f it is alright or don't**
	22	%tra:	-. **I don't know.**
			I don't know -. # they are looking for [//] i:f it is alright or
			don't -. I don't know.
	23	*UUU:	#0_6.
→	24	*MIQ:	<u>mira</u> <u>mira</u> <u>mira</u> <u>mira</u>!
		%tra:	look look look look!
		%add:	RES
	25	*UUU:	#0_2.
→	26	*MIQ:	la butxaca del davant.
		%tra:	the front pocket.

@Situation: MIQ takes form handed in by ENQ

	27	*MIQ:	más?
		%tra:	more?
	28	*MIQ:	**you have more**?
	29	*UUU:	#.
	30	*MIQ:	**you have another one**?
	31	*ENQ:	+ˆ **this is my my friend**.
	32	*MIQ	**you don't have any more**?
	33	*ENQ:	<u>uh</u>?
	34	*MIQ:	**you don't have any more**?

	35	*UUU:	#.
→	36	*MIQ:	*he estat a punt de tornar-l'hi a repetir però he pensat no et*
	37		*passis.*
		%tra:	I was about to repeat it again but then I thought don't overdo it!
		%add:	RES
	38	*RES:	*no ho ha entès* !
		%tra:	he did not understand
→	39	*MIQ:	*ja -! com no hi havia vingut ningú per aquí -. si arriba a*
	40	%tra:	*vindre algun amic d'ell no li agafo.*
			I know –! as there was nobody around -. if a friend of his had come I would not have taken it.

The enquirer hands only one application over to the official, who asks him twice whether he has any other applications for checking (see lines 4 and 6). The enquirer does not respond verbally to any of the Miquel's questions, although it is possible that he provided a nonverbal response. At any rate, as we have noted previously, in this sequential context, the value of positive answers as indicators of mutual understanding is weak. In spite of this uncertainty, Miquel moves on interactionally. In subsequent stretches of talk, we observe how the enquirer's command of both English and Spanish is extremely limited.

When the enquirer feels that his first request has been satisfied, he produces a new application for checking. Miquel then directs my attention to the enquirer's behaviour (lines 24 and 26). His repetitions of the verb *mira* 'look' evoke an interpretive framing of actions in which the official believes he has caught the enquirer red-handed. That is to say, the official interprets the enquirer's actions as sneaky breaches in the mutual alignment established. Yet the way the enquirer behaves – taking out this new application from his front pocket – does not seem to indicate that he is trying to conceal his actions. Why is it interpreted in this way by the official and what does that interpretation index in terms of his perception of the group of enquirers?

Miquel's interpretation makes sense if understood in the light of a generalised lack of trust towards his interlocutors. This perception is widespread in bureaucratic encounters on the whole, but more specifically in those involving migrants (Jacquemet 2005). At the research site, it manifests itself in various ways in officials' discursive practices. In spite of all this, Miquel decides to check his interlocutor's new application, though not without trying to embarrass him beforehand. He asks him up to four times whether he has any other applications for checking. Miquel's tone of voice is loud and his asking of the same information four times echoes a cross-examination session. The official himself acknowledges that he has overdone it a little bit (see lines 36–37). In line 38 I try to explain the enquirer's behaviour by appealing to his lack of understanding of Miquel's suggested conversational organisation. Surprisingly, the official agrees with me and then provides an account of why he has decided to check the enquirer's new application.

Two elements are striking in this last turn (lines 39–40). One of them is Miquel's response to my comment about the enquirer's lack of understanding ("I know!"), which contrasts with his interpretation of the client behaviour in lines 24 and 26 as intentionally subversive. The second surprising element is Miquel's need to account for his way of proceeding. Strict as he usually is with regard to clients producing new applications in the late stages of the exchange, this time he is allowing the client to have a new one checked. He probably realises that I may question his equal and fair treatment of the client. Beyond these considerations, it is revealing to examine the kind of justification he provides. Although he agrees with me that the enquirer probably did not understand, non-comprehension does not enter into his decision-making process. He will check the enquirer's new application out of generosity provided the right circumstances are met, that is, that the enquirer has come alone. This way, Miquel makes it clear that despite appearances, it is not the enquirer who controls the game, in Bourdieu's sense (1991), but Miquel himself. He makes it apparent that he could have acted otherwise had he wanted to. It is still he who sets the rules. Whether that involves holding an enquirer unfairly accountable for something of which he is ignorant does not enter into the picture.

It transpires from this extract that the question of how legitimately actors can be held accountable for their actions when mutual understanding has not been ensured is a key issue. In this encounter we have been able to observe that the enquirer's understanding of the official's question is dubious. The official himself acknowledges that, and yet he treats the enquirer's behaviour as intentionally subversive, even if there is no evidence for this. The official's behaviour calls into question the extent to which participants' assessment of their interlocutors' intentions and motivations takes into account their local discursive productions. The official brings about an institutional frame of reference in which the enquirer's actions are not interpreted in the light of what is available in the interaction, but rather in the context of pervasive institutional ideologies about enquirer behaviour.

Another example of how few chances of participation in conversational management enquirers were allowed at the office is provided in the ensuing extract (57). In this dialogue, we see how any attempts to depart from officials' routine sequencing of conversational episodes are immediately thwarted. The interaction starts off with the enquirer's service request (here actually made by a

The wish for absolute control 171

somewhat more fluent friend who has accompanied the real petitioner). This is an unusual request, as the enquirer is not interested in the status of his application. He has already been granted a work permit, but there seems to be a problem with the Foreigner Identification Number he was given on a previous occasion. In broken Spanish, he formulates his demand for service (lines 1–4). The official does not align himself with the enquirer's framing of the encounter. In fact, he ignores the enquirer's request completely and proceeds by asking how many applications the enquirer wants to have checked. By means of this question, the official imposes his own judgement of relevance and pursues his own interactional agenda.

(57)

	1	*EN1:	hola perdón uh él dice que él tienes el la informe **letter** pero él
	2		voy a la: # oficina de: seguridad él dice que falta la aquí
	3		número -. voy a la otra vez ahí o hablar que dame correcto
	4		número -. número éste # falta la número este esto no correcto.
		%tra:	hello excuse me uh he says that he have the the report letter but he go to the: office o:f security he says that faulty the here number -. I go there again or talk that you give me the correct number -. number this # faulty the number this this not correct.
	5	*MIQ:	a ver tú cuántos traes?
		%tra:	let's see how many do you have?
	6	*EN2:	tres.
		%act:	three.
	7	*MIQ:	uno do:s tres.
		%tra:	one two:: three.
		%add:	talking to himself
	8	*MIQ:	a ver éste es éste?
		%tra:	let's see is this this one?
→	9	*EN2:	xxx este número no -. malo.
		%tra:	xxx this number no -. bad.
		@Situation: MIQ checks status of first application in computer		
	10	*MIQ:	a ver *noranta quatre nou sis*.
		%tra:	let's see ninety -our nine six.
	11	*MIQ:	este número está malo i *aquesta correcció* ?
		%tra:	this number is bad and this correction?
		%add:	EN2/himself

            12 *ENQ: *ah està malament mira.*
                %tra: oh it's wrong look.
                %add: RES

            13 *MIQ: *lo que hi ha és un expedient més.*
                %tra: there is a file too many.
                %act: checks computer
                %add: himself

→   14 *MIQ: **the letter uh is not yet sent -. you have to wait three weeks**
        15   **for the letter okay?**

            16 *EN2:   **okay.**

→   17 *MIQ: **+ˆ this is the right number.**

            18 *EN2:   *sí vale gracias.*
                %tra: yes okay thanks.

The enquirer's attempts at formulating his service request are ignored by the official twice. Neither his first request (lines 1–4) nor his second attempt at making his needs explicit (line 8) is acknowledged. This illustrates the limited extent to which enquirers are allowed to intervene actively in the structuring of the interaction.

My final remark in this section concerns the format of the official's provision of service turns (lines 14–17). We can see how he provides the specific piece of information he has been asked for only at the end of this segment (line 17). This shows how, besides conversational organisation, judgements of interactional relevance are also clearly controlled by the institutional representative. By ordering the information he provides in the way he does, the official makes it evident, once again, that the enquirer is not allowed to shape the unfolding of the interaction in any way. Even though the request in this encounter is atypical, the bureaucrat still imposes his routine ordering of information. That is, he informs his client of the administrative status of his application first, and then furnishes whatever "exceptional" piece of information he has been asked for.

3. Ramon's idiosyncratic forms of language use

So far we have seen how officials' controlling efforts at the immigration office went beyond the close monitoring of the amount and type of information to be provided. We have shown that information control was but one aspect of a larger enterprise aimed at regimenting a social and a moral order in this office.

In the previous section we have depicted some habitual procedures for exerting generalised control over enquirers' behaviour, such as the strict regulation of the use of public space and bureaucrats' one-sided management of conversational organisation. The aim of this section is to examine in detail the interactional behaviour of one of the officials involved, namely Ramon. For this purpose, I shall be using concepts from pragmatic theory along with Goffman's understanding of role management and routine in public establishments.

The most pervasive characteristics of Ramon's turns were his use of a very informal register, especially in his choice of words and forms of address, and the abundant backstage comments he would make about his interlocutors. These comments were significant for three reasons. First, they tended to contain stereotypical negative characterisations of immigrants' actions and behaviour. Second, they represented Ramon's attempts at defining and regimenting the moral order of the office. Third, though characteristically backstage in style and content, Ramon's comments were not made backstage, but frontstage, that is, they were usually inserted into his service talk. Admittedly, Ramon's particular use of language was not comparable in any way to the manner in which the other officials in this and related settings spoke. But in spite of the exceptionality of Ramon's behaviour, it is of interest to analyse it for two reasons. First, because it sheds light on some of the key issues discussed in this chapter; secondly, because despite its clearly offensive nature and the fact that there were repeated complaints from immigrants, Ramon's conduct was largely tolerated by the institution. This indexes either the neglect or the downright racism of the institution Ramon was working for. This is why I devote a specific section here to examining Ramon's linguistic behaviour.

The first aspect that I shall discuss is the way in which Ramon played with register. His particular use of language is best exemplified by looking at the unusual ways in which he would start his interactions with enquirers (see extract below). The forms of address that he deployed conventionally index a social relationship of close familiarity between speakers. However, this was clearly not the relationship holding between Ramon and his interlocutors.

(58)

1   *ENQ: por favor.
     %tra: please.

2   *RAM: +ˆ tú qué quieres chato?
     %tra: +ˆ what do you want dear?

The form of address *chato* 'dear' is only employed in informal situations among very close friends, between partners or in the context of buying and selling at a market. In that context, sellers may want to establish a close relationship with buyers in order to create an atmosphere of solidarity that boosts sales. In this institutional setting, by contrast, service encounters were enacted as first time exchanges, that is, as interactions taking place between strangers who meet only for the purposes of exchanging information.[17] The degree of social distance existing between interlocutors was very high and forms of address indexing lack of solidarity between speakers were therefore logically to be expected.

Instead, Ramon employed a range of colloquial forms of address which anchored the exchange, as it were, in a contextual field of symmetrical social relations which had in fact nothing to do with his actual perception of the situation as indexed by his regular degrading remarks. Thus, there is evidence to argue that, in using informal terms of address his intention was not to challenge the office's routine implementation of bureaucrat–client communication as fundamentally unequal; he was not attemptting to bring about a socially close relationship which would enable clients to participate more actively in the shaping of the process of information exchange. Rather, my claim is that this particular official was manipulating speakers' pragmatic expectations on the solidarity axis to cause bewilderment to his audience, both addressees and bystanders. He was deliberately flouting conventions of language use to create a playful atmosphere that would enable him to distance himself from the detached, impersonal mode of behaving he was expected to adopt as a public bureaucrat, and at the same time, from a job which, from what I could gather during fieldwork, he found dull and unmotivating. In my interpretation, Ramon was not trying to promote a closer relationship with his interlocutors than would be expected. In keeping with this, I interpret the use of the word *chato* above as an element of Ramon's language games whereby he attempted to provoke his audience – real or imagined – by intentionally subverting the sociopragmatic conventions at play.

However, Ramon's manipulation of conventional language use was always one-sided; it was *his* prerogative. Though there were no examples of similar floutings of sociopragmatic norms on the part of enquirers, Ramon's comments and behaviour would lead us to surmise that, had it occurred, such behaviour would have been immediately challenged by this official.

Ramon's flouting of conventions was largely made possible due to the asymmetrical distribution of linguistic resources that existed among the interlocutors at this office. Most enquirers did not have the command of Spanish that would enable them to comprehend the talk being addressed to them. Even if they did understand what was being said, they usually lacked the resources to be able to challenge the way in which they were categorised and socially positioned by their interlocutor. In addition, their limited command of Spanish was likely to interact with their perception that challenging a public official would be detrimental to the outcome of their petition.

Ramon took advantage of this structural asymmetry not just to bewilder his audience but more significantly, to make demeaning remarks about enquirers' circumstances, and about their social and linguistic behaviour. These remarks went beyond what might have been considered a playful mode of talk and became offensive characterisations of immigrants' talk and actions. Indeed, Ramon's idiosyncratic language use fluctuated between the playful subversion of pragmatic expectations and his attempts to exert his power by foregrounding negative features of clients' behaviour.

The initial turns in the extract below (59) contain another display of Ramon's ostensibly playful interactional mode. In this case, the service exchange involves him and an enquirer of Chinese origin. In line 2 we can see how the official greets his interlocutor very emphatically. (I remember getting the impression at the time that they knew each other. When I later asked the official, however, he disconfirmed my guess.) To his particular intonation of the greeting device "*hola*" 'hello' – clearly resembling the intonation one would use when bumping into an acquaintance one has not seen for a long while – Ramon adds the use of the informal question "*qué hay*?" 'what's up?'. The official is, again, playing with language conventions and speakers' expectations (as evidenced by my mistaken assumption about their relationship).

As noted, an outsider to the setting might have interpreted the Ramon's moves as trying to create a friendly atmosphere. When enquirer–official communication becomes more conversational, it becomes potentially less "bureaucratic" (Sarangi and Slembrouck 1996). However, a close analysis of subsequent talk reveals how under Ramon's conversational geniality lurks a ridicule of the enquirer's linguistic abilities which draws on stereotypical constructions of immigrant identity. Conversationalisation can be used as yet one more strategy of social control, as Fairclough (1992) has pointed out.

(59)

	1	*ENQ:	hola.
		%tra:	hello.
→	2	*RAM:	hola:: [=! emphatic]!
		%tra:	hello:: [=! emphatic]!
→	3	*RAM:	qué hay?
		%tra:	what's up?

	4	*ENQ:	es eh para + ...
		%tra:	it's uh for + ...
→	5	*RAM:	pala qué -? pala qué?
		%tra:	what fol -? what fol?
→	6	*ENQ:	ma español sólo un poco.
		%tra:	my Spanish only a little.
→	7	*RAM:	poco español -? y cómo te las apañas en el restaurante?
		%tra:	little Spanish -? and how do you manage in the restaurant?
	8	*ENQ:	+ˆ sí chino xxx.
		%tra:	+ˆ yes Chinese xxx.
	9	*RAM:	aha.
		%tra:	uh huh.
	10	*RAM:	qué para mí -? qué es para mí -? para mí.
		%tra:	what for me -? what is for me -? for me.
	11	*ENQ:	ser eh + ...
		%tra:	be uh + ...
	12	*RAM:	inglés?
		%tra:	English?
	13	*RAM:	hablas inglés?
		%tra:	do you speak English?
	14	*ENQ:	español poco.
		%tra:	Spanish little.
	15	*RAM:	y inglés?
		%tra:	and English?
	16	*ENQ:	**English is <small> [>] [?].**
	17	*RAM:	**<English> [<].**
→	18	*RAM:	menos -. habla chino sólo.
		%tra:	less -. speaks chinese only.
	19	*RAM:	www.
	20	*PEN:	www.
→	21	*RAM:	qué me traes # chinín?
		%tra:	what are you bringing me little Chinaman?
	22	*RAM:	a::h -! esto vas allí vas allí.
		%tra:	o::h -! that you have to go there have to go there.

23 *ENQ: dónde?
   %tra: where?
24 *RAM: a las mesas # de allí.
   %tra: to the tables # there.

Apart from Ramon's specific greeting forms, there are other features of this encounter that deserve discussion. After greetings are exchanged, we can see the enquirer trying to formulate his service request (line 4). He seems to experience some difficulties, which the official makes fun of in line 5. In particular, he mocks his pronunciation of the preposition *para* 'for', thus discrediting his language competencies. In the official's caricature of the enquirer's linguistic abilities, the enquirer pronounces "*pala*" instead of "*para*". I myself could not hear the *l* sound in the enquirer's productions, which indicates that the official seems to be drawing on stereotypes rather than on actual speech forms to construct his interlocutor as a non-competent speaker.

It was a feature of Ramon's interactional behaviour that he would deviate rather frequently from a routine sequencing of events, contrary to, for example, his colleague Miquel. Yet Ramon's deviations did not serve to allow enquirers greater chances of participation. Instead, his frequent side sequences enabled him to make all sorts of offensive remarks about his interlocutors. In the example under examination, for instance, the official's aside serves to ridicule the enquirer's speech, which forces the latter to avow limited command of Spanish (see line 6). This is no trivial matter, as in this particular context, confessions of linguistic incompetence are especially face-damaging. Command of the majority language (Spanish) has a symbolic value in that it is ideologically treated as indexing the immigrant's will to integrate into the recipient community. Since this is an immigration office, what is at stake is precisely whether a given individual should be given the chance to become a regular member of the host society. By exposing the enquirer's linguistic inabilities, Ramon undermines whatever positive self-image the enquirer has been striving to present.

The official's ensuing turn (line 7) draws again on stereotypical images of Chinese immigrants (i.e. they all work in restaurants), as Ramon was in reality unaware of the enquirer's occupation. In fact, it is not until line 21 that Ramon examines his documents. By stereotyping the enquirer's pronunciation of Spanish sounds and assuming he works at a Chinese restaurant, Ramon foregrounds his ethnicity as the key defining trait of his identity. He is doubly categorised as an incompetent speaker of Spanish and as a stereotypical member of the Chinese immigrant category. His right to a distinct individual identity, uncoloured by ethnic stereotyping, is thereby symbolically denied to him.

But Ramon's demeaning actions do not stop here. Lines 12 to 18 contain another side sequence initiated by the official, who tries to find out whether his interlocutor speaks English or not. It may seem like a language negotiation sequence, but it is not. The official's command of English was deficient and he was eager to avoid using this language whenever possible. On this occasion, his interest in the enquirer's language competencies may have been motivated by my presence there, as he knew I was interested in enquirers' language use. As can be seen, Ramon does not miss the opportunity to expose his interlocutor's inadequacy again: not only does his client not speak Spanish he also does not speak any international language like English either. (Ramon himself doesn't speak English, but that does not prevent him from highlighting the inadequacy of his interlocutor).

Ramon makes his final statement in line 18: "*habla chino sólo*" 'he speaks Chinese only'. Two features of this turn are worth noting. One is Ramon's emphasis on *sólo* 'only' in "*chino sólo*" 'Chinese only' to highlight the enquirer's inadequacy. The second element is his use of the third person singular. This qualifies his turn as evaluative metatalk on the enquirer's words. It is significant that the negative characterisation of his interlocutor in "*chino sólo*" is not undertaken as an aside, but gets inserted into the flow of conversational interaction. This was a regular characteristic of Ramon's behaviour, as the examples below will further illustrate.

Before completing the analysis of this extract, it is important to note the form of address Ramon uses in line 21. He employs the diminutive form *chinín* 'little Chinaman' to refer to his interlocutor. Apart from the offensiveness of the choice of words, I want to remark on how the enquirer is positioned by Ramon.

Diminutives (here the *-ín* suffix) are regularly used in Spanish when talking to or about young children (Melzi and King 2003). By using the diminutive, Ramon positions the client as as child and appropriates for himself a parental voice. As with *chato*, diminutives carry connotational meanings of affection. Yet, in Ramon's turns, diminutives sounded not affectionate but condescending. This is because these forms were used alongside open expressions of mistrust towards clients and remarks on the need for physical violence (see examples [64] to [68] below). In fact, Ramon's talk echoes the two classic expressions of bigotry: the ostensibly charitable but essentially patronising view of the "bleeding heart" liberal, and the overtly contemptuous hostility of the hard-core racist.

The use of the diminutive indexes a type of relationship, i.e. parent–child, which is not that of bureaucrat–client, but which shares with it an asymmetrical nature. That asymmetry positions Ramon as the figure of authority, and more significantly, as someone who is entitled to reprimand, punish, and more generally, tell his interlocutor how to behave. This is in line with, and in fact adds up to, previously discussed mechanisms for enforcing a strict regimentation of the social arena in this site.

Far from being exceptional, Ramon's use of diminutive forms when talking to/about his interlocutors was pervasive. Another instance is provided by his use of the word "*caritas*" 'little faces' in (60) below.

(60)

    1   *RAM: y vosotros [/-] mira mira mira estos mira qué espectadores
    2   %tra: que tengo -! xxx mira qué caritas ponen!
                    and you [/-] look look look at these look at the spectators I have -! xxx look at their little faces.

A similar type of social relationship is indexed by Ramon's use of the term "*campeón*" literally 'champion', 'ace' in the ensuing extracts (61) and (62). As a term of address, *campeón* is mostly directed at small children, in particular boys, by fathers. It may also be heard in banter among young male friends. The similarity with previous exchanges leads us to think it is the former social relationship rather than the latter that is being evoked. As regards its contents, *campeón* conveys the idea that there is some real or imagined challenge that the person must face, and that his interlocutor believes he will rise to it. The patronising tone of the expression speaks for itself.

(61)

    1   *RAM: trámite también venga campeón!
           %tra: being processed too there you go ace!

(62)

    1   *RAM: +ˆ todo trámite <# campeón> [>]!
          %tra: +ˆ they are all being processed <# ace> [>]!

To sum up, through the recreation of specific voices (Bakhtin 1981) in service discourse, Ramon manages to convey a number of social meanings and projects a clearly hegemonic view of social relations in the bureaucratic field. He regularly appropriates for himself the voices of figures of authority, while simultaneously positioning his immigrant interlocutors in unmistakably subordinate roles.

As noted above, another characteristic of Ramon's speech was his frequent backstage remarks on clients' behaviour and talk. Goffman (1959) argues that it is common for members of a team who are presenting a performance *frontstage* to go *backstage* and derogate the audience in a way that is inconsistent with the face-to-face treatment given to them. In service occupations this may include ridiculing, caricaturising and criticising customers. As we have seen in example (59), this is precisely what the official does to the Chinese immigrant. The crucial difference is that the official makes these comments while interacting face-to-face with the enquirer.

Goffman (1959: 4) also claims that when an individual enters the presence of others s/he will modify his/her activity so that it conveys the impression that it is in his/her interest to convey. I would add, though, that this will only be the case if s/he either values the others in some way or wants to avoid the social sanctions that might derive from his/her inappropriate behaviour. These two ideas are intimately related. Sanctions are only effective if they are detrimental to the speaker's interests. One of these interests may be to foster a good social impression, that is, to present a positive self-image to one's interlocutor. That will only be a social goal if the impressions one's interlocutor receives are valued in some way. Thus, sanctions are only understood as such if there is the perception that the actor who displays the sanctioning behaviour is legitimised to do so, and legitimisation is attached to positions of speaking that are socially and contextually powerful. This is clearly not the type of position immigrant clients at the immigration office were in any way allowed to inhabit.

The way in which Ramon acted in his service communication with immigrants showed that he had complete disregard for the service impression fostered. As was observed earlier, though, his often verbally offensive behaviour could go largely unchallenged because of his clients' lack of linguistic competence and also because of their subordinate social and situational position. The official knowingly drew on those structural asymmetries to subvert the careful staging of service provision that some of his colleagues, like Miquel, attempted to undertake.

For Goffman, backstage conduct among colleagues is "one which allows minor acts which can easily be taken as symbolic of intimacy and disrespect for others present" (1959: 128). Among these he cites "playful aggressivity" and "inconsiderateness for the others in minor but potentially symbolic acts". Backstage is the social space for non-service relaxation. But it is also a space where equal social relations are actualised, where individuals step out of their social roles, where "playful aggressivity" can be resorted to. Embedding this sort of behaviour in unequal relationships of power where participants are structurally constrained to not act freely only works to reinforce their subordinate social position. The different layers of meaning and implicatures contained in Ramon's turns are examined in detail in the extracts below.

In example (63) the official describes the granting of a permit as a matter of good luck, as if the procedure whereby decisions on entitlements are made could be likened to a lottery. The official's comments do not work to sustain the image of objectivity and rationality a public institution ought to project. In addition, there is a sense in which the official's remarks may construct the enquirer as a potential cheater. If the bureaucratic process is a lottery, then it might happen that, in dumb luck, an applicant who does not legitimately fulfil the requirements is given legal residency in Spain. Implied in the official's talk is the idea that the enquirer may not have met those requirements. Any degree of enquirer control over the situation is metaphorically and symbolically taken away from them.

(63)

    1   *RAM: concedido éste-. fíjate has tenido suerte!
          %tra: this one is granted -. you've been really lucky!

In the example presented below (64), the immigrant client is, again, negatively categorised. I shall focus on the turn in line 4, in particular on Ramon's remark "*que amigos que sóis!*" 'you are all such good friends!'.

Ramon's talk is a comment on the enquirer's previous turn (line 3), where the enquirer puts forward a particular description of the world when he claims that the application he has handed over is from a friend. The enquirer's claim to reality is not believed by Ramon who nevertheless does not have evidence to the contrary. This is why he challenges the client's description only indirectly by means of an ironic remark. This remark is not intended to be answered. Rather, it belongs to the realm of the backstage, where officials work at discrediting enquirers' words. With this comment, Ramon conveys the idea that he does not believe a word of what the enquirer has just said, thereby constructing him as a liar.

(64)

        1   *RAM: de quién es éste?
             %tra: whose is this one?

        2   *RAM: de quién es?
             %tra: whose is it?

        3   *ENQ: es de ami [//] mío amigo.
             %tra: it's from a fri [//] a friend of mine.

→   4   *RAM: amigo no -? qué amigos que sóis!
             %tra: friends right -? you're all such good friends!

The practice of categorising enquirers in a negative light is also illustrated by example (65). In this encounter, however, Ramon goes beyond making ironic comments and challenges the enquirer openly by asking him if his documents are forged. For the first time in the extracts we have examined, we see an enquirer refuse to back down in the face of a challenge by this official. Instead, the enquirer insists on his initial presentation of reality.

(65)

	1	*RAM:	buenos días dígame.
		%tra:	good morning how can I help you?
	2	*ENQ:	traigo falta.
		%tra:	I am bringing my missing [documents]
→	3	*RAM:	es lo mismo que éste a que sí!
		%tra:	it's the same as this one I bet!
	4	*ENQ:	sí.
		%tra:	yes.
	5	*RAM:	lo mismo!
		%tra:	the same!
→	6	*ENQ:	todos habéis ido: <#> [>] al mismo médico # al mismo
	7		aboga(d)o # os ha cobra(d)o lo mismo con el mismo médico: -,
	8		os entró a todos una diarrea de narices o qué?
		%tra:	you've all been <#> [>] to the same doctor # to the same lawyer # he charged you all the same with the same docto::r -, did you all come down with a hell of a diarrhoea or what?
	9	*ENQ:	<eh sí > [<] [=! laughing].
		%tra:	<uh yes> [<] [=! laughing].
→	10	*ENQ:	pero pruebas # esto de:: esto seguro.
		%tra:	but evidence # this from this insurance.
→	11	*RAM:	pero qué trabajáis todos en la misma empresa?
		%tra:	but do you all work for the same company?
	12	*ENQ:	sí esto de mutua.
		%tra:	yes this from medical insurance.
	13	*RAM:	mutua de la empresa.
		%tra:	the company's medical insurance.
	14	*ENQ:	para + ...
		%tra:	for + ...

→ 15 *RAM: no será falso esto?
     %tra: this wouldn't be forged by any chance?

→ 16 *ENQ: no esto no falso no -. # esto original.
     %tra: no this not forged no -. # this original.

  17 *RAM: xxx.

  18 *RAM: ya está pues.
     %tra: alright then done.

The first significant turn is in line 3. Ramon claims to be able to predict the enquirer's behaviour (note his final "*a que sí!*" 'I bet'). The implicature is that all enquirers are liars trying to cheat the procedure by submitting forged documentation. His interlocutor responds with a simple "yes", not picking up on the official's implied accusation. Ramon persists in his strategy but now the tone of his talk becomes downright offensive (lines 6–8). The enquirer keeps responding in a calm manner, insisting that his documents are valid (line 10). Finally, the official voices his suspicions openly (line 15), accusing the enquirer of having submitted forged documents. But once again, the enquirer insists on the validity of his papers (line 16). Finally, Ramon has no choice but to accept the enquirer's documents and the interaction ends there.

One element to be pointed out is that Ramon's provocative behaviour is completely gratuitous. It is not up to him but to back-office staff to make decisions on entitlements on the basis of the documentary evidence presented. His job is to take in enquirers' documentation; yet this does not stop him from asserting his powerful position and trying to exercise social control over his interlocutors by repeatedly constructing them as morally reprehensible individuals.

Ramon's comments may also occur as echo remarks on his colleague Miquel's interactional contributions. Sometimes, as in example (66), Ramon simply mocks his colleague's talk. This contributes to sustaining the atmosphere of ostensible playfulness that I have argued Ramon recreates to relieve the boredom of his job.

(66)

  1 *RAM: **yes but now it's okay okay** -? **but not** concedido -. **wait two**
     %tra: **or three weeks but okay**.
            yes but now it's okay okay -? but not granted -. wait two or
            three weeks but okay.

  [...]

→   2   *ENQ: **not** concedido.
        %tra: not granted.
        %com: speaker puts on an English accent

At other times, Ramon employed his backstage remarks while Miquel was dealing with a client to reinforce his colleague's reprimanding tone (see line 4 in example [67] below). Particularly illuminating of Ramon's perception of his social function is his appeal to physical force in example (68) below (in particular, see comment in line 10 "when you leave I hope they give you a good beating").

(67)

   1   *EN1:   sí está aquí -. <u>ay</u>!
       %tra: yes it's here -. oops!

   2   *MIQ: trae el pasaporte:.
       %tra: bring the passport:.

   3   *MIQ: deprisa!
       %tra: quickly!

→ 4   *RAM: deprisa leche!
       %tra: quickly damn it!

(68)

   1   *EN1:   <u>uhm</u> maintenant #0_1 esto quel número?
       %tra: <u>uhm</u> now #0_1 this which number?

   2   *MIQ: esto el número del # ordenador.
       %tra: this the number in the # computer.

   3   *EN1:   <u>ah</u> ordenador #0_3 vale [=! soft].
       %tra: <u>ah</u> computer #0_3 okay [=! soft].

   4   *EN2:   entonces yo amigo.
       %tra: now me friend.

   5   *MIQ: <amigo> [=! shouting] -? te he dicho uno -? uno -? uno sólo -?
   6   <nadie más> [>1] -? no amigo -? no nadie -? no -. sólo uno -.
   7   pues sólo <uno> [>2] -. adiós.
       %tra: <friend> [=! shouting] -? I have told you one -? one -? only
                one -? <nobody else > [>1] -? no friend? no nobody -? no -.
                only one -. then only <one> [>2] -. good bye.

   8   *EN2:   <yo amigo> [<1].
       %tra: <me friend> [>1].

9   *EN2:   <vale> [<2].
    %tra: <okay> [<2].

→ 10   *RAM: au -. i ara cuando salgas que te den un viaje *a fora*.
       %tra: right -. and now when you leave I hope they give you a good beating.

4. Concluding remarks

In this chapter I have argued that the social and physical space of this office was highly regulated and normativised. I have shown how there seemed to be a number of spoken and unspoken rules of "appropriate" conduct that immigrant clients were expected to abide by. Normativisation was, however, one-sided: norms of appropriateness were defined by officials and imposed on clients; they were not open to negotiation; they concerned only clients' behaviour. This is in accordance with a perception of the office as a space managed by officials and essentially belonging to them.

The existence of these norms, which remained in the background and become foregrounded only when immigrant clients deviated from them (Garfinkel 1967), was highly operational for officials. Norms, or rather, their non-observance, allowed for the exposure of clients' behaviour. Norms constituted the backdrop against which clients were constructed as cheaters and liars. Negative categorisations and the discredit to which clients were subject also served to justify the far from adequate service bureaucrats provided to them.

Clients were categorised as unruly and crooked individuals, and were held accountable for the "subversive" nature of their actions. This picture is, as it were, fairly homogeneous. Although, if directly asked, officials would admit to existing variation within the client group, it was their generalised negative perception of foreign interlocutors which informed and shaped their discursive practice. In keeping with this, it is officials who, in the public discourse of service communication, assessed clients' mode of proceeding; the opposite could not happen. This evaluative prerogative, and the contextual circumstances which allowed for it in this social situation, constructed public officials' discursive and social position as dominant (Thornborrow 2002), and in turn, reinforced a hegemonic representation of social relations in this field.

The data in this chapter lends further support to the idea that the enactment of roles and speaking positions in this office as dominant–subordinate, with bureaucrats playing the dominant role and immigrant clients the subordinate one, was never negotiated or evened out in any way. On the contrary, it was constantly worked at by officials and only feebly contested by clients. This is not strange given that, as we have seen, their fundamentally unequal relationship was constructed on the basis of and drew on the multiple asymmetries defining these exchanges: bureaucrat versus lay person; local versus foreigner; legal versus illegal resident; Spanish/Catalan native versus non-native, etc. I have mentioned linguistic asymmetry last, not because it was least unimportant, but because it links up nicely with the analytical themes of the following chapter.

I argued in Chapter 3 that many of the practices that could be observed at this particular office are common currency in the Spanish public administration, and so did not take place in this site only because the clients in this case were foreign. Yet, in many ways, the shape of such practices was different at the immigration office and their frequency of occurrence much higher due to clients' limited opportunities for challenge and contestation. Another factor was officials' lack of accountability, which I would claim may have been more significant there than elsewhere on account of the foreign origin of the office's clientele. This is not surprising in the context of a public administration office where discrimination was institutionalised, as I shall illustrate in the following chapter in connection with the institution's policy for employing language interpreters.

Chapter 6
Language choice and multilingual practice

1. Introduction

My first impression of this office was that it was significantly more multilingual than the other sites I had observed and which also belonged to the immigration services. It was not that clients were served in their native languages though that would seem reasonable enough for this sort of service. The kind of multilingualism I am referring to involved using mostly English and some French alongside the two local languages, that is, Catalan and Spanish.

The reason why the linguistic practices differed at this office was the geographical origin of its clients, with the number of enquirers coming from the South Asian region (Pakistanis mostly, but also Indians and Bangladeshis) being significantly higher here than in other offices, where Latin American and North Africans predominated. Some of them spoke Spanish fluently, but the general impression was that the majority preferred to use English. I must admit, though, that it was difficult to know how proficient they were in Spanish because they were very often addressed directly in English by public officials, and clients tended to accommodate to officials' linguistic choices whenever they could.

It is interesting to note that the multilingual practices I have mentioned reflected in no way the linguistic means formally set up by the institution to facilitate communication with its clients. As I explained in Chapter 1, two of the desk staff, Miquel and Juan, had been officially hired as interpreters of Arabic and Russian respectively. The choice of these two languages, as I shall discuss later, was the result of the combination of a rather deficient analysis of language needs and the institution's discriminatory policy for hiring language specialists. The practical consequence was that these so-called interpreters conversed in Arabic and Russian very rarely and that, by contrast, they ended up needing to use English quite often. But paradoxically, apart from the supposed interpreters, none of the bureaucrats in this office was required to have any foreign language skills.

All this gives an idea of the complexities involved in describing the practices of multilingualism observed. Much could be said about how speakers used the different languages available to them. Multilingualism as a defining feature of this context could be looked at from many different angles. In this chapter, however, I shall choose only one of these possible approaches; I shall concentrate on the relationship between the three main languages employed (i.e. Catalan,

Spanish and English) and the social spaces they constructed, regulated and gave access to. I will examine multilingualism from this standpoint because it allows me to visualise and show the connections between particular language practices and processes of social exclusion. The analysis that I present shows that language is a valuable resource that is fought over by speakers and access to which is tightly controlled. Particular forms of language use are claims to symbolic capital and group membership, yet it is not forms alone that count but the particular speakers that produce them.

In this chaper, I examine who controlled language choice at the office, with what consequences and for whom. To understand this, it is necessary to look both at what happened in situated communication, and also go beyond the immediate realities of face-to-face talk to examine the ways in which the ideologies of the social and institutional orders played a prominent role in explaining some of what actors did, and crucially, *were able* to do.

2. Spanish and Catalan: Different languages, different spaces

Both Spanish and Catalan have the status of official languages in the Spanish Autonomous Community of Catalonia, where the city of Barcelona is located. The use of each language, as well as the nature of the bilingual practices observed, vary enormously depending on the type of speech activity, the social class of speakers, and the geographical area and socioinstitutional domain involved.

Catalan is the language of instruction in school and thus the predominant language of use in the public discourse of the classroom. By contrast, in peer talk produced by school children both inside and outside the classroom, Spanish seems to be preferred to Catalan, though this is clearly more the case for home-speaking Spanish speakers than for Catalan ones. The latter seem to have more balanced patterns of language choice than the former, who use Spanish predominantly (Generalitat de Catalunya 2004).

By law, Catalan is also the language of the local and regional public administrations. By contrast, within services and institutions run by the Spanish central government, like the railway, mail service and revenue office, the use of Spanish has traditionally tended to predominate. In some state institutions, official forms and informative leaflets are now in both languages. However, the administration that manages immigration (under the Spanish Ministry of the Interior) is one institution where this change has not yet taken place; here written communication is conducted exclusively in Spanish. It is probably assumed that the immigration service's clientele are not Catalans, but rather foreigners, who are more likely to be able to read and write Spanish than Catalan. However, this may be a bit of a simplification, as in fact, the number of Catalan solicitors and paralegal agents I saw seeking some kind of service from these offices was significant and on the increase. There is a broader sense, I would argue, in which the exclusive use of Spanish indexes that entitlement to nationality or, as in this case, legal residence is a prerogative of the national government and symbolises the exclusive power of the nation-state over the control of immigrant flows.

Spoken communication within the immigration service was another matter. Here Catalan did have a role in speaking. Among staff members, the use of Catalan varied depending on the sociolinguistic composition of the office examined, that is, depending on the number of habitual Catalan/Spanish speakers. In the setting studied, Catalan speakers happened to be the majority. This gave rise to interesting bilingual practices whose examination revealed the existence of a clear division of labour between the two languages.

Three of the four desk staff, namely Miquel, Ramon and Teresa, were Catalan speakers. The language of communication among them was Catalan. The fourth person (Juan) was a regular speaker of Spanish. Following the norm of *linguistic etiquette* (Woolard 1989), which is generalised in the Barcelona area, the other three spoke to him in Spanish, although in general they tended to interact very little. Catalan was also the language the manager employed when she first took me to meet her employees, and this is also the language I used in my interactions with Miquel, Teresa and Ramon. (I am myself a Catalan native speaker.)

In contrast to their habitual use of Catalan to talk to one another, when it came to addressing their foreign clients, Miquel, Ramon and Teresa employed Spanish. This is in line with what Pujolar (2007a) calls "the commonsensical sociolinguistic comportment", that is, the naturalised idea in Catalonia that foreigners are spoken to in Spanish. Spanish functions as the habitual language of intergroup communication, that is, as a kind of lingua franca, while the use of Catalan is restricted to public uses in certain institutional domains or for in-group communication among native Catalans.

In this office, Catalan worked as the language of the locals, the *we-code* in Gumperz' terms (1982b), which consisted of fellow colleagues and the researcher. The use of each language indexed different addressees (Auer 1984, 1995, 1998) and participation frameworks. Thus, the choice of Catalan indicated that a given comment was meant for fellow colleagues, whereas the choice of Spanish indicated that a stretch of talk was addressed to clients. Each language created a separate social space which included some speakers and excluded others. Interestingly, that division proved to be highly functional in service talk.

One of the ways in which that division was operational is in separating the different regions or spaces that framed talk, activities and behaviour in service contexts, that is, essentially, in separating the frontstage from the backstage. Catalan was not just the we-code but also the language of the backstage. This means that it was the language which was employed to talk about immigrant enquirers, that is, to make metadiscursive and evaluative comments on their language and behaviour, but was never used to talk to them. Spanish was employed for that purpose. This gave rise to interesting bilingual practices where in the same turn and without pausing, some talk was meant to go on stage, to count as public discourse, whereas the rest was meant for private, backstage consumption. The use of a different language for each space enabled officials to move unproblematically from one space to the other. The assumption that most clients do not know Catalan (or not much anyway) facilitated and explained the mutually exclusive nature of these sociolinguistic spaces.

The following example (69) illustrates very clearly the distinct, and more importantly, impassable social spaces constructed for/by actors in this setting. The client, a North African male who was an extremely fluent speaker of Spanish, had come to the office to accompany his sister, who had applied for legalisation. He initially addressed officials in Spanish. Throughout the exchange he employed a variety of strategies to establish rapport with the officials (and the researcher – I was sitting behind the counter). He tried to make small talk by remarking on the long queues and the large number of people waiting to be served. Then at one point in the exchange, the computer system broke down. It was at this point that the stretch of interaction shown in the excerpt below took place.

(69)

	1	*MIQ: %tra:	bueno pues a veure si sortim. well let's see if we can get out of here.
	2	*RAM: %tra:	ara a més s'haurà bloquejat i un merder ! now the system will be down and it'll be a mess!
	3	*RAM %tra: %add:	se han estropeao! they've broken down! EN1
→	4	*EN1: %tra:	i què ha passat ? and what's happened?
	5	*MIQ %tra:	<pues a ver si vuelve> [>] + ... <let's see if it comes back on> [>] + ...

6   *RAM   <los de www> [<] cuándo tocan allí no sé qué aquí se jode.
    %tra: <those on www> [<] whenever they touch something there they fuck things up here.
    %com: www is street where central office is located.

As can be seen in lines 1 and 2, Catalan is the language Miquel and Ramon employ to talk to one another. This choice ratifies their membership of the service provider group. In line 3, Ramon switches over to Spanish to address the client. As we have discussed, this is in keeping with habitual language practices in Catalonia in general and in this office in particular, but also with the client's previous interactional preference for Spanish. What is significant is that, in the following turn, the client responds to Ramon's comment not in Spanish but in Catalan ("*i què ha passat?*" 'and what's happened?'). His unexpected use of Catalan, the in-group language, and his earlier attempts at making small talk make us think that the client is using his turn not just to find out information; he is using it as a means to establish rapport with his interlocutors, to show alignment with the Catalan-speaking population, and in general, to create a positive image for himself as a "good" immigrant who has integrated himself well into Catalan society. Significantly, the client's use of Catalan is neither acknowledged nor taken up by either Miquel or Ramon in their ensuing turns. Rather, in line 6, Ramon responds to the information-seeking aspect of the enquirer's turn in Spanish. To do so, he uses his usual colloquial tone, examined in detail in the previous chapter.

The officials' refusal to respond to the client's attempt at language convergence – something that Catalan bilinguals do unproblematically on a regular basis – indexes the separate social spheres that each language constructed in this setting, and how speakers might legitimately belong to one sphere but not to the other. The different spaces that Catalan and Spanish created reflect and construct the social values attached to the two languages (Pujolar 2001). The idea that Catalan is not a language foreigners may ordinarily speak is grounded on a conception of Catalan as an identity language that only natives may choose to employ, and more significantly, may legitimately be allowed to employ (Pujolar 2007a). There is yet another sense in which Catalan is not a language that may "belong" to foreigners. Given that the language is a cultural and symbolic capital of basically the Catalan middle classes, for immigrants to speak Catalan is somehow perceived to be incongruent with the marginal space they occupy in the social arena and with their low position on the social ladder. The contradiction lies in the fact that, socially, speaking Catalan is taken to be the clearest indicator of a foreigner's will to integrate. However, that association works only on the symbolic axis. When it comes to speaking the language for everyday communication, Catalan is not a language Catalan native speakers will address foreigners in. That means that foreigners are expected to know and use Catalan to be able to participate fully in Catalan society, but the naturalised *habitus* (Bourdieu 1991) of Catalan speakers prevents them from being ordinarily exposed to it.

The excerpt above shows very clearly that, just as we saw in Chapter 5 that the physical space at the office was strictly controlled, the sociolinguistic space was also highly regulated. Thus far, we have only discussed the role of the two local languages, namely Spanish and Catalan, and the ways in which they were handled by actors, but we have already seen how only certain individuals and not others were considered to be legitimate speakers of certain languages. Once again, it was officials and not clients who decided; it was officials who imposed a sociolinguistic regime which was not inclusionary but exclusionary, which positioned immigrants peripherally in the social arena and which reinforced existing social inequalities.

3. The other languages

Apart from English, languages other than Spanish and Catalan had a limited presence in the office. Booklets with information on the legalisation campaign and application forms were published in Russian, Chinese, Arabic, English and French, though they did not seem to be widely distributed; in fact, they lay piled in the corridors for weeks. As for spoken communication, I mentioned before that Miquel and Juan had been hired as interpreters of Arabic and Russian respectively, but used these languages only occasionally. By contrast, English, though not officially supported, turned out to be the second most frequently spoken language in service talk (after Spanish).

The question arises of why certain languages received official support in the form of interpreters and others did not. One might imagine that the origin and linguistic background of clients would determine the institution's choice of languages. In that sense, having an interpreter for Arabic would seem appropriate, taking into account that North Africans formed the largest client group. With respect to Russian, the number of potential beneficiaries of the service, that is, applicants from Russia, other former members of the Soviet Union or Eastern European countries was rather small; in fact, they formed the smallest client group. However, in 1999, the year before I carried out my research, individuals coming from former Soviet Union Republics as well as the Balkan region had constituted one of the largest immigrant groups arriving in Barcelona, with a significant number of them seeking political asylum. The political asylum factor gave this group of migrants high institutional visibility (although their petitions were denied in the majority of cases) and this may explain the choice of Russian as one of the languages to receive official support. By way of contrast, the linguistic needs of enquirers from the South Asian region (Pakistanis, Indians and Bangladeshis), who were the second largest migrant group to seek legalisation from this office, were not catered for. This quick examination of the site's linguistic ecology reveals that institutional language provisions did not seem to be shaped by real communication needs. Let us therefore determine what other factors might come into play.

One of these factors was the availability of qualified professionals in the job market. In this respect, a relevant institutional constraint must be highlighted. In my informal conversations with office staff, I was told that, when it came to hiring interpreters for the civil service, priority was given to Spanish nationals over foreigners. This was especially the case if, apart from working as interpreters, they were also expected to handle work permit applications, as was generally the case. When I asked them why there was nobody who could speak Urdu, Hindi or Punjabi in the office, given the number of South Asian petitioners that were served every day, all the informants consulted agreed in attributing this absence to the fact that managers did not like to employ members of non-European ethnic groups.[18] Because at the time recruiters were unable to find Spanish nationals competent in South Asian languages, interpreters for these languages were not available in the office. In that connection, the senior manager who gave me permission to conduct my research once said in reference to South Asians, "they speak a language that nobody understands". The use of "nobody" is significant in that it shows very clearly that he did not consider employing "somebody" from the community who spoke that language (to say nothing of his use of the singular form "the language" to refer to a community where many different languages are spoken). This comment suggests that disdainful attitudes towards foreign ethnic groups informed the institutional order framing the provision of service.

Occasionally, foreigners did get hired as interpreters. When that happened, though, if there was another interpreter for the same language who was a Spanish national, s/he was appointed to work the morning rather than the afternoon shift. This was because the morning shift was regarded as the more important of the two, as a larger number of clients were served in the morning than in the afternoon. This is another index of the institution's generalised mistrust of foreigners, regardless of whether they were immigrants seeking legal status or staff members.

The choice of local professionals to work as interpreters had an effect on the languages officially supported, but also on the usefulness of that support. A case in point is provided by Miquel, the interpreter of Arabic. He held a first degree in Arabic from the University of Barcelona. He had a thorough grounding in Classical Arabic and could speak Modern Standard Arabic. He was also acquainted with the colloquial variety spoken in Iraq, where he had lived for two years, but was not proficient in Moroccan Arabic, the variety spoken by the majority of his Arabic-speaking clients at the office. This made him feel totally inadequate.[19] As a result, he tried to restrict the use of Arabic to occasions when it was absolutely essential. This is one of the reasons why the use of Arabic was so rare in this office. Another of the reasons for the limited use of Miquel's and Juan's language competencies was organisational. There were no notices or signs to let enquirers know that certain members of the information staff were language specialists. That is, officials' linguistic competencies were not made public. This made it difficult for enquirers to take advantage of them and thus restricted their usefulness. Finally, the third reason for this limited use of other languages like Arabic, I would argue, was the clients' reluctance to use them. This reluctance was not an individual matter, but a reflection of the ideologies of language and immigration which are hegemonic in the social sphere.

In one of the sites I observed (different from the information desk), it was common currency to see North African information seekers conversing in Spanish with an official – also North African – who had recently been hired. Clearly, they had the perception that speaking their own language (and, crucially, not speaking Spanish) was frowned upon by other staff members and taken to index their reluctance to integrate. This shows the extent to which the ideological assumption according to which language competence was a requirement for full membership in the recipient community was also present in this office (the same ideology was observed, for example, by Blommaert and Verschueren [1998] in the Belgian context). I would claim that, in many ways, the only *legitimate* language (Bourdieu 1991) to be spoken in this setting was Spanish.

One of the elements that indexes the significance of this ideological assumption was the position of the institution with regard to foreign language abilities. Competence in a given foreign language was a skill that only interpreters were expected to have (but only in the language for which they had been hired). The remaining information-providing officials were not required to know any foreign languages. It was not the case, as one might think, that these bureaucrats had had this job for a long time; these were newly employed staff members.

The consequences of this policy were, on the one hand, that bureaucrats' proficiency levels in foreign languages varied greatly, but were in general rather low. None of the desk officials at the various immigration offices I observed – apart from the interpreters – could speak/understand any of the immigrants' languages. Most of the immigration officials could not even speak an international language like English or French fluently. The majority knew just a few words or phrases that they were able to insert – whenever absolutely necessary – into their regular communication routines in Spanish.

But perhaps more important than actual competence was the bureaucrats' perception that in speaking a foreign language they were going beyond their professional duties as defined by the institution they were working for. From their perspective, then, speaking English or French became an act of "goodwill", something they did to help immigrant clients communicate, but not something they were expected to do and for which they could be held accountable. This explains the nature of some of the multilingual practices observed, which I shall describe in detail shortly.

I have argued so far that very little was done by the institution to adjust itself to the new demands of its heterogeneous clientele. Its ideological position with regard to languages framed and accounted for some of the phenomena that could be observed in face-to-face service talk and cast light on the interconnectedness and the mutually implicated nature of the interactional, the institutional and the social orders. With the immigration service being a key institution in foreigners' migrant experience, the language policy of the immigration office is but one index of a larger and deeper societal stance on the relationship between newcomers and the host society. The ideology of Spanish as the only legitimate language is but one facet of the ideology that places the onus to adjust on immigrants; it is they who have to speak the right language, behave in appropriate ways and integrate. At the same time, it is not they but the host society that decides what counts as speaking the right language, as displaying appropriate behaviour; in sum, as integrating. This is the same ideology that ranks people's knowledge and that frames, for example, the need to teach immigrants courses on nutrition and healthcare (Pujolar 2007a) on the assumption that foreigners will not know anything about nutrition and healthcare – unlike locals.

We have noted that in this particular office Catalan worked as the language of the backstage. Business in the frontstage was conducted in Spanish. I have claimed that this is in line with the established habitus in Catalonia, according to which foreigners are spoken to in Spanish. Here I want to argue that this "commonsensical" way of proceeding became intertwined with the institutionally supported ideology according to which Spanish was the only legitimate language of this office. This assumption surfaced, for example, in officials' ways of speaking about the procedure; it accounted for why they systematically employed key institutional words in Spanish, no matter what language they were speaking. This was highly visible when they employed Catalan. With Catalan and Spanish being closely related languages, the translation into Catalan of key institutional terms would have been straightforward. But indexing as they did the realm of institutional processes and procedures, these words were kept in the only language that legitimately represented the institutional order, that is, in Spanish. The codeswitched utterances that officials produced as a result indexed the different social orders that entered into their production and showed, once again, that situated talk cannot be fully understood without the careful examination of the mid-level institutional framing of social action.

The first two excerpts that I want to present come from petitioners' discourse. One of them is taken from the interview with Hussain, where not speaking Spanish is equated with not speaking at all (see lines 6 and 11).

(70)

	1	*RES:	vale -. y si tú no entiendes algo que te dicen -, eh # por
	2		ejemplo qué haces preguntas -? o:: <mira no> [>] entiendo
	3		me lo puedes repetir o me lo puedes explicar o no?
		%tra:	okay -. and if you don't understand something they tell you -, uh # for example what do you do do you ask -? or <please I don't> [>] understand could you repeat that or could you explain or you don't?
	4	*HUS:	<no porque> [<].
		%tra:	<no because> [<].
→	5	*HUS:	no porque cuando así preguntas ell dicen por ellos tráelo una
	6		persona lo que sabe hablar -. por ello lo que esta gente <que
	7		está ahí> [>].
		%tra:	no because when you ask the say bring a person that can speak -. it's them the people <that are there> [>].
	8	*RES:	<ah sí::> [<]?
	9	%tra:	<really> [<]?
→	10	*HUS:	sí -. es circas circas lo que hay circas mira si hay alguien
	11		que sabe hablar -, y llamas ellos.
		%tra:	yes -. it's near near that's near see if there is anybody who can speak -, and call them.
	12	*RES:	ah pero ellos no te lo explican.
		%tra:	oh but they do not explain.

	13	*HUS:	sí -. si no hay nadas no te dicen -. te dicen oyes habla su
→	14		idiomas hablas español dicen que ah vale no sabe nadas
	15		viene para aquí -. no sé para qué vienes -.vale pero esa
	16		persona si xxx vayas -. no hacemos nada.
		%tra:	yes -. if there is nothing they don't say -. they say listen speak your language speak Spanish they say oh okay you know nothing you come here -. I don't know what you come for -. okay but this person if xxx go -. we do nothing.
	17	*RES:	o sea si no hablas español ellos consideran que que es tu
	18		problema no?
		%tra:	so if you don't speak Spanish they think it's it's your problem right?
	19	*HUS:	sí.
		%tra:	yes.
	20	*RES:	no no se esfuerzan para explicarte + …
		%tra:	they don't make any effort to explain + …

In this excerpt Hussain shows how aware immigrant enquirers are of the linguistic ideology I have discussed above. He recounts in a very vivid manner (lines 13–16) how public officials do not value enquirers' competencies in languages other than Spanish ("you know nothing"), how enquirers are generally dismissed because of their non-mastery of Spanish ("I don't know what you come here for", "go") and how it is up to immigrants to look for help to communicate with officials (lines 5–6: "bring a person that can speak").

The second excerpt (71) comes from service interaction. I would like to comment on line 7, where the foreign interlocutor makes an unexpected statement about his proficiency in Spanish.

(71)

1	*ENQ:	bueno buenos días.
	%tra:	good good morning.
2	*MIQ:	buenos días.
	%tra:	good morning.
3	*MIQ:	estos todavía no están -. estamos por el día dieciocho de
4		mayo.
	%tra:	these are not [available] yet -. we are still doing the eighteenth of May.
	%act:	sorting out documents

	5	*ENQ: %tra:	vale. alright
	6	*MIQ: %tra:	estos faltan dos semanas para que estén aquí. these will be available in two weeks' time.
→	7	*ENQ: %tra:	vale -. yo hablo español perfectamente <de verdad> [?]. okay -. I speak perfect Spanish <honestly> [?].
	8	*MIQ: %tra:	bueno te lo he dicho en español no? okay I've said it in Spanish, have I not?

The enquirer's metacomment on his linguistic abilities (line 7) comes as unexpected in this sequential context. There is nothing in the preceding turns (such as simplification in the official's talk) that explains why the enquirer feels the need to state so clearly that he is "perfectly" competent in Spanish. Why then does he say it? What is he responding to? He may have different motivations. Some may be of a symbolic nature and others rather practical. The practical ones may have to do with his trying to obtain more information than is routinely provided by officials. The reference to his proficiency in Spanish may be an attempt to deroutinize the minimalist information provision practices of these officials and thus obtain more details. The symbolic reasons, in turn, may have to do with the wish to present himself in a positive light and to distinguish himself from other applicants. This connects up with and responds to the generalised negative construction of clienthood in this office, as discussed in the previous chapter. However, in claiming to speak Spanish (and not Catalan, for example), the enquirer is presenting himself not just as a "good" immigrant but as an institutionally appropriate one, in that he fulfils the basic norm of institutional behaviour in this context; that is, he speaks Spanish.

3.1. Lingua franca English

We mentioned earlier that, as no minimum standards were required by the institution, officials' foreign language competencies were quite variable but in general tended to be fairly low, in keeping with national standards.[20] The Pakistani immigrants I interviewed at the language school, for example, were eager to learn Spanish because they perceived English to be useless as a language of communication.

(72)

	1	*ST4:	can you not eh:: eh: teach us this language in free time?
	2	*RES:	oh dear!
	3	*ST4:	because you know you know in this country English is not accepted.
	4	*RES:	why why do you say that?
	5	*ST4:	in this country English is not recognised English is not a
	6		major language a lot of people cannot speak it.
	7	*RES:	it is not useful it is not useful -. if you go for example I
	8		am just interested if you go for example to the hospital
	9		or to an institution to get the papers done or do you have
	10		the impression that can you use English or + ...
→	11	*ST4:	English will not make a better impression for them.

In the information service, the official that I have called Teresa could speak near-native French due to a period of residence in France, but her knowledge of English was restricted to a few key words. Her colleague Ramon's command of English was better than Teresa's, but still very limited. As for French, I never heard him use it but I imagine he was able to understand and speak it minimally – as is common among Catalans over thirty-five. The third official, namely Miquel, could communicate quite fluently in English, though his range of structures and vocabulary was rather small. His grammatical accuracy was also fairly weak.

In this section I want to focus on the use of English for service talk in this office because, after Spanish, it was the most frequently employed language by officials and immigrant clients. Despite this, its use was not unproblematic. Here I want to explore some of the issues which framed the use of English and which questioned its viability as a fully operational language of communication in this setting.

When asked about their competencies in English, officials generally claimed that they were limited. However, their poor linguistic skills did not prevent them from making negative assessments of their interlocutors' competencies. That is to say, one of the key features that defined English language use at this site was bureaucrats' generalised dismissal of clients' competencies. This is clearly shown in the extract below, which is part of a reconstructed conversation between Ramon and myself:

(73)

	1	*RES:	*Ramon però tu parles anglès no?*
		%tra:	but you speak English, Ramon, right?
	2	*RAM:	*poc poc molt poc.*
		%tra:	little little very little.
	3	*RES:	*ja però pel que necessites aquí sí no?*
		%tra:	yes but it's enough for your needs here right?
→	4	*RAM:	*sí perquè ells encara el parlen pitjor que jo!*
		%tra:	yes because they speak even worse than I do!

Though Ramon acknowledges that he speaks very little English, it is interesting that he frames his little knowledge in the context of the even more limited competencies of clients. Their "even worse" English serves somehow as justification for his poor language skills.

There is no doubt that individual proficiency levels varied enormously among the South Asian clients of the office (the only ones that employed English regularly), and that in some cases, knowledge of the language was rather limited, but it is also true that there was a huge disparity of backgrounds and migration trajectories which made generalisations difficult if not clearly unfair. Yet the tendency to routinise all bureaucratic work practices led in this case to group-based evaluations of competence which hindered the realisation of individual language potentials.

One of the elements that worked to devalue the linguistic capital of South Asian clients was the variety of English they spoke (South Asian or Indian English). This raises interesting questions with regard to the "linguistic angloglobalisation" of the world depicted by some authors (Prcic 2003), as well as the actual mobility of linguistic resources. Even though the process of cultural and economic globalisation seems to have reinforced the position of English worldwide as an international lingua franca, as Blommaert (2003) discusses, perhaps only a few varieties of English (i.e. those spoken in first-world countries) are being globalised.

One of the problems that arose in connection with the kind of English clients spoke was that Miquel, Ramon and Teresa were not familiar with it. This was added to the fact that, as I noted in Chapter 3, officials did not receive any kind of linguistic training at the initiation of their employment. In the case of English, awareness of the differences between South Asian varieties and, say, British or American English could have facilitated bureaucrats' understanding of the situation and enhanced service communication in significant ways.

Instead, what happened was that the comprehension difficulties that arose were attributed by bureaucrats to clients' limited knowledge of the language. In this way, the generalised dismissal of clients' English became operational for bureaucrats because it allowed them to blame clients for any disfluencies that might occur in communication. It is true that not all of their South Asian clients' command of English was particularly sophisticated. However, bureaucrats' deficit evaluations of clients' skills to a large extent derived from their own difficulties in understanding, either because they were unfamiliar with Indian English (I would say mainly as a result of clients' dissimilar pronunciation of certain sounds, and specific prosodic and intonational features), or because their own English skills were low. Yet any reflection about their own limited language skills was absent from bureaucrats' accounts. This dismissal of immigrants' English was congruent with and sustained by the idea that English was not a language that "belonged" to Pakistanis or Indians, as Blommaert (2003) puts it, but a language "owned" by Americans, Britons, Canadians, Australians or New Zealanders. In addition, as a kind of linguistic capital valued on the international arena, and on a more local level as a kind of capital associated with the Spanish upper and middle classes, competence in English was not the type of skill immigrants from developing countries were expected (I would even say allowed) to have (Unamuno and Codó 2007).

The following reconstructed interaction bears witness to this. Here Ramon is complaining that it is very difficult to understand what enquirers are trying to say in English. He is referring to enquirers of South Asian origin. So I point out that this is due to their accent, which is different from the varieties of English Catalans are familiar with. Ramon disagrees with my understanding of the situation, and attributes his comprehension difficulties to clients' poor competence in the language. Even though I am considered to be the expert in English, and as such, often called upon to help in service talk, in this particular case, Ramon pays no heed to my explanations. As I argue above, blaming enquirers' lack of competence in English was useful for officials, because it relieved them of all responsibility for communication problems. Unsurprisingly, any explanation that ran counter to that expectation would be roundly dismissed.

(74)

    1   *RAM: *és que costa molt entendre'ls* !
              %tra: it is very difficult to understand them!

    2   *RES: *és clar és que tenen un accent diferent*!
              %tra: of course because they have a different accent!

3   *RAM: *no és que no en saben gaire!*
    %tra: no the problem is they know very little!

The devaluing or undervaluing of immigrants' proficiency in English was not specific to this office but quite generalised in the immigration service. I heard similar remarks in the other offices I observed and which served as the contextual framing for this study. The extract below comes from the recordings I made at one of these other sites. In it, Rosa and Loli discuss clients' competencies (see especially lines 5 and 7–8).

(75)

    1   *ENQ   <**speak English**> [<]?
    2   *ENQ: **do you speak English?**
    3   *LOL: no.
    4   *LOL: *es igual!*
        %tra: it doesn't matter!
        %act: ENQ hands documents over to LOL
→   5   *ROS: *no y además aunque le digas que sí no lo hablan ellos, eh?*
        %tra: no but even if you say you do they don't speak it,you know.
    6   *LOL: *pero mejor que le <conteste que no que no xxx> [>].*
        %tra: but it's better if I <say that I don't I don't xxx> [>]
→   7   *ROS: <*se pegan el pegote*> [<] *y les empiezas a*
    8   *conversar y ya no saben por donde salir ## una pasada!*
        %tra: <they pretend they do> [<] and then when you start talking they don't know how to continue ## amazing!

The extract begins with the enquirer trying to negotiate the use of English for the interaction. In line 3, Loli avows lack of competence. Loli remarks on the absence of any reaction on the part of the enquirer ("it doesn't matter"), suggesting that he did not actually care whether she could speak English or not. In an attempt to prevent Loli's possible feelings of inadequacy for not speaking English, Rosa, who is the manager and a senior member of staff, reassures her that speaking the language would not make any difference. The reason is, she claims, that despite appearances immigrant information seekers are not competent in it.

The comments made by Rosa throw light on a number of relevant issues. First, Rosa's remarks shows that multilingual competence is not an objectively definable object, but rather, always vulnerable to subjective appreciation (Blommaert et al. 2005). It is the interactional space, and in particular the differential position of speakers with regard to the possibility of attaching value to linguistic resources, that determines who counts as competent in a given language. Secondly, Rosa's competence assessments are not based on her interlocutors' production skills, but on their listening abilities, that is, on their capacity to understand *her*. She is a rather fluent non-native speaker of English, but her grammar is inaccurate and she has a very strong Spanish accent. It is not unlikely, therefore, that her turns are hard to understand for someone not acquainted with Spanish-sounding English. Yet not only does Rosa not question her own language abilities, but she assesses others' competence on the basis of their understanding of her English. Finally, Rosa even accuses enquirers of trying to deceive bureaucrats by claiming to be able to speak English, when –according to her– in fact they cannot. Here we see that language practices become one more facet of the process of negative construction to which these immigrants were constantly subjected. Such practices are influenced by and feed into the "ideology of mistrust" that defines the way in which the relationship between bureaucrats and the public is constructed in bureaucratic domains in general and whose application was particularly visible at this particular site.

Yet mistrust worked both ways. If we examine immigrants' discourse, we see how keenly aware they were of the devaluing process to which their linguistic capitals were subject. We also observe that they did not go along with their being categorised as non-competent speakers of the language and that they actually resisted that categorisation. In their discourse, clients presented a totally dissimilar scenario to the one depicted by officials. Interestingly, however, they tended to use the same arguments as their institutional counterparts. That is, like officials, clients also highlighted the idea that their interlocutors' language practices were deceitful because they were oriented to making clients believe they were proficient in a language when in fact they were not, and emphasised the thesis that it was the others' poor language competence that was at the root of their intercomprehension troubles.

The extract below comes from the long interview with Hussain. It is interesting to observe how aware he is of what was really happening in exchanges with immigration officials, and how vividly and accurately he describes the dismissal process to which clients were subjected.

(76)

→ 1 *HUS: dicen que normalmente es porque ellos tampoco de gente de
    2   España no sabe hablar inglés -. por esto dicen oye tú qué
    3   está hablando que yo no entiendo nadas no tú no sabe inglés
    4   tampoco -. si ellos no saben -. esto no que él otra persona no
    5   sabes -. lo que está diciendo sabes oyes ah vale!

		%tra:	they say that usually it's because they either people from Spain cannot speak English -. this is why they say listen what are you speaking I don't understand anything no you cannot speak English either -. if they can't -. this is it not that somebody else can't -. the one that's speaking can hears that okay.

6 *RES: ah en realidad o sea los de aquí no saben pero dicen a los de
7   tu país ah tú no sabes.
    %tra: oh okay so in fact people here cannot [speak English] but they tell people from your country oh you don't know.

8 *HUS: tú no sabes de qué no entiendo nada de lo que tú quieres
9   decir -. porque primero hablan inglés estos estos no dicen
10   con español.
    %tra: you can't [speak English] I don't understand anything of what you're trying to say -. because first they speak English these these don't say in Spanish.

11 *RES: quién esto -? quién?
    %tra: who does that -? who?

12 *HUS: <gente de aquí> [>].
    %tra: <people here> [>].

13 *RES: <la gente que acaba de llegar> [<]?
    %tra: <the people that have just arrived> [<]?

14 *HUS: no no gente de aquí -, primero preguntan tú sabes inglés -?
15   si dicen sí.
    %tra: no no the people here -, first they ask can you speak English -? if they say yes.

16 *RES: a la gente de tu país les preguntan siempre si saben inglés?
    %tra: do they always ask the people from your country if they can speak English?

17 *HUS: no no por ejemplo un paisano mío -,.
    %tra: no for example a fellow countryman -,.

18 *RES: sí::.
    %tra: ye::s.

19 *HUS: llegas vayas esta oficina.
    %tra: arrive go to this office.

20 *RES: sí::.
    %tra: ye::s

The other languages 205

→ 21   *HUS: preguntas # o dicen español gente de aquí los que
  22   trabajadores están ahí trabajandos este despacho -, ellos
  23   preguntan español -? no -. inglés -? dicen que otra persona
  24   dice yes pero ellos dicen preguntan un dos palabras lo que
  25   ellos saben después hablandos después no hablan inglés -.
  26   habla español que él no sabe nada inglés así diciendo
  27   siempres -. porque ellos no sabes -. pero después dice vale
  28   ya toma.
       %tra: ask # or they say Spanish people from here the workers are
                there working this office -, they ask Spanish -? no -.
                English -? they say that another person says yes but they
                say ask one or two words whatever they know afterwards
                speaking afterwards they don't speak English -. they speak
                Spanish he cannot speak English they always say -. because
                they don't know -. but afterwards they say okay right there
                you go.

In his last intervention (lines 21–28) Hussain's comments are focused on the language practices of the bureaucrats in the immigration services ("the workers working this office"). The interactional behaviour depicted (bureaucrats claiming to speak English but then only being able to produce a couple of words and resuming in Spanish) is the same as what Rosa attributed to clients in extract (75). In what follows, I will show how accurate Hussain's perception of the situation is by examining actual practice in service talk. But before that, it is important to remark that, beyond speakers' mutual accusations of incompetence, what mattered in these clearly asymmetrical exchanges is that it was bureaucrats' and not clients' perceptions of the others' language abilities that were made to count; it was bureaucrats' understanding of the space of interaction (that is, of who the actors were and of what their competencies were) that shaped service talk in crucial ways. In sum, it was officials' framing of service practice that determined how much information would be provided, on which terms and in which language.

Officials' crucial position is illustrated in the next extract in which, following a rather tense beginning to the exchange, a client's accusation of incompetence is fiercely contested by an irritated official.

The contextual background for this extract is important. As will be recalled, one of the requirements of the legalisation was that applicants had to provide documentary evidence that could prove their arrival in Spain before 1 June 1999. On this occasion, it appears that the evidence submitted by this particular enquirer has not been accepted by the institution (hence the use of *falta* in line 1). Consequently, he demands that his name be erased from the institution's database ("this my name finito finish"). In view of the exceptionality of the request, the official (Miquel) repeatedly avows lack of understanding. At one point, the enquirer reacts by blaming Miquel's lack of understanding on his poor language skills (line 8).

(77)

	1	*ENQ:	**but look look this** falta.
		%tra:	but look look this missing.
	2	*MIQ:	<falta sí> [>].
		%tra:	missing yes.
	3	*ENQ:	<understand> [<] ?
	4	*ENQ:	falta <u>hm</u> **okay** <no> [>] falta **no okay # you understand -? but**
	5		**this my name #** <u>finito</u> **# finish.**
		%tra:	missing hm okay no missing no okay # you understand -? but this my name finished # finish.
	6	*MIQ:	**<oka::y>** [<] ?
	7	*MIQ:	**I don't understand**.
→	8	*ENQ:	**you what is the English you speak** xxx ?
→	9	*MIQ:	**I speak English you don't speak English!**
	10	*ENQ:	**yes**.
→	11	*MIQ:	**my name** <u>no</u> <u>finito</u>!
	12	*ENQ:	+ˆ **yes finish**.
	13	*MIQ:	**finish what** -? # **finish** ?
	14	*ENQ:	**yes this immigration** #0_2 <**finish**> [>1] **but** <**you understand**> [>2]?
	15		**<no>** [<1].

There are several elements in this exchange that deserve close attention. First, it is surprising that the enquirer makes an overt metalinguistic judgement on the skills of his situationally more powerful interlocutor. Secondly, it is interesting that what seems to be a problem with Miquel's understanding of the nature of the enquirer's service request is presented as a linguistic problem. Faced with communication asynchronies, actors tend to problematise what is immediately accessible to them. As a result, language skills often become their object of scrutiny. There is no doubt that for a lay actor like this client it is easier to problematise language competencies than the way in which his lay knowledge and talk are being converted into a bureaucratic case, for this would require in-depth knowledge of the institutional arena and close monitoring of the turns at talk, all outside the grasp of this client. Thirdly, the two interlocutors approach the issue of their respective language competencies in remarkably different ways. That is, while the client phrases his challenge in terms of the "quality" of the English spoken by Miquel ("what is the English you speak?"), the latter presents it in absolute terms, that is, as speaking or not speaking English. It is also significant that Miquel presents a codeswitched sentence (line 11) as evidence that his interlocutor "does not speak English". According to Miquel, being competent in English entails being able to separate it completely from other linguistic codes. In his view, codemixing and hybridity amount to absolute lack of competence. Miquel's statement must have at least astonished his interlocutor, since mixing and switching are everyday currency in the "Outer Circle" where English is used alongside a number of linguistic codes (Kachru 1990). Miquel's perception of competence is laden with views about the purity of languages and the separatedness of linguistic codes.

What is quite clear from this exchange is that when clients question bureaucrats' competences –as bureaucrats do all the time– they only manage to create more trouble for themselves. The irritated mode in which the official responds and his categorical rejection of the client's challenge show that overt criticisms of professionals' competencies are unfailingly dismissed. Hardly ever does clients' resistance discourse find its way into public service talk, and when it does, it is bitterly contested. This example shows, once again, that evaluative moves are only allowed in one direction.

Thus far, we have concentrated on participants' mutually judgemental approaches towards each other's competencies in English. In what follows, I would like to shift the analytical focus towards an examination of what happens in the minute-to-minute unfolding of service communication. Having spelt out what factors conditioned the role of English as a fully operational language and thus made language choice another highly constrained space at the immigration office, I would like to explore how this was made evident in situated talk.

One of the general claims that can be made with regard to the viability of English as a communicative resource in this context is that in one sense it was unpredictable because its functionality depended largely on the linguistic skills of the specific institutional interlocutor that immigrant clients happened to encounter. In another sense, however, the viability of English *was* predictable. This is because, on the one hand, the generalised lack of foreign language skills amongst the local population, and on the other, the institutional view of foreign language provision as not being part of bureaucrats' ordinary service obligations inevitably resulted in officials having limited proficiency levels.

Due to their limited abilities in English, both Teresa and Ramon tried to avoid employing this language as much as possible preferring instead Spanish, which was constructed as the default language of interaction. This obviously worked to the detriment of those enquirers who were not competent in Spanish. The following encounter illustrates Teresa's habitual language practices.

(78)

→ 1   *TER: eso qué es para entregar papeles o para mirar ordenador?
      %tra: is this to submit documents or to check computer?

2   *EN1:   xxx.

3   *TER: <u>eh</u>?

4   *EN1:   0
      %act: hands TER some documents

5   *TER: te sacan aquí un montón de papeles y no sabes para qué.
      %tra: they take out a pile of documents and you don't know what for.

6   *TER: es para entregar -? para mí -? ## sí?
      %tra: is this for submission -? for me -? ## yes?

7   *EN1:   sí.
      %tra: yes.

8   *TER: esto no está presentado -. esto no está presentado no tiene el sello.
9   %tra: this has not been entered -. this has not been entered -. it doesn't have a stamp.

10   *UUU: #0_3.

11   *TER: sello?
      %tra: stamp?
      %act: exemplifies word with her hands

12   *TER: resguardo con el sello?
      %tra: copy with a stamp?

13   *TER: sí sí sí.
      %tra: yes yes yes.

14   *TER: tú tú lo tienes # tú?
      %tra: you you have it # you?

15   *UUU: #0_2.

	16	*TER:	a ver ## la primera # primera vez?
		%tra:	let's see ## the first # first time?
→	17	*TER:	tú hablas inglés verdad?
		%tra:	you speak English don't you?
		%add:	RES
	18	*EN2:	<xxx> [>].
		%com:	talks to EN1 in a South Asian language
	19	*RES:	<sí> [<].
		%tra:	<yes> [<]
	20	*TER:	qué es la primera vez que lo presenta?
		%tra:	is this the first time he presents it?
			EN2
	21	*EN2:	xxx.
		%com:	talks to EN1 in the same South Asian language
	22	*EN1:	eh::.
	23	*TER:	esto lo ha presentado alguna vez?
		%tra:	has he submitted this before?
	24	*EN2:	xxx.
		%com:	talks to EN1 in the same South Asian language
	25	*EN2:	eh nada.
		%tra:	uh nothing.
	26	*TER:	eh -? no lo ha presentado nunca -. le falta el sello como que
	27		ha entrado o que me lo ha traído.
		%tra:	uh -? he has never entered it -. the stamp showing it has been entered or brought to me is missing.
→	28	*EN2:	xxx **want entry in registration** xxx.
			EN1
	29	*EN1:	no **but** eh xxx.
	30	*TER:	no -. es la primera vez porque ya veo que viene preparado con
	31		se con las fotos y todo ese tiene que:: tiene que hacer cuatro es
	32		que no tenías que haber cogido número no necesitabas número -.
	33		el número es para mirar por ordenador.
		%tra:	no -. it is the first time because I can see that he has everything ready with the pic with the photographs and everything this one has to he has to make four you didn't have to take a number you needed no number -. the number is to check with the computer.

	34	*EN2:	xxx.
		%com:	talks to EN1 in the same South Asian language
	35	*TER:	dile que haga los cuatro impresos o si quiere puede hacer
→	36		fotocopias pero a lo mejor ahora está cerrado ya -. que haga los
→	37		estos cuatro igual # cuatro iguales **the same** -. **four the same**
→	38		**okay** -? y los presentas allí en las mesas # aquí no allí # <**okay**>
	39		[>] ?
		%tra:	tell him to fill in the four forms or if he wants he can make photocopies but it might be closed already -. he needs to do the these four of the same # four of the same the same -. four the same okay -? and you enter them there at the tables # not here there # <okay> [>] ?
	40	*EN1:	<**okay**> [<].
	41	*EN2:	xxx.
	42	*TER:	eh -? sí -? pues allí -. todo allí vale?
		%tra:	uh -? yes -? okay there -. everything there right?

Throughout the exchange, Teresa is trying to ascertain the nature of the two enquirers' service request. In line 28, one of the enquirers tries to formulate in English what the purpose of their visit to the office is. Teresa does not seem to understand. At last, she uses the information she is able to obtain visually from the documents the enquirers are handing out to her to infer what they want. Even though the enquirer has suggested the use of English, Teresa does not codeswitch into this language, as she does not speak it (in line 17, she even suggests that I might be needed to help). In one of her final turns, though, Teresa uses English and we can see how limited her competence is. In fact, she only uses certain pivot words/phrases she knows ("the same", "four" and "okay") and adds them to her turn to facilitate enquirers' understanding. She uses gestures and Spanish to communicate because these are the only resources she has available. This is a clear example of how pervasively the institutional order at the immigration office, which did not require bureaucrats to know any foreign languages, bore upon the realities of situated encounters.

The language practices of the other official, namely Ramon, were fairly different. Apart from Spanish, the only other language he employed with enquirers was English. This happened only occasionally. However, unlike his colleague Teresa, Ramon claimed to speak English. As was shown in example (73), he sometimes even claimed his competence to be higher than that of his interlocutors. In local discursive practice, however, he made every effort to avoid using English. This generalised reluctance to use English at the site was the second

The other languages 211

factor which, I would argue, undermined the communicative value of English in this context. As was suggested earlier, the origins of this attitude can be directly traced to the ideological positioning of the institutional order, which did not require service providers to be competent in any foreign languages. As a consequence, some public servers felt they had no "obligation" to speak English. The practical implications of this were far-reaching in terms of migrants' having to struggle to understand officials' talk.

The following examples illustrate the interactional practice just described. As will be observed, Ramon's codeswitches into English have to be explicitly requested by his interlocutors. When that happens, he changes over to that language but reverts to Spanish as soon as he thinks fit.

(79)

    1   *RAM: to:dos todos -. venga.
          %tra: a:ll all of them -. come on.

    2   *EN1:   0.
          %act: hands applications over to official

    3   *RAM: trae -! cuarenta -. trae:.
          %tra: come on -! forty -. give them to me.

    4   *RAM: no -. esto esto no esto.
          %tra: no -. this this not this.

    5   *UUU: esto sí y esto también.
          %tra: this yes and this as well.

    6   *RAM: esto no.
          %tra: not this.

    7   *EN1:   esto sí.
          %tra: this yes.

    8   *UUU: xxx.

    9   *RAM: mayo no:.
          %tra: not May.

   10   *EN1:   no?

   11   *RAM: mayo no: -. # mayo no tengo # mayo no.
          %tra: not Ma:y -. May I don't have # not May.

→   12   *EN1:   **not yet**?

→   13   *EN1:   **computer** sí -. # **please**.

| | 14 | *RAM: | no:: éste éste sí -. éste no -. éste no. |
| | | %tra: | no this this one yes -. not this one -. this one no. |

| | 15 | *RAM: | éste no. |
| | | %tra: | this one no. |

	16	*RAM:	ya estamos aquí cuarenta tí:os # empujando en la barra a ver si
	17		nos metemos en la calle siguiente # # <cojones ya> [=! putting
	18	%tra:	on an Andalusian accent] !
			here we're forty mates already # pushing at the bar see if we get to the next street ## bloody hell [=! putting on an Andalusian accent] !
		%add:	clients waiting

| | 19 | *RAM: | *bue:no -! d'aquí cinc minuts torno a cridar* ! |
| | | %tra: | right -! in five minutes I shall be shouting again ! |

@Situation: RAM is checking status of ENQ's application

→ 20 *EN1: **speak English -. speak English** sí?
       %tra: speak English -. speak English yes?

→ 21 *RAM: venga: **speak English.**
       %tra: oka::y speak English.

   22 *RAM: qué?
       %tra: what?

   23 *EN1: 0.
       %act: indicates he wants to ask a fellow countrymen to help him

   24 *RAM: sí sí.
       %tra: yes yes.

   25 *RAM: uno eh?
       %tra: one right?

   26 *RAM: éste -. uno -. uno-. tú pa(ra) (a)llí -. uno.
       %tra: this one -. one -. one -. you move over there -. one.

   27 *EN1: uno.
       %tra: one.

→ 28 *RAM: **the last day you can check in computer are ten of May.**

   29 *EN2: **May?**

   30 *RAM: **ten # of May.**

   31 *EN2: xxx.

   32 *RAM: **seven seventeenth.**

	33	*RAM:	**after one week, okay**?
	34	*EN2:	**yes** xxx **after one** <week> [>] -. **after one**?
	35	*RAM:	<a̲i̲> [<]!
	36	*RAM:	**<after>** [<] **one week today no.**
	37	*EN2:	<una> [<]?
		%tra:	<one> [<]?
→	38	*RAM:	éste trámite.
		%tra:	this one being processed.
	39	*EN2:	tramite.
		%tra:	being processed.
		%com:	stresses word on second syllable.
	40	*RAM:	+ˆ ya le puedes ir contando lo que es tramite.
		%tra:	+ˆ you can start telling them what being processed is.
		%com:	stresses "tramite" on second syllable.
	41	*EN2:	cómo trámite?
		%tra:	what being processed?

In this example, the enquirer's evident lack of understanding of what is going on interactionally (lines 4–11) together with his use of English in lines 12 and 13 do not prompt Ramon to negotiate or change the language of interaction. The enquirer is finally forced to make his linguistic request explicit (line 20). Ramon responds with a reluctant "*venga*" 'okay'. Ramon's reluctance is indexed by his lengthening of the last vowel in this word. The enquirer indicates that he wants to ask an English-speaking friend to help him communicate with the official, and Ramon accedes to this request. Significantly, this negotiation takes place in Spanish and not in English. Interaction between the enquirer's friend (EN2) and Ramon starts off in English, as requested (line 28). Yet Ramon takes advantage of the first occasion in which EN2 uses Spanish, even though the only word he utters is *trámite*, to codeswitch back into this language. The conversation then proceeds in Spanish. The official's linguistic behaviour is not guided by a desire to facilitate communication with his interlocutors. On the contrary, his own needs are made to prevail, as using Spanish involves less effort for him. Besides, as illustrated in the previous chapter, he can exploit the linguistic asymmetry established by the use of Spanish to pass overt judgement on his interlocutors and act as the gatekeeper of the moral order of the office.

Example (80) illustrates the same practice again. After being asked to translate a word into English (line 4), Ramon provides this translation (line 5), and

214   *Language choice and multilingual practice*

continues in Spanish (line 8). This official's mode of behaviour in relation to language choice seems to be the rule rather than the exception and fits exactly into Hussain's description presented earlier. What is significant about this example is that Ramon is the official who claimed in example (79) that his linguistic skills in English were "adequate" because immigrants' abilities were even more limited than his.

(80)

		1	*RAM:	concedido éste -. fíjate has tenido suerte.
			%tra:	this one's granted -. you've been really lucky.
		2	*ENQ:	éste?
			%tra:	this one?
		3	*RAM:	concedido.
			%tra:	granted.
→		4	*ENQ:	pero en inglés [?] ?
			%tra:	but in English [?] ?
→		5	*RAM:	**accepted**.
		6	*ENQ:	**accepted**?
		7	*RAM:	**hu.**
→		8	*RAM:	de quién es éste?
			%tra:	whose is this one?
		9	*RAM:	de quién es?
			%tra:	whose is it?
		10	*ENQ:	es de ami mío amigo.
			%tra:	it's from a fri a friend of mine.
		11	*RAM:	amigo no -? qué amigos que sóis!
			%tra:	friends right -? you're all such good friends!

It is interesting to examine the languages other than English that South Asian enquirers employed, as they bore the traces of their migration trajectories. Many of them, for example, had arrived in Spain after having lived in France, Italy or Germany and used the linguistic abilities they had acquired in those countries (basically French, but also some German and some Italian, as in encounter [77] above) to communicate with officials. Particularly interesting is the case of a South Asian enquirer who communicated in English with a strong German accent. He was not only quite fluent in English but also a particularly articulate client. This case indicates that transnational migration seems to be opening up opportunities for individuals to have access to valuable communicative resources, like lingua franca English. I wonder whether the enquirer's German accent was due to his having learnt the language in Germany or the result of the modification of his phonology to adjust it to the norms of appreciation of German society (similarly to what was happening in this office).

The remainder of this chapter is devoted to the examination of Miquel's language practices. Holding a university degree in Arabic, this official was the most language-minded of the staff. On several occasions he made comments on his interlocutors' linguistic practices. He was aware, for example, that his South Asian interlocutors pronounced some English sounds in a special way, in particular, the sounds /w/, /θ/ and /eɪ/, which South Asians pronounce /v/, /t/ and /e:/ respectively, and he tried to incorporate his interlocutors' phonology into his own linguistic productions to facilitate mutual understanding. This interest also motivated him to experiment with language. At one point he found out that the temporal phrase "three weeks more" was easier for enquirers to understand than the standard "three more weeks" and decided to use the former. Nonetheless, in spite of his linguistic awareness, there were a few elements in Miquel's linguistic behaviour which worked to hinder rather than facilitate service communication.

One of these elements was his rather uncreative use of codeswitching. By uncreative I mean that, by and large, he tended to stick to the monolingual norm, whereby only one language of interaction is used at a time. He produced frequent inter-turn but very few intra-turn switches (that is of course if we exclude the turns containing the word *trámite*, which was always uttered in Spanish in this office, and Miquel's routinised repetition of *tres semanas* 'three weeks' in Spanish and English in provision of service moves). By contrast, his interlocutors sometimes employed up to three languages in their turns to get their message across.

One reason to explain interactants' divergent practices as regards codeswitching may be that enquirers were more aware of their limited abilities and therefore mobilised all their linguistic resources to make themselves understood. They had a bigger investment in successful communication than officials did. However, this alone falls short of providing a complete explanation for this phenomenon. Long-standing linguistic ideologies and/or speakers' different linguistic *habituses* (Bourdieu 1991) may be another part of the explanation for their different practices. For instance, as is well-known, codemixing involving English is well-rooted in the linguistic practices of South Asians but rare in the Catalan sociolinguistic context.

The second element to be pointed out and a key factor in constraining the functional value of English as a contact language in these institutional encounters is the non-negotiated character of Miquel's language choices. This, I would argue, stemmed from and is another index of the generalised lack of interactional synchrony that characterised these interactions and which I have amply described in Chapters 3 and 4. In the following paragraphs, I shall explain my understanding of the relationship between interactional synchrony and language choice.

Miquel was the only institutional representative who employed English regularly. Analysis of the service exchanges in which he engaged shows that it is difficult to define regularities in his language choices. Even though he regularly adopted Spanish to open his service interactions with enquirers, with South Asian clients his opting for either English or Spanish appeared to be random. His choices did not seem to have a clearly identifiable motivation or follow a regular pattern.

More significant than the language Miquel chose to start an exchange was is the way in which the interaction would then proceed. Explicit language negotiation sequences (Codó 1998) were infrequent (there were in fact only nine in the whole corpus). Significantly, most of them (66%) were initiated by enquirers, not by bureaucrats. By and large, lack of uptake was the most frequent "method" used by clients to show the inappropriateness of officials' linguistic choices and attempt to change the language of interaction. In view of officials' restricted use of explicit language negotiation sequences, it could be hypothesised that language negotiation took place in an implicit way. That is to say, officials would interpret enquirers' linguistic choices for their turns as displays of linguistic preference and converge to them (Auer 1984, 1995, 1998).

In general, an analysis of the data disconfirms this hypothesis. This is what is referred to above as the non-negotiated character of language choice. Admittedly, the lack of convergence can partly be attributed to the frequent breaks characterising the encounters under analysis, but not exclusively. Implicit language negotiation sequences demand that participants be highly attuned to the needs of their interlocutors and monitor their own linguistic productions closely. Routinisation and lack of interactional synchrony, which are the defining traits of these service interactions, work against these demands. Nowhere was routinisation more evident than in the provision of service turn. This turn tended to have a standard codeswitched format regardless of the established language of interaction. This routinised practice is illustrated in extract (81) below.

(81)

	1	*MIQ:	hola.
		%tra:	hello.
	2	*ENQ:	0.
		%tra:	hands copies of several application forms over to MIQ
	3	*MIQ:	éste nada -,.
		%tra:	this one no -,.
		%act:	goes through applications first
	4	*MIQ:	éste todavía no -,.
		%tra:	this one not yet -,.
	5	*ENQ:	éste no?
		%tra:	not this one?
	6	*MIQ:	hola::!
		%tra:	hello::!
		%add:	unknown
	7	*MIQ:	vamos por el tres de julio.
		%tra:	we've got until July third.
	8	*ENQ:	a ver xxx cinco de julio.
		%tra:	let's see xxx July fifth.
		@Situation: MIQ checks status of application	
→	9	*MIQ:	en trámite -, **three weeks more**.
		%tra:	being processed -, three weeks more.
	10	*ENQ:	perdón pero esto muchos # día!
		%tra:	sorry but this many days!
	11	*MIQ:	sí -. # en el ordenador en trámite -. yo.
		%tra:	yes -. # in the computer being processed-. me.
		%act:	shrugs his shoulders
	12	*ENQ:	[=! laughs].

The whole interaction takes place in Spanish except for the provision of service turn (line 9), where for no apparent reason, the official produces codeswitches from Spanish into English. As was pointed out earlier, the frequent breaks in the interaction motivated by officials' searching routines facilitated switches in the language of interaction. An extreme case is presented in the extract below:

(82)

	1	*ENQ:	0.
		%act:	hands copies of application forms over to MIQ
	2	*MIQ:	éste todavía no está faltan dos o tres semanas para que esté
	3		aquí.
		%tra:	this one is not available yet in two or three weeks it'll be here.
	4	*ENQ:	**thanks.**

@Situation: MIQ checks status of application

→ 5 *MIQ: éste está concedido -. # tienes pasaporte?
      %tra: this one is granted -. # do you have a passport?

  6 *ENQ: sí.
      %tra: yes.

@Situation: MIQ fills in an official form certifying work permit has been granted

→ 7 *MIQ: **in three weeks we send him a letter to come here with photos to fingers**.
      %tra: makes gesture indicating what he means by 'fingers'

→ 8 *ENQ: **thank you sir.**

@Situation: MIQ checks status of following application

→ 9 *MIQ: éste está en trámite -. **three weeks**.
      %tra: this one is being processed -. three weeks.

  10 *ENQ: gracias.
      %tra: thank you.

There are three breaks in this interaction, and after each break a different language is chosen. Spanish is chosen after the first break (line 5), disregarding the enquirer's previous display of preference for English (line 4). The enquirer converges to the official's language by uttering the adverbial *sí* 'yes' in Spanish (line 6). However, after the second break, English is chosen. The enquirer again converges to the language chosen by his interlocutor (line 8). After the third break the official starts off in Spanish again, although the routinisation of his responses leads him to switch back into English to provide the usual temporal adverbial phrase. The enquirer converges to his interlocutor's language yet one more time. Clearly, the enquirer is more attuned to the linguistic displays of the official than vice versa. This is surprising but not completely unexpected. It seems to be yet another example of the same underlying pattern: the non-negotiated character of the verbal exchanges under examination.

The final extract in this chapter shows an illuminating instance of an enquirer accommodating to the official's interactional preference for English despite the client's fluency in Spanish.

(83)

	1	*ENQ:	0.
		%act:	hands application forms over to MIQ
→	2	*MIQ:	**only one**?
	3	*ENQ:	**no two -. only** <**it is not**> [>].
	4	*MIQ:	<**where is**> [<]?
	5	*ENQ:	**the name is** <u>eh</u>:: # <**twenty five**> [>].
	6	*MIQ:	<**bring me**> **all the papers**.
	7	*ENQ:	+ˆ **no only paper one**.
	8	*MIQ:	**only one**?
	9	*ENQ:	**one paper**.
			@Situation: MIQ starts checking status of applications
→	10	*ENQ:	usted bolígrafo o no me entiendes [?]?
		%tra:	you pen or don't you understand me [?]?
	11	*ENQ:	por favor un boli -? un boli?
		%tra:	please a pen -? a pen?
		%add:	RES
	12	*RES	un?
		%tra:	a?
	13	*MIQ:	qué?
		%tra:	what?
	14	*RES:	boli?
		%tra:	pen?
	15	*ENQ:	boli sí -. # una.
		%tra:	pen yes -. # one.
	16	*ENQ:	gracias.
		%tra:	thank you.

220 *Language choice and multilingual practice*

@Situation: ENQ writes name of a person whose application he wants to have checked

17 *MIQ: **if you don't have this paper I don't look # anything** -. ##
18   **okay**?

19 *MIQ: en trámite -. <#> [>] **you have to wait three more weeks**.
   %tra: being processed -. <#> [>] **you have to wait three more weeks**.

20 *ENQ: <tienes> [<].
   %tra: <you have to> [<].

21 *ENQ: uh huh eh:: xxx **three** -? **three week** eh?

22 *ENQ   **yes <the end of the week>** [?] -. # **twenty-nine** [?].

23 *ENQ: por favor # eh:: **twenty five to May** -. mayo mayo.
   %tra: please # eh:: **twenty five to May** -. May May.

24 *MIQ: +ˆ **twenty five may is not here.**

The enquirer is initially addressed by Miquel in English (line 2). He responds in English as well, and the interaction continues in this language. However, we see how in line 10, the same enquirer now addresses me in Spanish. When Miquel addresses him again, he does so again in English. As in the previous stretch of talk, the enquirer converges to this language until the interaction is brought to an end. This interaction shows that the enquirer's use of English is not motivated by his lack of competence in Spanish (in fact, in line 23, he seems to be more at ease using Spanish than English), but by his desire to converge to the official's choices. In doing so, the client is contributing to the construction of the official's socially and interactionally dominant position.

The effect of the non-negotiated nature of bureaucrats' choices at the site was that rarely did a conversation proceed entirely in English. This certainly restricted the functionality of the code. More than a fully operative language, English seemed to hold the status of an "supporting" language. Apart from the frequent changes in the language of interaction which took place as a result of bureaucrats' reluctance to speak English or their losing track of enquirer's displayed preferences, the well-established routine of always using all the bureaucratic terms describing the administrative procedure in Spanish (e.g. the use of *trámite* in the extract above) severely restricted the functionality of English. Service seekers needed to have at least some knowledge of the key words service providers regularly employed to be able to gain a tentative understanding of the stage in the process their applications were at. As we have argued earlier, knowledge of the meaning of *trámite* alone did not solve the problem, but the idea that English was not a fully functional language and that Spanish was the code to be spoken was successfully transmitted to South Asian immigrant clients.

4. Concluding remarks

As a complement to Chapter 5, the present chapter has provided new arguments and data to support the claim that this office was a highly controlled space. An examination of the strict regulation to which language choice was subject allows for the visualisation of how little room there was for negotiation. In fact, these two chapters have focused on the symbolic dimension of the gatekeeping process examined, which was connected with the need to socialise migrants into becoming proper Spanish citizens.

We have seen how even the use of a "global" language of communication like English, which some authors (e.g. House 2003) have claimed makes it possible for speakers to interact on a more equal footing than the native speaker versus non-native speaker relationship allows for, is not unproblematic. What is more, our examination of English language use at the immigration office has unveiled how pervasive certain ideological conceptions concerning the nature of language and language use still are. Against the postulates of utilitarian views of English, the data has shown that being considered competent in English is a matter of not just speaking the language but speaking the appropriate variety of it and being a legitimate speaker (Bourdieu 1991). We have seen that language choice in these service encounters is closely tied up to the specific configurations of power and linguistic and cultural capitals that define these encounters.

As outsiders to Catalan society, foreigners are quickly socialised into the rules of "appropriate conduct" in this bilingual community. They are positioned in the orbit of the Spanish-speaking population by Catalan-speaking bureaucrats themselves, who as employees of an institution run by the Spanish state "commonsensically" push Catalan into their private, backstage practices. Language choice allows them to construct two distinct interactional and relational spaces, spaces defined by particular forms of language use. Language choice serves local purposes but the specific associations made between the private and the public, the frontstage and the backstage are informed by and in turn reinforce the social meanings attached to Catalan and Spanish in present-day Catalan society.

The picture that emerges from the analysis of the multilingual practices observed is sharply defined. It speaks of clients having to fit into the limited spaces which are created for them by bureaucrats and where there is very little room for manoeuvre. But above all, it is not different from the broader picture of the social order, where hierarchies of knowledge, languages and cultures define and construct the unequal position of actors in the social arena and where there seems to be no space for negotiating the basis on which to construct social relations on a more equal footing.

By way of conclusion

A lot has been said in this book about language, transnational migration and bureaucratic control. My purpose has been to show how these three concepts intertwine and bear on one another in explaining service provision at a state immigration office.

There are some limitations to this study, which are mainly related to the length and scope of the ethnography undertaken, and my limited access to clients' perspectives and understandings. I believe, however, that these limitations do not undermine the sociolinguistic relevance of the data presented, which has enabled us to examine in very close detail the multiple ways in which local discursive action feeds into processes of social stratification.

This study has examined how the immigration agency of a Western European country copes with the fundamental contradiction which stems from the state's commitment to the values of pluralism, justice and equality on the one hand, and its function as the main regulator of access to valuable socioeconomic resources on the other. I have discussed the many ways in which what happened in the verbal interactions that took place between state bureaucrats and immigrant petitioners over a counter was not about the provision of information but about the enactment of the regulation of access to Spanish citizenship. The close regimentation of attitude and conduct to which migrant petitioners were subject not only reproduced but actually reinforced their subordinate position in the social arena.

My story has presented an account of the daily realities of individuals seeking to find a place for themselves in the so-called developed societies they come to live in and struggling to gain access to important socioeconomic resources. A close examination of the multiplicity of microencounters in which immigrants engage is, as Goffman (1983: 14) claims, fundamental. Migrants' occasions of interaction with the host population form the fabric of their experience in the host society and give them a sense of place in the wider community. Yet the social encounters I have discussed in this book are not just any kind of encounters. They are of a very important sort, as the state agency where they took place plays a key role in the structuring and development of petitioners' migration process.

This is because having legal status changes immigrants' relationship with the host society in a number of ways. The most obvious one is, quite simply, recognition by the state of the very existence of those individuals, since they are thereafter counted as official members of the country's population. As legal citizens, immigrants are also entitled to a number of social and welfare benefits to which they previously did not have access. Yet they are much more subject than before to different forms of bureaucratic and administrative control.

This change in status also brings about a change in the host community's perception of immigrants. Indeed, it is often the case that having entered the country using backdoor methods or residing illegally in it are equated with assumptions about immigrants' dubious behaviour and moral worth. The link between the political and social regulation of immigration and immigrants' moral goodness emerges very clearly in the discourse of right-wing politicians and media groups. What is never discussed, however, is why so many people resort to the use of illegal means to enter our so-called developed societies in the first place.

In spite of the socially sensitive nature of the site studied, I have not intended to use this research to simply "sniff out political incorrectness from the huge complexities of institutional life" (Roberts 2001: 323). This is too easy to do and of little explanatory value. What I have tried to show is how particular individuals try to make sense of their local circumstances, what spaces are open for them to do so, what resources they draw on, and what the consequences are for themselves and others.

The data has shed light on some hot issues on the current sociolinguistic scene. I have discussed some of the ways in which transnational migration and globalisation are changing the societies we live in by challenging accepted views of citizenship and group membership based on homogeneity and uniformisation. Although transnational migrations are increasingly calling into question the authority of the nation-state and its status as the main regulator of people's lives and identities (Pujolar 2007b), the data has shown that nation-states still strive to maintain their hegemonic position and to protect the interests of their national population.

As sociolinguists, we try to come to terms with the new globalised social order by focusing on situated occasions of contact between people from diverse sociocultural backgrounds and their linguistic practices, and by examining how those contacts result in highly hybrid and mixed forms of communication (Rampton 1995, 2001). From a critical standpoint, we try to account for how these new forms of language combine with traditional communicative means, and how they are all mobilised by speakers in situated social interaction, for what ends, and with what kinds of meanings. The study of transnational migrations and the sociolinguistic phenomena associated with them allows the visualisation of the ways in which processes of social inclusion and exclusion continue to be reproduced in and through occasions of assessment of linguistic performance embedded in social situations which are defined by asymmetrical distributions of power and capitals.

The story I have told here is the story of when the global meets the local. It is the story of how people coming from a multiplicity of backgrounds come to encounter a national bureaucracy with homogeneous and homogenising views of citizenship and culturally rooted forms of service practice; it is also the story of a whole country which is failing to acknowledge the increasingly heterogeneity of its population.

As a country of emigrants until rather recently and a fairly homogeneous society in terms of race and religion, Spain is finding it hard to come to terms with the social and cultural changes brought about by foreign immigration. By and large, Spanish society wavers between the realization that the influx of immigrants that the country faces is not only inevitable but needed, and the difficult task of removing from public and private spheres deep-rooted forms of racism that stigmatise cultural, religious and ethnic differences.

An understanding of the social role of the bureaucracy studied is central to explaining the nature of the service practices observed. Bureaucracies are instruments of the state, and as such, they are the means whereby the state pursues its goals. As a liberal democratic society, Spain has to abide by the principles of justice, equality and democracy; but at the same time, the state has as its duty to protect the interests of those it serves, that is, the Spanish population. This is one of the contradictions that needed to be managed in this context. The second one is connected with the realisation that immigrants are necessary for Spain's economic growth. Yet while the country must give a considerable number of foreigners access to citizenship, the state also wants to act as a gatekeeper, and therefore strictly limits access. There are several reasons for this. One of them is the desire to make this socioeconomic resource seem scarce, because that way it seems more valuable. The second reason has to do with the fact that the state wants to be seen in the eyes of locals and foreigners alike as controlling the rules of the game. The management of all these contradictions is central to the work of the bureaucrats observed in this study. Their ambivalent positions emerged clearly in their discourses and practices, but with different emphases depending on individual persons. Teresa, for example, sometimes empathised with her immigrant clients and felt pity at their miserable material and economic circumstances; at other times, she disregarded their need for respectful and professional forms of service provision. Similar comments could be made of the other bureaucrats. One of the things this clearly shows is that an immigration office is not located in a social vacuum; no institutional domain is. But I have shown how, because of its social function and role, this site was a particularly privileged arena in which to examine how social discourses on immigration and diversity informed and legitimised certain forms of social and institutional practice.

One key element in the process of safeguarding the interests of the indigenous population is the state's vested interest in protecting those elements that have traditionally defined Spanish identity. Language is one of the most important ones. The ideology of Spanish as the common language that unites all Spaniards informs discourses on language from a Spanish nationalist perspective, and surfaces regularly in the media in connection with the role and function of Basque, Galician and Catalan, the three minority languages in the country.

In the immigration office, the only legitimate (Bourdieu 1991) language to be spoken was, in keeping with that ideology, Spanish. The language policy of the institution left no doubt as to where it stood. By not requiring its bureaucrats to be competent in languages other than Spanish, the institution was constructing the structural conditions that protected the value of Spanish as a form of capital at this site. However, the message that was being sent was not just that competence of Spanish is an essential requirement for dealings with the Spanish public administration, but rather, that it is a fundamental prerequisite for becoming a full-fledged member of Spanish society. In connection with this, Hussain, for example, discussed in the interview how, in ordinary talk, not speaking Spanish was equated with not speaking at all. Another index of the central role socially accorded to Spanish is the fact that not speaking Spanish is often presented by politicians and many media commentators as an index of the lack of desire to "integrate" (sic), and thus, a key element in the continuous process of categorisation (between good and bad immigrants) to which foreigners are subject.

Yet, as is often the case, speaking Spanish was not sufficient in itself at the office studied. Knowledge of Spanish is often the basis upon which many arguments connected with opportunities for integration are constructed. Yet it is also the element that masks the reality that foreigners' full-fledged participation in the host society depends on the availability of opportunities that will allow them to do so. Knowledge of Spanish is just an initial screening mechanism, because after this requirement is fulfilled, other obstacles will be placed in the way. In the particular case of this office, the data has shown that access to an understanding of the bureaucratic procedure was also refused to those who did speak Spanish. This proves the extent to which social and institutional participation is not jut about speaking Spanish, but about something more.

In spite of the fact that the service discussed was the information counter of an immigration office, service provision was not about making information accessible, or even available. What was it about, then? I have claimed that it was about enacting the regulation of access to citizenship and about safeguarding the institution and protecting it from criticism. As a bureaucracy of the state, this agency was not just an administrative body in charge of the practical implementation of the law. In multiple ways it also played an active role in the regulation, both real and symbolic, of immigrants' entitlement to citizenship.

One of such constraints on access had to do with the definition of the types of documents accepted to prove arrival in the country by 1 June 1999. Allegedly, the criteria employed to establish the suitability of certain documents were more restrictive in Barcelona than in other provinces, and so was the way petitions were examined. As a result, a more limited range of documents was accepted as evidence and it was much more difficult to gain access to legal status in Barcelona than elsewhere. This would explain why, as I mention in Chapter 1, so many of the applications submitted in the province of Barcelona were rejected. This is an example of how the valuable resource dispensed by this official institution was made to appear scarcer than it actually was. Besides, the criteria established showed that the state protects its own regimes of truth, since it rejected as untrustworthy any documents not issued by state agencies or highly bureaucratised corporations like banks. The fact that most of the petitions rejected in 2000 were finally accepted in 2001 as a result of the loosening of the criteria for entitlement supports the idea that what this agency was really doing was acting out regulation and control.

The gatekeeping function of this bureaucracy, however, was not limited to regulating elements of the legal procedure. The practical organisation of work was another index of its investment in making legal citizenship appear like a rare object of desire. The way paperwork was processed did not seem to have been carefully planned or to be organised efficiently and rationally. Though much of what I observed connects up with established forms of practice in Spanish bureaucratic agencies, the blunt sloppiness and carelessness of this particular institution was astonishing and has to be interpreted against the idea that the function of this agency was not, as I noted, to serve clients (Verschueren p.c.) but to enact the control of the state.

The complete disregard for accurate information was another index of the same phenomenon. On the face of it, the institution followed democratic principles by allowing petitioners to demand details on the progress of applications. But the truth is, as I have shown, that no relevant information was in fact provided, and that immigrants were kept mostly in the dark about the fate of their applications and about when a final decision would be made. Because the institution disregarded the process of information exchange, it did not provide any kind of professional training to its employees. Officials were left to their own devices as regards information provision. They had to decide what to say, how to act and what to do.

This book has, thus, highlighted the difficulty of describing the role of human agency in the constitution of socioinstitutional life. Yet at the same time it has pointed out ways in which such complexity can begin to be disentangled. I have combined the detailed examination of face-to-face communicative data with a thorough analysis of the institutional frame. The connections that have been brought to the fore provide new arguments for the claim that interactional phenomena and institutional contexts cannot be investigated independently of each other, but also, that their relationship is complex and multidimensional (Sarangi and Roberts 1999).

I have avoided simplistic analyses of the institutional arena; that is, I have moved away from dichotomies that classify some actors as the "good guys" and some others as the "bad guys". It is all too easy to overemphasise the role of individual agency, especially front-line workers, in institutional domains, without acknowledging the way in which structural inequalities are built into administrative procedures and processes as they are defined in present-day Western bureaucracies. As Blommaert (2001) argues, believing in the justice of the liberal democratic state is a typical ideology of the middle classes. According to this ideology, the system is not intrinsically unfair; it is just a matter of investing more money and resources on training schemes for front-line bureaucrats so that they learn how to represent information more accurately and how to be more respectful with clients. Why is it, then, that problems continue to arise, that implicit and explicit forms of racism persist, and that institutional processes are so often disadvantageous to minority group members?

The data has borne witness to the constructed nature of bureaucratic events. Bureaucracy is not, as I have discussed, a given, but something that is constructed out of the ways in which actors take up certain social roles, sanction specific modes of behaviour and make particular sense of the talk produced. One of the aspects that I have tried to underline is the ways in which actors at this site understood the institutional constraints to which they were subject, and how there was variation in how they positioned themselves with respect to them, with specific consequences for their practices and for the lives of others.

In that sense, Miquel and Ramon, two of the main characters of this story, embodied two different ways of behaving, and of understanding their duties and their social position in the office.

Miquel had a real investment in defining standard forms of service provision for the office. He wanted to keep a unified front because he was concerned with not giving the show away, aware as he was that what they were doing was giving a performance in the strict sense of the word. Miquel was fully aware of his subordinate position in the institutional hierarchy and justified his compliance with institutional guidelines by highlighting his interest in having access to a permanent contract. He was the institutional actor who most carefully managed his interactional identity, constructing himself as a computer checker to distance himself from certain institutional practices while at the same time not losing professional face. It seems, thus, that Miquel felt somehow uneasy about the office's service practices, but that, at the same time, he had an investment in them as the only way of protecting himself from criticism and making sense of what he was doing.

Ramon was probably the only bureaucrat who spoke the truth (Heller p.c.). This is why his service practices were so shocking. Ramon mistreated immigrant clients openly. He shouted at them, criticised and insulted them, and questioned their honesty and moral worth. It is significant that the majority of these actions were (or were connected with) occasions of categorisation. We observe in Ramon's turns how he constantly passed judgement on his interlocutors. In most cases, his categorisations were stereotypical and negative, but in some cases they were positive, as when he stated that a particular service seeker was a "better person" than the rest because he had admitted to not having valid evidence to support his petition, or when he described another client as being good-mannered because he was European. It is difficult not to establish parallels between Ramon's instances of categorisation and the practices of the state, which defines norms of inclusion and exclusion, and assesses immigrants' adequacy by reference to those norms.

It will be recalled that, in spite of his abusive behaviour, Ramon retained his job, while Miquel was made redundant. Although Miquel's redundancy had nothing to do with his service practices, it is interesting to note that they did not help his case, and that Ramon's position was not affected by the numerous written complaints he received from clients. This fits in with our argument that Ramon's behaviour was in line with state expectations of him. However, it would also be fair to claim that Miquel's conduct appeared to be more appropriate in professional terms than Ramon's. This is because Miquel was more skilful than Ramon – who did not actually care much about the issue – at masking the real social function of this agency. It was not the case, as the data has shown, that Miquel furnished more information to clients than Ramon. But he came across as being less offensive because, by and large, he was careful to stage service practice as if its function were the satisfaction of clients' service needs, that is, in this case, to provide information.

Ramon and Miquel assessed institutional constraints in different ways and understood their position differently. Ramon's exclusionary practices were blunt, whereas Miquel's were more subtle. Yet they both reproduced socially hegemonic ways of being and acting in bureaucratic spaces, ways which were not just asymmetrical but clearly unequal. The role relationship of bureaucrats and clients was constructed on the domination–subordination axis, where bureaucrats exerted their power, and thus enacted a socially dominant position, and clients were pushed into a subordinate mode of being, without forgetting, of course, the role of the subordinate actor, fragile and contingent as her or his compliance may be, in constructing the bureaucrat's dominance.

In response to a question about whether any clients had complained about Ramon's behaviour, Miquel once asked me, "Would you dare speak up to a policeman?" Miquel's comment was framed in such a commonsensical manner that it left no doubt as to where he stood. His equation of the status and social function of bureaucrats with that of policemen was highly revealing and was an indication that, although he was general more polite and respectful than Ramon in service practice, he also had clear ideas about what the nature of his institutional duties was.

It was the highly evaluative behaviour of bureaucrats' that defined their authoritative position and explained what these encounters were about. Their assessments may seem gratuitous, as decisions on clients' cases were made elsewhere and not on the basis of how clients performed in situated interaction. Yet they were not gratuitous if we take them to be the situated performance of the gatekeeping function of this bureaucracy. In Chapter 5, I have argued that certain instances of Ramon's provocative forms of language use, besides effecting social control, were a way for him to have fun, that is, to relieve the boredom of a job he found unmotivating. But beyond that, the general discredit of immigrants' conduct which emerged as a result of bureaucrats' assessment processes crucially gave them a sense of ontological security in what they did. In other words, the idea that immigrants did not deserve better treatment legitimised the bureaucrats' terribly uninformative practices, and reinforced stereotypical constructions of migrants' behaviour. But at a broader level, officials' evaluative mode has to be understood as one more index of the generalised evaluation to which immigrants are subject in the social sphere, where they constantly have to prove their value and adequacy as individuals. In this scenario, the practices that we observed in the agency which regulates immigrants' legal access to citizenship were legitimised by socially hegemonic ways of understanding the relationship between locals and foreigners, but also by ideological conceptions of the role of the state as the regulator of social life and as the main protector of the interests of its national population.

Officials' evaluative actions and attitudes (as for society's similar stance) found their justification in the ideology of mistrust which Sarangi and Slembrouck (1996) discuss and which I have shown informed bureaucratic practice at many levels. This same ideology informs relationships between immigrants and the host society at a broader level. That means that immigrants in this bureaucratic context found themselves subject to a double process of mistrust: they were mistrusted as clients of a bureaucratic organisation, and they were, crucially, mistrusted as foreigners coming from a developing country and from a different sociocultural and religious milieu. Immigrants strove hard to present themselves as adequate individuals. They chatted with officials and even sympathised with the hardness of their job, provided information about their marital status (in particular, about having Spanish spouses), stated their profound knowledge of Spanish, or used Catalan to index their will to integrate (Chapter 6). Unconnected as these metacomments may seem, they sought to overcome the continuous process of negative stereotyping to which immigrant clients were subject in this bureaucratic context.

If we change perspectives and look at what happened in these encounters from the perspective of clients, mistrust was also the word that defined best their relationship with the institution and its representatives. Clients' feelings of mistrust were rooted in experiences of discrimination in the host society and were fed by the specific institutional practices that they experienced at this office. Chapter 4 has illustrated how immigrants perceived that the information they received was contradictory and seemed dependent on the specific bureaucrat they happened to deal with. This, added to their lack of comprehension of how the institutional procedure was organised and where and when decisions were made, fostered feelings of uncertainty about the rationality and fairness of the institution. I have also illustrated how mistrust got voiced in public service discourse, but crucially, how little was done by the institution to reassure clients.

In my story I have shown that some immigrants learned how to be "good" clients, like Hussain, who waited longer than advised, spoke fluent Spanish and did not bother officials with unnecessary questions. Others actually resisted being pushed into the background; they actively sought more knowledge, contested the scarce information they were given and tried to get bureaucrats to perceive the world through their eyes, as we have seen in Chapter 4. Or they voiced a discourse that rejected the devaluing of their linguistic capital undertaken by bureaucrats, as we noted in Chapter 6. Yet all this seemed to meet little success. Migrants did not manage to obtain more information or to make their linguistic skills count. It is true that these resistance moves did, at least for some time, question or even contest bureaucrats' dominant positioning of themselves, that is, they suspended the unequal enactment of roles in these encounters, but this suspension was, unfortunately, short-lived. We have seen that, in their practices, bureaucrats did not open up spaces for clients to participate more equally in the construction and definition of these events, but I have also tried to show that that was not what they were expected to do. Such behaviour would have amounted to acting "uninstitutionally" and would have threatened their position in the agency. This does not mean that it was all strategically planned, and that institutional representatives chose, intentionally, to proceed in that fashion.

On the contrary, both as bureaucrats and as clients of bureaucracies, they were socialised into ways of acting, doing and believing that reproduce practices of categorisation and forms of exclusion which, in turn, feed into processes of social stratification. In the particular case of this office, those practices were informed by homogeneous views of Spanish identity, and by criteria of inclusion based on uniformity and founded on the mistrust of difference.

Notes

1. Source: Newspaper *El País* (Madrid), 2 February 2000.
2. One of these problems comes from the fact that a person wanting to register with a municipality does not need to be physically present at the time of registration. Another problem is how to keep track of foreigners who decide to return to their countries of origin. Although non-EEA foreigners without permanent residence in Spain must now renew their registration every two years, there is no way of knowing how accurate figures are at a particular moment in time.
3. Source: *Anuario Estadístico de Inmigración. Año 2004* (Observatorio Permanente de la Inmigración 2005).
4. Although not members of the European Union, Swiss nationals are included within this group by virtue of the agreement signed on 21 June 1999 between Switzerland and the European Union.
5. According to data from the newspaper *El País* (Madrid), 20 March 2000.
6. Source: *Anuario Estadístico de Extranjería 2000* (Ministerio del Interior 2001)
7. Source: Newspaper *El País* (Madrid), 3 August 2000.
8. This was the list of documents required for standard cases. Of course, depending on the type of applicant, different documents might be necessary. For example, foreigners whose applications for political asylum had been rejected could then apply for legal status like regular economic migrants, in which case they were asked to present a copy of the official notification of refusal of asylum. In the case of relatives of applicants or legal residents, they needed to provide a legal document proving their kinship relationship.
9. This requirement excluded, of course, any criminal offences related to the applicant's illegal situation in the country. For instance, many immigrants had *órdenes de expulsión* (deportation orders) in their police records as a result of a previous unsuccessful work permit application process. Such *órdenes* had to be repealed before the application could make progress. This took a particularly long time when the *órdenes* were issued in a province different from the province where the application was being processed.
10. It must be noted, however, that the motivation for journalists' reports seems to stem from the grievances of the neighbours, who often complain about noise and garbage (see newspaper *El Periódico* 29 December 2001) rather than from a genuine interest in the social conditions of immigrants in Catalonia.
11. "Blaming the machine" is a favourite strategy to escape responsibility in many bureaucratic contexts.
12. This may also have applied to Teresa and Juan, but I did not have the chance to converse with them on this issue.

234 *Notes*

13. The original version of the email message, in Catalan, goes as follows:

    Hola abans del pont, maqbul i mahfuz amb la u llarga son concedido i denegado, això que poses que deiem el Ramon i jo no tinc ni idea del que és, el Ramon és de vacances i fins la setmana que ve no se li pot preguntar, això de bilifits ni idea tarabya pot ser algo de àrab (arabiya) i bakawuab tampoc ho sé baka sol vol dir falta, pero wuab ni idea o sigui que o ho portes o res, però això desprès del pont, *per cert que aquí estem tots espantadíssims perquè ens volen fotre al carrer perquè diuen que s'ha acabat la feina i estem tots bastant fotuts.*

14. It is significant that Miquel pointed out that Ramon and Teresa had retained their jobs in spite of service seekers' complaints. Miquel was likely to have assumed that the chances of his retaining his job were dependent on his professional performance, whereas for Ramon and Teresa this association was not apparent. This latter approach is in line with Nieto's (1996) remarks that in the Spanish bureaucratic system promotion is not dependent upon the worker's professional performance.

15. The expressin *fase vuitanta-tres* 'phase eighty-three' that Rosa mentions in the interaction was another institutional label for the "proposed for rejection" stage.

16. Note the use of the impersonal place adverbial "here" or "there" to avoid personalising the enquirer's choice.

17. The use of the word "enacted as" is intentional here. Even when enquirers dealt with the same bureaucrat on various occasions, the latter would avoid showing signs of acquaintance or familiarity. In that vein, Miquel produced the following backstage comment after one interaction (boldface is mine):

    *MIQ: ... *i que jo li havia dit que portés el passaport i ara el portava però com allà no estava apuntat si hagués sigut jo aquest matí li hagués posat setze del sis o si no que vingui* el amigo *i que m'ho demostri* **però a la majoria ni els miro**!

    %tra: ... [according to him] I told him to bring his passport and now he had it, but since it was not written there [on the form]... If he'd been here this morning I would have written sixteenth of June. [If he wants me to believe him] he should ask his friend to come and prove it to me but **I don't look most of them in the face** anyway!

18. For example, on one occasion, a bureaucrat from one of the other immigration offices I visited voiced the mistrust of the institution towards paperwork-handling officials of Moroccan origin in the following way: "*A veure què tal va, perquè els d'aquí no se'n fien*" 'let's see how it goes, because the people from here [the managers] don't trust them'. This comment was made in reference to a recently hired member of staff.

19. Miquel's view of his inadequacy is revealed in the extract below. On one of the last days of the legalisation campaign, the official was asked to appear on TV to give an institutional message in Arabic but refused to do so. This is how he accounted for his refusal:

*MIQ: *imagina't per la tele* [diu unes quantes paraules en àrab] *i tots els marroquins ha ha ha!*

%tra: imagine me on TV [utters a few words in Arabic] and all the Moroccans going ho ho ho!

20. See for example the article by Mercè Beltran in the newspaper *La Vanguardia* (Barcelona), 11 March 2007, or the article by Carles López in the newspaper *El Periódico de Cataluña* (Barcelona), 28 October 2007.

References

Administración General del Estado
    2000   *Guide to the Aliens Regularisation Procedure. From 31 March to 31 July 2000*. Madrid.

Agar, Michael
    1985   Institutional Discourse. *Text* 5(3), 147–168.

Alcalá Recuerda, Esther
    2006   Aprendiendo a comportarse: normas y evaluación en la interacción en el aula. Unpublished doctoral dissertation, Universidad Autónoma de Madrid.

Arango Vila-Belda, Joaquín
    2002   La inmigración en España a comienzos del siglo XXI: Un intento de caracterización. In: García Castaño F. J. and C. Muriel López (eds.), *La inmigración en España: contextos y alternativas*. Granada: Laboratorio de Estudios Interculturales, 57–70.

Atkinson, J. Maxwell and John Heritage (eds.)
    1984   *Structures of Social Action: Studies in Conversation Analysis*. Cambridge: Cambridge University Press.

Auer, Peter
    1984   *Bilingual Strategies*. Amsterdam and Philadelphia: John Benjamins.
    1995   The pragmatics of code-switching: a sequential approach. In: Milroy, L. and P. Muysken (eds.), *One Speaker, Two Languages*. Cambridge: Cambridge University Press, 115–135.

Auer, Peter (ed.)
    1998   *Code-Switching in Conversation*. London: Routledge.

Auer, Peter and Aldo di Luzio (eds.)
    1992   *The Contextualization of Language*. Amsterdam and Philadelphia: John Benjamins.

Bakhtin, Mikhail
    1981   *The Dialogic Imagination*. Austin: University of Texas Press.

Barry, Brian M.
    2001   *Culture and Equality: An Egalitarian Critique of Multiculturalism*. Oxford: Polity Press.

Blommaert, Jan
    1999   The debate is open. In: Blommaert, J. (ed.), *Language Ideological Debates*. Berlin and New York: Mouton de Gruyter, 1–38.

2001   Investigating narrative inequality: African asylum seekers' stories in Belgium. *Discourse and Society* 12(4), 413–449.
2003   Comentary: A sociolinguistics of globalization. *Journal of Sociolinguistics* 7(4), 607–623.
2005   *Discourse*. Cambridge: Cambridge University Press.

Blommaert, Jan, James Collins and Stef Slembrouck
2005   Spaces of Multilingualism. *Language & Communication* 25, 197–216.

Blommaert, Jan and Jef Verschueren
1998   *Debating Diversity. Analysing the discourse of tolerance*. London: Routledge.

Boden, Deidre and Don Zimmerman (eds.)
1991   *Talk and Social Structure*. Cambridge: Polity Press.

Bourdieu, Pierre
1977   *Outline of a Theory of Practice*. Cambridge: Cambridge University Press.
1985   *¿Qué significa hablar?* Torrejón de Ardoz: Akal/Universitaria.
1991   *Language and Symbolic Power*. Cambridge: Polity Press.

Bremer, Katharina, Celia Roberts, Marie-Thérèse Vasseur, Margaret Simonot and Peter Broeder
1996   *Achieving Understanding: Discourse in Intercultural Encounters*. London: Longman.

Chouliaraki, Lilie and Norman Fairclough
1999   *Discourse in Late Modernity*. Edinburgh: Edinburgh University Press.

Cicourel, Aaron V.
1992   The interpenetration of communicative contexts: Examples from medical encounters. In: Duranti, A. and C. Goodwin (eds.), *Rethinking Context*. Cambridge: Cambridge University Press, 291–310.

Codó, Eva
1998   Analysis of language choice in intercultural service encounters. M.A. thesis, Universitat Autònoma de Barcelona, Bellaterra, Barcelona.

Collins, James
1987   Conversation and knowledge in bureaucratic settings. *Discourse Processes* 10, 303–319.

Cook-Gumperz, Jenny
2000   Cooperation, collaboration and pleasure in work. In: Di Luzio, A., S. Günthner and F. Orletti (eds.), *Culture in Communication. Analyses of Intercultural Situations*. Amsterdam and Philadelphia: John Benjamins, 117–139.

Delanty, Gerard
1995   *Inventing Europe: Idea, Identity, Reality*. London: MacMillan.

de Lucas, Javier
    2006   La inmigración en España: Una obsesión desbordada. In: *Le Monde Diplomatique (Spanish version)*, January 2006.
Díez Nicolás, Juan and María José Ramírez Lafita
    2001   *La inmigración en España. Una década de investigaciones*. Madrid: Instituto de Migraciones y Servicios Sociales.
Drew, Paul and John Heritage (eds.)
    1992   *Talk at Work. Interaction in Institutional Settings*. Cambridge: Cambridge University Press.
Duranti, Alessandro
    1997   *Linguistic Anthropology*. Cambridge: Cambridge University Press.
Duranti, Alessandro and Charles Goodwin (eds.)
    1992   *Rethinking Context*. Cambridge: Cambridge University Press.
Erickson, Frederick
    1975   Gatekeeping and the melting pot: Interaction in counselling encounters. *Harvard Educational Review* 45, 44–70.
    2001   Co-membership and wiggle room: Some implications of the study of talk for the development of social theory. In: Coupland, N., S. Sarangi and C.N. Candlin (eds.), *Sociolinguistics and Social Theory*. London: Longman, 152–181.
Erickson, Frederick and John Schultz
    1982   *The Counsellor as Gatekeeper. Social Interaction in Interviews*. New York: Academic Press.
Fairclough, Norman
    1989   *Language and Power*. London: Longman.
    1992   *Discourse and Social Change*. Cambridge: Polity Press.
Foucault, Michel
    1977   *Discipline and Punish: The Birth of the Prison*. New York: Vintage.
    1984   The order of discourse. In: Shapiro, M. (ed.), *Language and Politics*. Oxford: Basil Blackwell, 108–138.
Fraser, Nancy
    1988   *Unruly Practices: Power, Discourse, and Gender in Contemporary Social Theory*. Minneapolis: University of Minnesota Press.
García Jorba, Juan M.
    2000   *Diarios de campo*. Madrid: Centro de Investigaciones Sociológicas.
Garfinkel, Harold
    1967   *Studies in Ethnomethodology*. Englewood Cliffs, NJ: Prentice Hall.

Generalitat de Catalunya
    2004   *Pla per a la llengua i la cohesió social*. Barcelona: Departament d'Educació. http://www.xtec.es/lic/documents.htm

Giddens, Anthony
    1979   *Central Problems in Social Theory. Action, Structure and Contradiction in Social Analysis*. London: MacMillan Education.
    1984   *The Constitution of Society*. Cambridge: Polity Press.

Giménez Romero, Carlos
    2003   *Qué es la inmigración*. Barcelona: RBA.

Goffman, Erving
    1959   *The Presentation of Self in Everyday Life*. New York: Doubleday.
    1981   *Forms of Talk*. Oxford: Blackwell.
    1983   The Interaction Order. *American Sociological Review* 48(1), 1–17.

Gordon, Colin (ed.)
    1980   *Michel Foucault. Power/Knowledge. Selected Interviews and Other Writings 1972–1977*. London: Harvester Wheatsheaf.

Gould, Robert
    2005   The European paradox: Swiss discourses of identity between dependence and xenophobia. In: Mar-Molinero, C. and P. Stevenson (eds.), *Language Ideologies, Policies and Practices*. London: Palgrave, 162–176.

Gramsci, Antonio
    1971   *Selections from the Prison Notebooks* (ed. and transl. by Q. Hoare and G. Nowell-Smith). London: Lawrence & Wishart.

Gumperz, John J.
    1982a   *Discourse Strategies*. Cambridge: Cambridge University Press.
    1982b   *Language and Social Identity*. Cambridge: Cambridge University Press.
    1992a   Contextualization revisited. In: Auer, P. and A. di Luzio (eds.), *The Contextualisation of Language*. Amsterdam and Philadelphia: John Benjamins.
    1992b   Contextualization and understanding. In: Duranti, A. and C. Goodwin (eds.), *Rethinking Context*. Cambridge: Cambridge University Press.

Gumperz, John J. and Celia Roberts
    1991   Understanding in intercultural encounters. In: Blommaert, J. and J. Verschueren (eds.), *The Pragmatics of Intercultural and International Communication*. Amsterdam and Philadelphia: John Benjamins, 51–90.

Hall, Christopher, Srikant Sarangi and Stefaan Slembrouck
    1999   The legitimation of the client and the profession: Identities and roles in social work discourse. In: Sarangi, S. and C. Roberts (eds.), *Talk, Work and Institutional Order. Discourse in Medical, Mediation, and Management Settings*. Berlin and New York: Mouton de Gruyter, 293–322.

Heller, Monica
  1999 *Linguistic Minorities and Modernity. A Sociolinguistic Ethnography*. London and New York: Longman.
  2001a Undoing the macro/micro dichotomy: Ideology and categorisation in a linguistic minority school. In: Coupland, N., S. Sarangi and C. N. Candlin (eds.), *Sociolinguistics and Social Theory*. London: Longman, 212–234.
  2001b Critique and sociolinguistic analysis of discourse. *Critique of Anthropology* 21(2), 117–141.

Heritage, John
  1984 *Garfinkel and Ethnomethodology*. Cambridge: Polity Press.

House, Julianne
  2003 English as a lingua franca: A threat to multilingualism. *Journal of Sociolinguistics* 7(4), 556–578.

Hutchby, Ian and Robin Wooffitt
  1998 *Conversation Analysis: Principles, Practices and Applications*. Cambridge: Polity Press.

Jacquemet, Marco
  2005 The registration interview. Restricting refugees' narrative performances. In: Baynham, M. and A. De Fina (eds.), *Dislocations/Relocations. Narratives of Displacement*. Manchester: St. Jerome, 197–218.

Kachru, Braj B.
  1990 World Englishes and applied linguistics. *World Englishes* 9(1), 3–20.

Kerekes, Julie A.
  2006 Winning an interviewer's trust in a gatekeeping encounter. *Language in Society* 35, 27–57.

Kymlicka, Will
  1995 *Multicultural Citizenship*. Oxford: Oxford University Press.

Lamoreux, Edward Lee
  1988/89 Rhetoric and conversation in service encounters. *Research on Language and Social Interaction* 22, 93–114.

Levinson, Stephen
  1983 *Pragmatics*. Cambridge: Cambridge University Press.

LIPPS Group
  2000 The LIDES coding manual: A document for preparing and analysing language interaction data. *International Journal of Bilingualism* 4(2), 131–270.

MacWhinney, Brian
  2000 *The CHILDES Project: Tools for Analyzing Talk*, 3rd ed. Mahwah, NJ: Lawrence Erlbaum.

Mar-Molinero, Claire and Patrick Stevenson
    2005   Language, the national and the transnational in contemporary Europe. In: Mar-Molinero, C. and P. Stevenson (eds.), *Language Ideologies, Policies and Practices*. London: Palgrave, 1–10.

Maryns, Katrijn
    2005   Displacement in asylum seekers' narratives. In: Baynham, M. and A. De Fina (eds.), *Dislocations/Relocations. Narratives of Displacement*. Manchester: St. Jerome, 174–196.
    2006   *The Asylum Speaker. Language in the Belgian Asylum Procedure*. Manchester: St. Jerome.

Maryns, Katrijn and Jan Blommaert
    2002   Pretextuality and pretextual gaps: On re/defining linguistic inequality. *Pragmatics* 12(1), 11–30.
    2005   Conducting dissonance: Codeswitching and differential access to context in the Belgian asylum procedure. In: Mar-Molinero, C. and P. Stevenson (eds.), *Language Ideologies, Policies and Practices*. London: Palgrave, 177–190.

Massey, Douglas S., Joaquin Arango, Graeme Hugo, Ali Kouaouci, Adela Pellegrino and J. Edward Taylor
    1993   Theories of international migration: A review and appraisal. *Population and Development Review* 19(3), 431–466.

Melzi, Gigliana and Kendall A. King
    2003   Spanish diminutives in mother-child conversations. *Journal of Child Language* 30, 281–304.

Merritt, Marilyn
    1976   On questions following questions in service encounters. *Language in Society* 5, 315–357.

Ministerio del Interior
    2001   *Anuario Estadístico de Extranjería 2000*. Madrid: Delegación del Gobierno para la Extranjería y la Inmigración, Ministerio del Interior. http://extranjeros.mtas.es/es/general/Anuario2000_ANEXT01.pdf

Moyer, Melissa G. and Luisa Martín Rojo
    2007   Language, migration and citizenship: New challenges in the regulation of bilingualism. In: Heller, M. (ed.), *Bilingualism: A Social Approach*. London: Palgrave, 137–160.

Niessen, Jan, Maria José Peiro and Yongmi Schibel
    2005   *Civic Citizenship and Immigrant Inclusion*. Brussels: Migration Policy Group. http://www.migpolgroup.com/multiattachments/2470/DocumentName/civiccitizenship.pdf

Nieto, Alejandro
    1984   *La organización del desgobierno*. Barcelona: Ariel.
    1996   *La "nueva" organización del desgobierno*. Barcelona: Ariel.

Observatorio Permanente de la Inmigración
    2004   *Anuario Estadístico de Extranjería. Año 2003*. Madrid: Ministerio de Trabajo y Asuntos Sociales.
            http://extranjeros.mtas.es/es/general/Anuario_de_Extranjeria_2003.pdf
    2005   *Anuario Estadístico de Inmigración. Año 2004*. Madrid: Ministerio de Trabajo y Asuntos Sociales.
            http://extranjeros.mtas.es/es/general/ANUARIO_INMIGRACION_2004.pdf

Parekh, Bhikhu
    2001   *Rethinking Multiculturalism*. London: Palgrave.

Pin, José Ramón, Luis López and Ángela Gallifa
    2004   *Libro Blanco sobre las Mejores Prácticas para la Integración del Trabajador Immigrante en las Empresas Españolas*. Navarra: IESE Business School, Universidad de Navarra.

Prcic, Tvrtko
    2003   Is English Still a Foreign Language? *The European English Messenger* XII(2), 35–37.

Pujolar, Joan
    2001   *Gender, Heteroglossia and Power: A Sociolinguistic Study of Youth Culture*. Berlin and New York: Mouton de Gruyter.
    2007a   African women in Catalan language courses: Struggles over class, gender and ethnicity in advanced liberalism. In: McElhinny, B. (ed.), *Words, Worlds and Material Girls: Language, Gender, Globalization*. Berlin and New York: Mouton de Gruyter, 305–347.
    2007b   Bilingualism and the nation-State in the post-national era. In: Heller, M. (ed.), *Bilingualism: A Social Approach*. London: Palgrave, 71–95.

Rabinow, Paul and Nikolas Rose
    2003   *The Essential Foucault*. New York: The New Press.

Rampton, Ben
    1995   *Crossing: Language and Ethnicity among Adolescents*. London: Longman.
    2001   Language crossing, cross-talk, and cross-disciplinarity in sociolinguistics. In: Coupland, N., S. Sarangi and C. N. Candlin (eds.), *Sociolinguistics and Social Theory*. London: Longman, 261–296.

Roberts, Celia
    2001   'Critical' social theory: Good to think with or something more? In: Coupland, N., S. Sarangi and C.N. Candlin (eds.), *Sociolinguistics and Social Theory*. London: Longman, 323–333.

Roberts, Celia and Srikant Sarangi
    1995   'But are they one of us?': Managing and evaluating identities in work-related contexts. *Multilingua* 14(4), 363–390.
    1999   Hybridity in gatekeeping discourse: Issues of practical relevance for the researcher. In: Sarangi S. and C. Roberts (eds.), *Talk, Work and Institutional Order. Discourse in Medical, Mediation and Management Settings* Berlin and New York: Mouton de Gruyter, 473–503.

Roberts, Celia and Pete Sayers
    1987   Keeping the gate: How judgements are made in interethnic interviews. In: Knapp, K., W. Enninger and A. Knapp-Potthoff (eds.), *Analyzing Intercultural Communication*. Berlin and New York: Mouton de Gruyter, 25–43.

Sacks, Harvey, Emmanuel A. Schegloff and Gail Jefferson
    1974   A symplest systematics for the organisation of turn-taking for conversation. *Language* 50, 696–735.

Sarangi, Srikant
    1996   Conflation of institutional and cultural stereotyping in Asian migrants' discourse. *Discourse & Society* 7(3), 359–387.
    1998   Rethinking recontextualisation in professional discourse studies: An epilogue. *Text* 18(2), 301–318.

Sarangi, Srikant and Celia Roberts
    1999   The dynamics of interactional and institutional orders in work-related settings. In: Sarangi, S. and C. Roberts (eds.), *Talk, Work and Institutional Order. Discourse in Medical, Mediation and Management Settings*. Berlin and New York: Mouton de Gruyter, 1–57.

Sarangi, Srikant and Stefaan Slembrouck
    1996   *Language, Bureaucracy and Social Control*. London and New York: Longman.

Schegloff, Emanuel A.
    1991   Reflections on talk and social structure. In: Boden, D. and D. Zimmerman (eds.), *Talk and Social Structure*. Cambridge: Polity Press, 44–70.

Schegloff, Emanuel A., Gail Jefferson and Harvey Sacks
    1977   The preference for self-correction in the organization of repair in conversation. *Language* 53(2), 361–382.

Silverman, David
    2000   *Doing Qualitative Research*. London: Sage.

Simon, Herbert A.
    1957   *Administrative Behaviour*. New York: MacMillan.

Smart, Barry
    1983   *Foucault, Marxism and Critique*. London: Routledge.

Stevenson, Patrick
    2005   'National' languages in transnational contexts: Language, migration and citizenship in Europe. In: Mar-Molinero, C. and P. Stevenson (eds.), *Language Ideologies, Policies and Practices*. London: Palgrave, 147–161.

Subirats, Joan
    2002   Cultura, ciutadania, identitat. *El País*, 5 December 2002, 6/Quadern.

ten Have, Paul
    1998   *Doing Conversation Analysis: A Practical Guide*. London: Sage.

Thomas, Jenny
    1986   The dynamics of discourse: A pragmatic analysis of confrontational interaction. Unpublished doctoral dissertation, Lancaster University, Lancaster.

Thornborrow, Joanna
    2002   *Power Talk. Language and Interaction in Institutional Discourse*. London: Longman.

Trinch, Shonna L.
    2001   The advocate as gatekeeper: The limits of politeness in protective order interviews with Latina survivors of domestic abuse. *Journal of Sociolinguistics* 5, 475–506.

Unamuno, Virginia and Eva Codó
    2007   Categorizar a través del habla: la construcción interactiva de la extranjeridad. *Discurso y Sociedad* 1(1), 116–147.
            http://www.dissoc.org/ediciones/v01n01/DS1%281%29Unamuno-Codo.pdf

Ventola, Elija
    1987   *The Structure of Social Interaction*. London: Pinter.

Weber, Max
    1947   *The Theory of Social and Economic Organization* (transl. by A.M. Henderson and Talcott Parsons). New York: The Free Press.
    1948   *Essays in Sociology*. London: Routledge & Kegan Paul.

Wodak, Ruth and Teun van Dijk
    2000   *Racism at the Top. Parliamentary Discourse on Ethnic Issues in Six European States*. Vienna: Austrian Federal Ministry of Education.

Woolard, Kathryn
    1989   *Doubletalk: Bilingualism and the Politics of Ethnicity in Catalonia*. Stanford, CA: Stanford University Press.

Index

accountability
   managerial, 96
   of clients, 66, 148, 155, 170, 185
   of bureaucrats, 9, 95, 104, 107, 123, 134, 147, 186, 195
Agar, Michael, 9, 10, 77, 88, 96, 98
agency, 10, 32, 34, 42, 74, 96, 107, 121, 227, 228
aliens. *See* immigration
alignment, 191
   avoidance of, 141, 146, 147, 171
   body alignment and social intercourse, 52
   breaches in, 169
   lack of, 136
   personal, 106
   social, 52
applications/petitions
   administrative processing of, 45–51
   review of petition outcome, 49
   stalling of, 47–49, 82
   submission of, 44–45
Arabic, 18, 25, 31, 44, 74, 98, 112, 187, 192, 194, 215
asymmetry, 79, 147, 175, 178, 186, 205. *See also* information exchange
   linguistic, 69–70, 151, 174, 180, 186, 213
   of capitals, 224
   of knowledge, 69–70, 129
   of power, 70, 129, 180, 224
   of rights and obligations, 137, 147
   of role relationships, 104, 186, 229, 231
asylum, 17, 21, 192
authority
   computer as, 122
   figures of, 178–179
   managerial, 96–98, 105, 107, 112
   subversion of, 104

back office, 20, 30, 43, 133, 136
   and information desk, 97
   staff, 45, 50, 95, 136–137, 144, 183
backstage, 25, 40–41, 180–181, 190
   and Catalan, 190, 195, 221
   comments/remarks, 25, 27–28, 40, 77, 107, 110, 121, 157, 173, 179–181, 184
bilingualism
   bilingual application forms, 44
   Catalonia as bilingual community, 188, 221
   Spanish-Catalan bilingual practices, 189–190, 191
Blommaert, Jan, 6–7, 13, 39, 194, 200–202, 228
Bourdieu, Pierre, 10, 32–33, 35–37, 161, 170, 192, 194, 215, 221, 226
bureaucracy. *See also* migration trajectories, rationality
   and credibility, 8, 108, 145, 165
   and equality/inequality, 83–85, 108, 111, 129, 228
   and expectations of transparency, 10
   and fairness, 103, 231
   and homogeneity, 42, 225
   and language use, 11–12
   and objectivity, 165, 181
   and social control, 11, 151
   and the state, 8–10, 151, 225–227
   as constructed, 11, 84, 228
   as distributor of rights and obligations, 9, 151
   as impersonal, 84, 174
   culturally-specific practices, 77, 225
   definition of, 84, 103
   hegemonic views of, 129, 179, 185, 229
   regulatory function of, 52, 151, 227
bureaucratic jargon, 11

bureaucratic/insider knowledge
    clients' access to, 87–88, 89–92
        control of, 126, 133–148, 151
    bureaucrats' representation of, 74–83
bureaucratic talk
    and assumption of relevance, 78–79
    and disciplinary dimension, 162
bureaucrat practices, general description of, 116–127. *See also* capital, information exchange
    appeals to violence, 178, 184–185
    avoidance of uninstitutional behaviour, 134, 140, 231
    blame on clients, 72, 127, 201
    institutional safeguarding, 72, 74, 94, 147, 226
    mistrust of clients, 139, 169, 178, 181–182
    professional role management, 115–118, 121–126, 132, 136, 147, 151, 225, 228
    regimentation/control mode, 78, 152–173, 179, 183, 185, 223, 230
    reprimands to clients, 156–157
    threats to clients, 127, 153, 161, 162
    use of disciplinary language, 152, 155, 162
    use of verbally offensive behaviour, 175–183
bureaucrats, characterisation of, 10–11, 29–30. *See also* language competence

capital(s), 3, 36, 67, 69, 85, 188. S*ee also* asymmetry, Catalan, English
    cultural, 221
    linguistic, 200–201, 203, 221, 231
        bureaucrats' devaluing of clients' linguistic capital, 35, 199–203, 231
Catalan, 25–26, 28–29, 31, 88, 162, 187, 188–192, 195–196, 198, 221, 226, 231. *See also* backstage, bilingualism
    and integration, 161, 191, 231
    as an identity language, 191
    as symbolic capital, 161, 191
    as we-code, 161, 189–190
categorisation, 226
    and practices of inclusion and exclusion, 12, 229, 232
    and social inequality, 39
    negative client categorisation/construction/characterisation, 151, 173–183, 185–186, 229
    self-categorisation, 160–161
    resistance to categorisation, 203
Chinese
    clients, 15, 71, 175–180
    language, 18, 44, 192
citizenship. *See also* difference
    and language competence, 6
    and homogeneity, 224
    and national identity, 6
    gain access to, 162
    civic citizenship, 6
    regulation of access to, 226–227, 230
clienthood, negative ideological constructions of, 151, 198
client practices, general description of, 127–146. *See also* resistance
    challenges to bureaucrats, 72, 84, 87, 88, 98, 104, 108, 117, 128, 132, 134, 136–137, 139, 144, 147, 174, 180, 186, 207
    cheating, 49, 71, 165
    complaining, 21, 64, 116, 126–127, 140–141, 145, 147, 173, 229–230
    making personal appeals, 65, 145–146, 147
    self-construction as knowledgeable participants 158–160
    self-construction as professional clients, 137, 140
    subversion of regimentation/control, 129–130, 155, 157, 165
    use of insider knowledge, 133–134
clients, characterisation of, 10, 29–30

codeswitching, 130, 196, 207, 210–211, 215–221
contestation, 37, 124, 127–146, 185–186, 205, 207, 231. *See also* information
contextualisation, 38–39, 120
  access to spaces of, 8
control, 36, 96, 129, 221. *See also* bureaucrat practices, bureaucratic/insider knowledge, client practices, information exchange
  bureaucratic/institutional, 9, 112, 115, 140, 151, 223–224, 227
  interpersonal, 147
  managerial, 97
  of information, 19, 36, 140, 146, 151, 172
  of interactions/service discourse, 12, 41, 51, 62, 66, 69, 84, 164–172
  of language use, 41, 187–222
  of migrant flows, 4–5, 18, 189. *See also* Spanish
  of relevance judgements, 171–172
  social control, 34, 41–42, 183, 230. *See also* bureaucracy, client practices
  and conversationalisation, 175
  and language use, 19, 78
conversation analysis, 37–39
culturalisation of migrants, 7

deception and language use, 203
difference, 6–7
  citizenship and recognition of, 85
  cultural, 5, 225
  depolitisation of, 5
  equality of, 5, 85
  ethnic, 225
  mistrust of, 226
  politics of, 5
  religious, 225
  stigmatisation of, 225
discourse(s), 105, 115
  bureaucratic, 78
  bureaucrats', 94, 99–107, 225

classroom, 188
clients' 196, 203, 207, 231
institutional, 38, 94, 96, 105–106
on immigration, 6, 224–225
in Spain, 14
on language, 226
discrimination, 108, 186, 231
domination and subordination, relationships of, 33–34, 229

eligibility requirements/conditions, 44, 49, 103, 107
  information on, 44, 51
English, 18, 23–25, 31, 44, 70, 74, 77, 79, 83–85, 89, 92, 112, 128–129, 144, 169, 178, 187–188, 192, 195
  as capital, 200–201
  as lingua franca, 15, 198–208, 200, 215, 221
  functional value of, 198–199, 215–221
  South Asian/Indian English, 200–201, 207, 215
entitlement, 43, 183, 189, 227
  arbitrary criteria, 49
  as good luck, 146, 180–181
European Economic Area, 18, 29
European Union, 13, 18, 29
  and migrants' civic rights, 6

fairness. *See* bureaucracy, heterogeneity, resources, routinisation
face, 37
  and miscommunication, 88
  face-redressive strategies, 125
  facework, 145, 147
  interactional face, 145
  keep face, 113, 115, 117, 147
  language incompetence as face-damaging, 177
  lose face, 78, 229
  positive face, 147
  professional face, 115, 117, 229
  threats to face, 78, 88, 98, 108
field, 36, 179, 185

250 *Index*

focused interaction, 24
footing, 40, 140–141, 146
forged documentation, 47, 49, 75, 95, 105–106, 162, 182–183
Foucault, Michel, 32, 35, 93–94, 162
frame, 121
    bureaucratic, 145, 146
    institutional, 104, 121, 126, 145, 147, 170, 196, 228
    interpretive, 11, 132, 167, 169
    legal, 4
    bureaucrats', 205
    political, 4
    clients' reframing potential, 129
French, 18, 25, 31, 44, 74, 112, 128–130, 187, 192, 195, 199, 214
front
    front region, 40
    unified front, 105, 107–112, 117, 228
front-line communication/talk. *See* information exchange
frontstage 25, 40–41, 157, 160, 173, 179
    and Spanish, 190–191, 195, 221

game, 117, 170, 225
    language games, 174
gatekeeping, 7–8, 13, 42, 74, 112, 146–147, 221, 227, 230
gaze, management of, 24, 86
German, 25, 26, 214–215
Giddens, Anthony, 32, 33–35, 37, 93, 120
globalisation, 14, 200, 224
Goffman, Erving, 25, 37–41, 84, 85, 108, 117, 173, 179, 180, 223
Gumperz, John J., 7–8, 38, 39, 120, 128, 189

habitus, 10, 32, 36–37, 192, 195, 215
Heller, Monica, 8, 39, 229
heterogeneity/diversity, 4. *See also* difference, immigration
    and equality/inequality, 5–7, 12
    and fairness, 5, 7
    and institutional practice, 7–8, 12, 83–85, 111, 195, 225

    in Spain, 14, 224–225
    linguistic, 7–8
hierarchies of knowledge, 195, 221
historicity of linguistic facts, 13
homogeneity. *See* bureaucracy, citizenship, identity, integration, nation-state, social cohesion
hybridity, 41, 207, 224

identity. *See also* Catalan, citizenship, immigration, power, social cohesion, and culture, 5
    and ethnicity, 177
    and face-to-face interaction, 122
    homogeneous views of, 232
    integrated foreigner identity, 160–161, 190–191
    national, 3
    Spanish, 226
ideology(ies), 37, 177, 194, 195, 226. *See also* nation-state, Spanish, state
    institutional, 49, 94, 170, 211
    linguistic, 72, 195, 197, 221
    of discipline and order, 155
    of mistrust, 72, 151, 203, 230
immigrants. *See* clients
immigration. *See also* discourse, social change
    and access to valuable communicative resources, 215
    and diversity, 5
    and national identity, 6
    and security, 5
    and the nation-state, 7, 189, 224
    and the state, 4, 8–9, 225–226
    networks, 7
    to Mediterranean countries, 13–14, 16–17
    to Spain, 13–17, 225
    undocumented, 5, 21, 26, 186, 224
        to Spain, 15–16, 19, 49

Index   251

immigration laws, 4–5, 8, 151
    in Spain, 13–14, 16, 17–19
immigration policies, 4, 6–7, 14
implicature, 133, 180, 183
indexicality of language, 39
inequality, 4, 7, 12, 74, 222. *See also*
    bureaucracy, categorisation, heterogeneity, routinisation, service exchanges, Spanish
    and information, 69
    and situated language use, 4, 8, 12, 33, 37–39, 74, 93, 129, 192, 229
informal language/register 173-185
information. *See also* control, eligibility, inequality, ontological security, service responses
    contestation of, 19, 56, 62, 115, 126, 128, 144, 231
    contradictory, 117, 130, 136, 231
    disembedding of, 73
    illusion of, 89–90, 93, 111
    written information as a resource, 72
information desk staff, 10, 29–30
information exchange. *See also* power, service responses
    and control, 11–12, 35, 69
    and speaking positions, 11
    as asymmetrical, 70, 79
    institutional disregard for, 86, 88–89, 112, 140, 227
    practices of information provision, 51, 74–83, 118–121. *See also* routinisation
institutions. *See also* truth
    and regulation of social life, 9
    as mid-level structures, 9, 196
    as systems, 10, 96
    institutional reproduction and situated action, 93
integration, 6–7
    and homogeneity, 7
    and language, 194. *See also* Catalan, Spanish

integrative research, 32
interactional synchrony, 145
    and language choice, 216
interpreters, 128–129, 187, 193–194
Italian, 25–26, 214

language choice, 56, 162, 187–188, 207, 214, 216–221. *See also* interactional synchrony
language competence. *See* also citizenship, face, Spanish
    assessments of, 199, 200, 203, 224
    bureaucrats' competence in foreign languages, 31, 187, 194–195, 198–199, 203–205, 210–211
    deficit approach to/problematisation of, 23, 86, 112, 201–202, 203–205
language negotiation, 56, 61, 178, 213, 216
language repertoire, 83
legalisation campaign, 14, 17–19, 21, 28, 44, 51, 192

magnet effect, 19
metadiscourse/metatalk/metacomments, 27, 165, 166, 178, 190, 198, 206, 231
migration trajectories, 200
    and bureaucracy, 10
    and language, 214–215
miscommunication, 80–81, 88–89
mistrust, 77, 139, 141, 145, 178, 193, 231, 232. *See also* bureaucrat practices, difference, ideology
mobility
    of migrants in Spain, 17
    of linguistic resources, 200
modes of talk, 141, 147, 175
multiculturalist approaches, 5–6
multilingualism, 187–222
    and social spaces, 188–192
    elite, 7
multimodal interaction, 72
mutual understanding, 70, 88, 169–170, 215

252   *Index*

nation-state(s), 12. *See also* immigration, Spanish
    as main regulator of identities, 224
    homogeneous conceptions of, 5, 7
normativisation, 151, 155–156, 161, 185

officials. *See* information desk staff
ontological security
    and bureaucrats' evaluative mode, 230
    and information, 69
    and routine, 34, 37
order
    interconnectedness of orders, 9, 12, 195, 228
    interactional, 37, 94, 112, 116–117, 120, 125, 210
    institutional, 11, 74, 94, 96–97, 107, 112, 120, 122, 125–126, 188, 193, 196, 210–211, 228
    moral, 37, 148, 152, 155, 172–173, 213
    social, 37, 93, 155, 157, 188, 196, 221, 224

participation framework, 27, 40, 189
pidgin, 76, 79
power, 32, 34–35, 37, 229. *See also* asymmetry, resources
    and access to context, 39
    and backstage talk, 180, 183
    and identity construction, 122
    and information exchange, 11, 69, 70, 88, 93–95
    and intentionality, 34–35, 93–94
    as a web, 35, 94
    configurations, 221
    disempowerment, 88
    reproduction, 129
    situational, 125, 180, 206
pragmatics, 38, 173. *See also* service exchanges
    and social analysis, 79
    subversion of pragmatic expectations, 152, 173–175
    pragmatic function of turns, 145
    participants' different pragmatic behaviour, 137, 147
procedural consequentiality, 38
Pujolar, Joan, 189, 191, 195, 224
Punjabi, 25–26, 193

racism, 173, 178
rationality
    and bureaucratic practice, 10, 103, 165, 181, 231
    rational work organisation, 78, 96, 97
regimentation. *See* bureaucrat practices, client practices
regions and forms of talk, 40–41, 189
resistance, 36. *See also* categorisation
    clients' resistance 203, 207, 231
resources, 35–36, 210, 224. *See also* immigration, mobility
    access to, 8, 12, 33, 36, 39, 85, 112, 223
    and fairness, 12
    and power, 36
    attach value to, 36, 203
    human, 45, 95
    interactional, 115
    legal status as a scarce resource, 88, 225, 227
    linguistic, 39, 69, 84, 88, 104, 112, 174, 188, 200, 207, 215
    roles as resources, 122
ritual, 37, 93
routinisation, 66
    and fairness, 83–85
    and inequality, 83–85
    deroutinisation/debureaucratisation, 134, 146, 198
    of service responses 51, 66, 77, 112, 218
Russian, 18, 31, 44, 74, 112, 187, 192–193

Sarangi, Srikant, 8, 11, 25, 32, 39, 72,
    78–79, 84, 86–87, 122, 137, 146, 151,
    161, 175, 228, 230
service activity(ies)
    definition of, 56
    description of, 56–66
    types of, 56
service episode(s), definition of, 56
service exchanges/encounters/interactions
    and sociopragmatic conventions,
        174–175
    and inequality, 174
    and social distance, 174
    as discontinuous, 52
    brevity of, 74
    characterisation of, 51–66
    enacted as first time exchanges, 174
    similarity of, 51
service responses. *See also* information
    exchange, routinisation, truth
    ambiguous, 82, 111
    brief, 74
    formulaic, 77, 90, 95, 130
    minimal, 74, 82, 85, 111–112, 117,
        128, 198
    scripted, 83–84, 112, 140, 146–147
    tokenistic, 89
    uncommitted, 64, 72, 77, 121
    uninformative, 77, 83, 86, 89, 112,
        115, 230
    vague, 88
simplification of language, 85–88, 93
Slembrouck, Stefaan, 151, 161
small talk, 53, 161, 190–191
social change, 37
    and immigration, 3
social cohesion
    and cultural identity, 6
    and homogeneity, 7
social exclusion, 4, 8, 12, 15, 33, 36, 38,
    42, 69, 85, 111, 129, 188, 189, 192,
    224, 229, 232. *See also* categorisation,
    state, stratification

social practice, 33–34
socialisation processes, 9–10, 21, 36, 117,
    221, 232
sociolinguistic regime, 41, 192
sociolinguistics, 37, 224
    interactional, 39
South Asians, 8, 30, 77, 79, 193, 200–205,
    214–215, 221
Spanish, 18, 25–27, 29, 31, 44, 53, 112,
    128, 130, 139, 140, 161, 162, 178,
    187, 188–192, 195–199, 205, 208,
    210–222. *See also* bilingualism,
    frontstage
    and integration, 177, 194, 226
    as common language, ideology of,
        226
    as only legitimate language, 194–196,
        226
    clients' low competence in, 70, 83,
        144, 169
        and inequality, 74, 85, 88, 92,
        129, 174–175,
    indexing nation-state control of flows,
        189
    use in service responses, 76–77,
        79–81, 89–92, 215
Spanish public administration, 9, 87–88,
    107–108, 186, 226–227
state. *See also* bureaucracy, immigration
    and means of coertion, 162
    and middle-class ideology, 228
    and norms of inclusion/exclusion,
        229
    and protection of national population,
        225, 230
    and protection of regimes of truth, 75,
        227
    as gatekeeper, 225
    regulatory function of, 42, 162, 225,
        230
stereotypes, 173, 175–177, 229–231

stratification
    and situated talk, 39, 42, 223
    and social exclusion, 232
structure and situated action, 32–34
structuration, 12, 32, 33–34
suspicion, 50, 66, 129, 151, 183

truth
    speak the truth about the institution, 229
    domains of, 35, 93
    objects of, 93
    rituals of, 93
    truthfulness of bureaucrats' responses, 75, 111, 117–118, 122, 129, 134, 136–137, 139
    as taken for granted, 78

voices, 41, 105, 178–179

Weber, Max, 43, 84–85, 103

www.ingramcontent.com/pod-product-compliance
Lightning Source LLC
Chambersburg PA
CBHW082104250426
43661CB00079B/2630